The Third
WomanSleuth Anthology:
Contemporary Mystery Stories by Women

edited by Irene Zahava

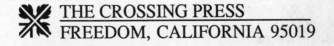
THE CROSSING PRESS
FREEDOM, CALIFORNIA 95019

Dedicated to my great-aunts,
Helen Hershowitz and Pauline Grife ...
they always enjoyed a good mystery.

Cover ilustration and design by Gary Carpenter
Book design and production by Martha Waters

Printed in the U.S.A.

Library of Congress Cataloging-in-Publication Data

The third womansleuth anthology : contemporary mystery stories by
  women / edited by Irene Zahava.
       p.   cm.
    Includes bibliographical references.
    ISBN 0-89594-414-6. -- ISBN 0-89594-413-8 (pbk.)
    1. Detective and mystery stories, American--Women authors.
  2. Women detectives--Fiction.   I. Zahava, Irene.
  PS648.D4T44   1990
  813' .0872089287--dc20   90-40975
                                                      CIP

Contents

The Adventure
of the Gioconda Smile[†]

Ellen Dearmore

I.

THIS ADVENTURE IS NOT, like Charles Dickens's great novel, a tale of two cities, but rather a story about two paintings, and about how one of them, Leonardo da Vinci's masterpiece, the *Mona Lisa*, was stolen from the Louvre in the year 1911. This adventure is also about how Gertrude, in order to solve the mystery of that theft, became a detective—indeed, this was her first case—and about how I became an astrologer, learning out of dire necessity how to use that ancient art. But I am getting ahead of myself. For this case was first of all about art, and about a painting that inspired so much passion that it almost caused the death of a man. And as I am speaking of Gertrude's dear friend, Pablo Picasso, I will begin with him.

I, of course, am Alice Toklas; Gertrude, Gertrude Stein.

Gertrude and Picasso met in 1905, appropriately enough in an art gallery in Paris where Gertrude and her brother Leo had gone to buy some paintings. And if it was not a marriage made in heaven, it was a friendship forged with steel, for from the very beginning, Picasso and Gertrude had understood one another. I was not a part of Gertrude's life then; I would not meet her until 1907. But I saw

---

[†]This is a work of fiction. Events and characters in no way depict real situations or events.

enough of her early friendship with Picasso to know its nature. I, who had absolutely no compunction about challenging the bond that Gertrude had with her brother Leo, knowing as I did that she would not be free to become herself until she was free from Leo, knew better than to challenge her feelings for Picasso. For if I had, I would have lost, as would have Gertrude. For in those early days in Paris, Gertrude and Picasso needed each other as they needed no other—to inspire, guide, support and challenge—until they were sure enough of themselves to claim that which they were—geniuses.

Picasso drew portraits of all of his friends; it was one of his ways of celebrating the friendship. And so it was only inevitable that in time, given his feelings for Gertrude, he would want to do her portrait. But for some reason Picasso put this off, and as the years passed, it became something of a problem. For Gertrude had become by then, for Picasso, a difficult subject. This became quite obvious early in the year 1911, when Picasso finally started to paint Gertrude's portrait. For it soon became clear that he could not do it. Gertrude would go daily for her sitting with Picasso, walking through the Luxembourg Gardens, up to the Odéon, where, catching the horse-drawn bus, she would go to Montmartre and Picasso's studio. But days passed and then months, as sitting followed sitting, with little accomplished, Picasso becoming more and more frustrated, reworking the canvas until it resembled not the portrait of a woman, but a giant battlefield. Gertrude, for her part, did not at first mind the fact that Picasso could not finish her portrait; to be in his company was satisfaction enough. But as the number of sittings mounted—seventy, eighty—even she began to question Picasso's art, her doubts unnerving Picasso even more. For he needed Gertrude's approval, and if she were no longer to believe in him, then maybe it was true. Maybe he was not the genius that he thought himself to be.

Things came to a head one afternoon, in the summer of 1911, when Gertrude, coming home from one of her sittings at Picasso's studio, finally voiced her opinions. She had just had an argument with Picasso over her portrait, and whether or not he was artist enough to do it, and he, in a burst of anger, had wiped her face completely out. He had looked at her for so long, he said, that he could no longer see her. Gertrude was an impossible subject to paint, and he was wasting his time with the effort!

I, of course, knew that it was only a passing moment in a friendship that could survive earthquakes. But I also knew something else—why Picasso had not been able to paint Gertrude's portrait.

Gertrude and I were sitting in the atelier at the rue de Fleurus, as we often did in the late afternoons, coming together sometimes for the first time in the day, I after my chores, Gertrude after her daily walk. Surrounded by her art collection, her paintings that stretched up almost to the ceiling, seated in her deep chintz chair that was before the fireplace, Gertrude was most herself here. And so it was, on this day, that I finally decided to speak my mind.

"Gertrude," I began, "it is quite clear what is wrong. Picasso cannot paint your portrait for one simple reason."

"And what is that?"

I braced myself. "Because he has not slept with you."

"What are you saying?" Gertrude asked, beginning to move in her chair.

"Picasso has not slept with you, Gertrude," I repeated. "And as that has not happened, he will never be able to paint your portrait."

"Alice, sex has absolutely *nothing* to do with it!" Gertrude said, getting up from her chair and beginning to pace the floor, a sure sign she was troubled. "Pablo has painted many portraits of people he has not slept with—Max Jacob and Apollinaire, to name two."

"But they were *men,* Gertrude! Picasso must sleep with a woman before he can paint her. It's his way of conquering, so he can be sure enough of himself to paint. You haven't submitted, and so he can't paint you!"

"Nonsense, Alice! Of course I haven't submitted to Pablo. It is why we are still friends. We are brothers—equals! It is a relationship that suits us both."

"Maybe so," I answered. "But don't expect a miracle then—your portrait."

"You are not suggesting that I sleep with Pablo?"

"Most certainly *not!*" I answered. "But something is going to have to give, Gertrude, if you want your portrait!"

If Picasso that summer was having trouble with Gertrude, he was soon to have difficulties of a far more serious nature. For he was about to become involved in a crime that would rock all of France. And as this part of the adventure involves the painting that I mentioned earlier, Leonardo's *Mona Lisa,* I must speak of it now.

3

The *Mona Lisa,* in the year 1911, was under a kind of seige itself, having come to stand for, at least to some, a kind of duplicity. Although painted by an Italian in the sixteenth century, the painting had, by the late eighteenth, become the property of the French people, in whose museum, the Louvre, it hung, if not proudly then at least a symbol of the beauty and power that France had once been. Possession, however, for some, was not proof of ownership, and in the early years of this century, the Italians began to assert their claim. The *Mona Lisa* belonged to Italy, Italian patriots in Paris began to argue, the painting had been stolen away from its rightful owners by the kings of France. Angry viewers in the Louvre began to attack the painting itself, shouting that if Italy could not have the painting, then no one would. One such attacker, an Italian, threw a rock at it, cracking its frame. The directors of the Louvre, fearing for the safety of the painting, covered it with glass, an action that caused a further outcry, this time from the French, who felt that the glass was an offense to the painting itself. No painting should be covered with glass, they argued, as the paint could not then breathe, and without breath, a painting would die. There was a riot outside the Louvre, the Italians attacking the French and the French attacking themselves—France was the only country in the world, one reporter observed, that would start a war over a painting—and the museum was closed for a week so that tempers could cool. But tempers did not cool, and on a hot day in August—the twenty-first, I remember—the *Mona Lisa* was stolen from the Louvre, an event that was to catapult Paris into the worst confusion she had experienced since the fall of the Bastille.

The theft, although shocking, did not at first affect Gertrude or me. The *Mona Lisa* was, to be sure, a great painting, and one that I had certain fondness for. But we had other things on our minds—planning our annual trip to Spain, for example—although it was a trip that, given the events that were about to transpire, would never take place. For two days after the *Mona Lisa* was stolen from the Louvre, Gertrude's dear friend Guillaume Apollinaire was arrested by the Paris police, charged with the theft of the painting, and put into the prison, La Santé. When his mistress, Marie Laurencin, had gone to visit him, in order to protest his innocence, she too, had been arrested.

It was at this point, with two of her good friends in jail, that Gertrude and I began to question our trip. But if we still had any hopes of going to Spain, they were all but dashed a day later, when there was a third arrest, this time, Pablo Picasso, who, like his friend Guillaume Apollinaire, was charged with the theft of the *Mona Lisa,* and imprisoned in La Santé. No longer having the luxury of indecision, Gertrude was at last shocked into action: we would definitely *not* be going to Spain this year. Before, however, Gertrude could decide what she was going to do to help Picasso, she received an urgent *petite bleu* from Fernande Olivier, Picasso's mistress, asking her to come to her at once. And thus began our involvement in what was to become one of our most remarkable adventures.

Picasso and Fernande were at that time living on the Boulevard de Clichy, the last home Picasso would have before he left Montmartre forever and moved onto finer things. His home there mirrored this transitional state. Characterized by just enough respectability to keep Fernande happy—a few pieces of heavy mahogany furniture, a maid who wore a white apron and answered the front door, Sunday afternoons when Fernande was "at home"—the apartment still retained the certain clutter, even disorderliness, that Picasso required in order to function.

On the day that Gertrude and I went to see Fernande, however, the state of her apartment was the last thing on her mind. Clearly and visibly upset, more so than I had ever seen her, she descended almost at once upon Gertrude.

"Is he still out there?" she asked Gertrude, almost before we were in the front door.

"Who?" Gertrude asked, turning around.

"The policeman across the street. He has been there since yesterday. He watches me wherever I go. I am under house arrest!"

Gertrude opened the door and peered out. "I see no one, Fernande."

"You will. Just wait. He will be back again."

Fernande led us past a row of canvases, stacked against the wall, and into the parlor. I noticed, as we passed, a number of portraits of Fernande. Picasso, obviously, had had no trouble painting *her* portrait. I started to say something to Gertrude, but then checked myself. It was obviously not a time for levity. Not even offering us tea, Fernande began at once, even before Gertrude and I were seated.

"I'm afraid for my life, Gertrude," she said, "afraid to go

anywhere, afraid that if I do they will put me in jail. Like Marie Laurencin. Did you see in the newspaper?"

"I did," Gertrude said, taking a seat.

"They have found out that Guillaume has an Italian mother," Fernande continued, "and are calling him a *métèque,* a wop, and saying that Pablo is the head of an international gang that has come to France to steal all her treasures! *La Bande à Pablo,* they call it. What am I going to do?"

"Fernande," Gertrude said slowly. "Please calm yourself. I can understand nothing of what you are saying. Take a deep breath, and then tell me what has happened."

"I'm not sure I can. But I do know one thing. It was Géry Piéret who started it."

"Géry Piéret?"

"You don't know him—Pablo keeps him hidden. He's a boxer, sometimes. From Belgium. He's been in America—California—the past few years. But now he's back. He does odd jobs, for his friends. For Pablo."

"Odd jobs?"

"I shouldn't tell you this, Gertrude. Pablo will be angry. But you will have to know. Géry has been stealing things from the Louvre for years, to make a little money."

"Someone has been stealing things *from the Louvre?*"

"Nothing serious. Small things, statues, carvings, anything he could get into his trousers—he had special pockets inside them. He had a joke. "I'm off to the Louvre," he would say to his friends. "Can I bring you anything?"

Fernande laughed. "It was all quite harmless," she went on. "Until Pablo needed the masks."

"What masks?"

"Two African masks in the Louvre. Géry got them for Pablo."

Fernande paused. "Géry was going to take them back," she went on, "I'm sure of it, after Pablo had finished with them. But then Géry went to America and forgot, until now, until the *Mona Lisa* was stolen. Then he decided to show off. He took several of the statues he had stolen to the newspapers, to show them how easy it is to steal from the Louvre. The police found out about it, and went to see Apollinaire, who also had a stolen statue."

"Apollinaire was in on this, too?"

"He was the first to do it. He thought it was a joke, too. But they

6

broke him down in prison. They stripped him naked, as part of the search. But you know Guillaume, Gertrude. So modest! He was mortified. He began to talk. He told them about Pablo. Then the police came here, and found the two masks. Then they arrested Pablo."

"And Piéret? Have they arrested him, too?"

"They weren't quick enough. He fled the country."

"Who has told you all of this, Fernande?"

"Max Jacob. He has been to see Pablo."

"Ummm," Gertrude said. "Go on."

"Pablo knew that the police would come for him. The night before, he spent walking up and down the Seine. He had the two masks in a suitcase. He wanted to throw them into the river. I told him to do it. It would have been so easy—just one toss, and he would be free! But he couldn't do it. He came back home, crying. 'Now they will get me, too,' he said."

"Fernande," Gertrude said slowly. "I want you to tell me the truth. Rest assured that I will tell no one. Do you think that Pablo stole the *Mona Lisa?*"

Fernande sighed, and began to twist a small white handkerchief that she held in her hand.

"Normally, no, Gertrude. He could not have done such a thing. But this has not been a normal time. He never brought the *Mona Lisa* here—I never saw it. I will testify to that in court. But Pablo has not been himself lately. He has been upset like I have never seen him before. He has not been able to paint, and when he cannot paint, he becomes a madman! *Le Fou!*"

Gertrude stood up, and began pacing the floor. "Fernande, we are going to have to do something! Pablo is in serious trouble. He may even be a thief!"

"That is why I called you, Gertrude. You are his best friend. He loves you!"

"I will begin tomorrow," Gertrude said. "By going to La Santé!"

"Gertrude," I interrupted. "I do not think that advisable. Haven't you been listening to Fernande? When Marie went to see about Guillaume, *she* was arrested! And now Fernande has a policeman outside her door. It is best to stay away."

"Max Jacob wasn't arrested, when he went!"

"You are not Max Jacob!" I said. "You are known to be one of

7

Picasso's best friends. You have discussed art with him on numerous occasions—you have even talked about the *Mona Lisa*. There is also your own art collection, which is known throughout Paris. If I had to say whom the police would arrest next, I would have to say you! You could very well be a member of Picasso's gang!"

"I may be many things, Alice, but I am not a member of Pablo's gang!"

"Tell that to the police!" I said.

Gertrude sighed. "All right," she finally said. "Then I will just have to think of something else. What, I am not yet sure."

It was a question still on Gertrude's mind, I remember, as we left Fernande's apartment that day—how she was going to help Picasso—but one that she was soon to answer. For we had not been three minutes out of Fernande's house, when I turned and saw him.

"Gertrude," I said. "Don't look now, but we are being followed. Behind us. Fernande's policeman!"

"I do not like to think that I am being followed!"

"In here!" I said, quickly pulling Gertrude into an open doorway. "Let him pass."

We stood there for a few minutes, catching our breath.

"That settles it, Alice," Gertrude said, once the policeman had passed. "I have been thinking about it for some time. But now I'm sure. I am just going to have to do it."

"What?"

"Become a detective."

"What?"

"Like Sherlock Holmes."

"Gertrude, he was in a *book!*"

"That doesn't matter. The principle's the same. Detection—the art of uncovering, discovering. That's easy. I will simply apply what I already know to that which I don't know. The known will lead me to the unknown, who stole the *Mona Lisa*. Which, of course, is known by someone.

"Who?"

"The thief, of course!"

The next three days, I remember, were unlike any Gertrude had ever spent before, she going to bed late at night, as was her custom, but also getting up early, indeed, sometimes even before I. I would come down into the studio, around six in the morning, and find

Gertrude there, as I had left her the night before, poring over newspaper accounts of the theft, taking copious notes, then arranging her material in great piles on her desk. Knowing that Gertrude did not like to be disturbed while she was working, I went my own way and said nothing. But on the third day when I, overcome with suspense, was just about to break silence, Gertrude finally spoke.

"Alice," she said excitedly as I entered the studio. "I was just about to call you. I have figured out the case!"

"You know who stole the *Mona Lisa?*"

Gertrude nodded.

"Picasso?" I asked.

"Please, Alice, sit. You know I can't talk while you are standing."

I moved toward a chair.

"No," Gertrude said, once I was seated. "The thief is not Pablo."

"But what about Fernande's story?"

"I must admit that what she said gave me pause. But now that I have calmed myself, and thought deeply about the case, I realize that Pablo could never have stolen the *Mona Lisa.*"

"Why not?"

"Because it just doesn't make any sense—Pablo being the thief. Why would he steal such a painting, when he has painted greater ones of his own? It would be like a cobbler stealing shoes. Admittedly, he *does* like the *Mona Lisa.* He and I have had arguments that lasted into the morning about it. As you know, I do *not* like the *Gioconda,* or her smile. Smiles belong on photographs, I have told Pablo a hundred times, never on serious paintings."

"Gertrude," I said. "None of this proves that Picasso did not steal the painting."

"No, but something else does. Logistics."

"What do you mean?"

"The painting was stolen on a Monday, Alice, the day the Louvre is closed to the public. In order to be in the museum on that day, Pablo would have had to hide in it overnight, somewhere safe and private, probably in one of the toilets. Now, if I put myself in Pablo's place, as all good detectives must do—*become* the criminal—and hide myself in one of the toilets all night, waiting for morning to come so that I can steal the *Mona Lisa,* then I immediately run into trouble. You know Pablo, Alice. He would have been too frightened. Even if by some miracle he had gotten as far as the toilets, he would have been so upset by morning that he would have been able to do nothing, much less, steal. No, Pablo isn't the thief."

"Then who?"

"I will tell you in a minute. But first I must give you the facts of the case. The thief, without the facts, will not make much sense. Now," Gertrude began, "the actual facts in the case are few in number, and very simple. Sometime between seven and eight, on the morning of August 21st, someone entered the Salon Carree in the Louvre, and took the *Mona Lisa* off the wall. Then the thief darted down one of the staircases, quickly removed the painting's heavy gold frame and glass—they were both found later at the foot of the stairs—and disappeared with the painting."

"No one saw him do it?"

"Of course not!"

"Then how do they know what time it was stolen?"

"From one of the workmen in the Louvre that day. He passed the *Mona Lisa* that morning, around seven o'clock. Then, about an hour later, when he walked by again, the painting was gone."

"Wasn't he suspicious?"

"That was the funny part. Paintings were taken off the walls all the time—to be cleaned, restored, photographed. So if a painting were not on a wall, no one would think anything about it. That was the case here. No one even suspected that the painting had been stolen, until the next morning, when an art student showed up and wanted to copy it. When he couldn't find it, he called a guard. Even then, it took them all morning to realize that the painting had been stolen. As you might expect, pandemonium followed, then curiosity."

Gertrude laughed. "More people now come to look at the empty spot on the wall where the *Mona Lisa* once hung, than used to come to see the painting itself. Five thousand people in one day! Now," Gertrude continued, "in spite of the enormity of the crime, there are only two small clues. One, a fingerprint—a clear thumb mark—that was found on the empty picture frame by the fingerprint expert, Alphonse Bertillon."

"That could be a very large clue."

"It wasn't. When Bertillon tried to match the print with those in his files, 700,000, he found nothing."

"And the second clue?"

"On the day of the theft, a baggage handler at the Gare d'Orsay saw a suspicious looking man with a beard board the train for Florence, with a flat, rectangular object under his arm. The *Mona Lisa,* the handler was sure, when he later heard of the theft."

I sighed. "That sounds more like a wish than a clue."

"I quite agree. That's why I called it small. Everything points to its being an inside job, an insight, I am sorry to say, that the Paris police have not yet had. They have assigned sixty special policemen to the case, on the mistaken belief that sixty heads are better than one. But they have done nothing but confuse one another! They have even arrested some poor German whom a woman saw eating peanuts outside the Louvre on the day of the theft, just because he had what she called 'un air sournois.' But I know better. It *had* to be an inside job, Alice. Only someone with a thorough knowledge of how the Louvre worked would have dared such a theft, or have been able to carry it off successfully."

Gertrude paused, and looked down at her notes. "There's another reason I think it was an inside job. The painting was fastened to the wall by four iron pegs that fit into the back of the picture frame. In order to get the painting off the wall, one had to remove its frame first. This was a rather complicated process, and one that only someone with special knowledge could have accomplished. There is the painting itself, an oil, done on wood. It is also rather large, twenty inches by thirty inches. It could not have been rolled up and concealed under the thief's clothing. The thief would have had to know that about the painting in advance, in order to get it out of the Louvre undetected."

"Who was in the Louvre that day?"

"A skeleton crew, as the museum was closed. Twelve men."

"One of them is the thief?"

"Yes."

"Which one?"

"I have been able to eliminate definitely five men. First, the museum director, and his assistant. Even though they have been fired for incompetence, they have sterling characters and reputations, and are really above reproach. There were also two guards in the museum that day, but neither of them seems likely. Between seven and eight, when the painting was stolen, they were together, cleaning up the cloakroom in the front lobby. There was also a porter there that day. But he spent the morning in one of the courtyards, sleeping behind a large red umbrella. He was observed there by the two guards. There was another guard, the one who usually watched the Salon Carré, where the *Mona Lisa* hung. But I have eliminated him also. He wasn't in the Louvre that day. He stayed home, sick with the flu."

"Isn't that suspicious?"

"What is suspicious about the flu?"

"The fact that he just happened to have it that day, and so wasn't in the salon on the one day that the most famous painting in the world was stolen from it. Maybe he knew something. Maybe even *he* was the thief."

"It would have been too risky. Someone might have recognized him. No, Alice, it has to be one of the remaining men. The seven workmen. I have made a list of their names."

"Could I see it?"

Gertrude handed me her list.

I looked at the seven suspects' names. An eighth name had a line drawn through it.

"Who is Joseph Homolle?"

"The guard I mentioned earlier. The one sick with the flu."

"So the thief is one of these seven men?"

"Yes."

"Which one?"

"I'm not sure yet. I have eliminated several of them, but I want to think some more."

"What will you do when you have him?"

"Go to the police, of course! But I must say this about the case, Alice. It hasn't been nearly as much fun as I thought."

"Why not?"

"It's been too easy! It's not at all like it is in my mystery books, where there are many more clues and false trails that lead nowhere. I just haven't had enough to think about! So once I have the thief, I think I will go back to my books. They are much more fun!"

If the case had been, according to Gertrude, less than sufficiently challenging, it was soon to change. For suddenly the story of the theft intensified, fueled by a letter that Picasso's thief, Géry Piéret, sent to the newspaper, the *Paris-Journal*.

Sent in two parts, first from Vienna and then from Rome, the letter detailed the way that Picasso, with the aid of Piéret, had planned, and then executed, the theft of the *Mona Lisa*. Claiming that the Louvre was as easy "to pick as a pocket," that there was a side door that was always open, even on Mondays, when the museum was closed, Piéret told how he and Picasso had stolen the painting from the Louvre, a theft, Piéret also claimed, that had taken less than fifteen minutes, and was easier to accomplish than an average house theft. Piéret also promised more to his readers, a final letter in which he would tell what Picasso had done with the *Mona Lisa,* after he had stolen it.

Piéret's letter, which caused a sensation, was to be followed by an even greater commotion. An enterprising reporter, upon reading Piéret's letter, decided to test its contents for himself. Entering the Louvre on a Monday, through the afore-mentioned side door, then simulating the theft according to Piéret's instructions, the reporter found that, indeed, such an act could have been accomplished in fifteen minutes, and could be done undetected; no one had seen the reporter carry out his surreptitious deed.

When the reporter's story was published, there was an immediate outcry, both against the museum officials, for being so lax in their security measures, and against Pablo Picasso, for being at last definitely identified as the thief. An angry mob of almost two hundred men, carrying torches and armed with pitchforks, stormed La Santé prison, demanding the thief Picasso, whom they wanted to hang. Breaking through the front door of the prison, they got as far as some of the inner offices before they were stopped. The police, no longer able to insure the safety of Picasso, transferred him, in the dead of night and under heavy guard, to a fortress prison, the Conciergerie, where he was put into a dungeon, impenetrable, save by cannons.

"Well," I said to Gertrude, on the morning of these new developments. "You've gotten your wish. The case has certainly become more complicated."

"Yes, but it's not nearly as much fun as I thought it would be."

"Apparently there were no toilets, as you thought. Just a side door. Anyone could walk into the Louvre, on any day."

"And apparently anyone did."

"What are you going to do now?"

"What I have been doing for the past two days. Rethink the case. And I don't like what I've found."

"What?"

"I have been thinking about it all morning, something that

13

Fernande said, when we talked to her. It didn't sink in then, but now it has. The two African masks. Why did Pablo want them so desperately, Alice, enough to steal them from the Louvre? He could have been content just to view them, but no, he wanted them closer. Why? And then suddenly, this morning, I had the answer! Of course, his painting, the *Demoiselles!*"

"What do you mean?"

"Don't you remember when Pablo was painting the *Demoiselles?*"

"Not really. It was some time ago."

"Four years. But I remember it quite well. Pablo had a terrible time with that painting, with the faces of the five women in it. He got three done right away. They were quite natural, and even looked like faces. But the other two caused him no amount of pain. He struggled and struggled with them, trying to get them right. And then one day he came and got me. He was so excited. He had finally been able to finish the painting! At the time I thought nothing of it, but now I see what happened."

"What?"

"The faces of Pablo's two women. They aren't human. They are like masks, wooden African masks! Pablo copied those faces *from the two stolen masks!* There is something even more disturbing here. We now know how Pablo works, Alice. I thought I knew everything there was to know about Pablo, but I obviously did not. He has been taking things from the Louvre for years, if he needed them for his work. He needed the two masks in order to finish the *Demoiselles,* and so he took them. This brings us to the case at hand. I think Pablo now needs another work from the Louvre, the *Mona Lisa.*"

"But why?"

"Have you forgotten, Alice? Pablo has been painting my portrait!"

"But that's been going on for months!"

"That's the problem! He hasn't been able to finish it! I have had to sit almost ninety times, and he still hasn't been able to get my face right!"

"Are you saying that Picasso stole the *Mona Lisa* in order to finish his portrait of you?"

"I am."

"But Gertrude! You look nothing like the *Mona Lisa!*"

"Perhaps to Pablo I do!"

I sat there, stunned, unable to speak.

Gertrude looked at me. "Of course," she said, "there's an easy way to find out. Come, Alice, we must go to the Bateau-Lavoir! The evidence is there!"

Picasso's studio, the Bateau-Lavoir, in Montmartre, was as I had remembered it, shabby beyond repair, its tin walls pockmarked and streaked with grime, its roof sagging so in the middle that it looked as if it might cave in.

"It has to be shabby, Alice," Gertrude said, after I had commented on the studio's condition. "Or else Pablo can't work in it. He has several of these studios scattered throughout Paris, each one more disreputable than the other. Pablo's a peasant at heart. It's one of his great strengths. Any kind of elegance intimidates him. It will always be so—no matter how rich he becomes!"

"But won't it be locked?" I asked, as we walked toward the door.

"There are no locks here, Alice. Who would want Pablo's paintings?" Gertrude laughed. "Several years ago thieves broke into Pablo's apartment and stole some of his clothes. Don't you remember, Alice? Pablo was devastated. 'When will they know who I am?' he lamented. 'When will my paintings be more valuable than my clothes, something that thieves will want to steal?'"

Gertrude pulled open the studio's sagging wooden door, struggling with it as it scraped against the ground.

"What are we looking for?" I asked, as we stepped into the room.

"The *Demoiselles,* first. You know the painting, Alice. Five nudes, several of them standing, against a background of white. It shouldn't be hard to spot. It is large, among other things."

I immediately saw the painting, resting against a side wall. I walked over to it.

"Pablo's first masterpiece," Gertrude said, as she joined me. "The world does not yet know it, but someday it will."

I looked at the five women, several of them staring out of the canvas at me, their faces twisted into unnatural shapes, two of them almost animal-like in their features.

"But it's so ugly," I said.

"It has to be ugly, Alice, because it is a complete break with the

15

past, and in order to break you must do violent things. It will eventually be beautiful, once it has become the thing that others must break from. But that will not happen in our lifetime! But it is as I remembered. See—the two faces on the right?"

I nodded.

"Those are the ones that Pablo stole from the Louvre. Look! They aren't faces, but masks. They are the two African masks! Now," Gertrude said, beginning to move around the studio, "we must find my portrait."

I began flipping through a stack of canvases that were leaning against a wall.

"Not there—it won't be with the others. It's thick with paint, about ninety layers," Gertrude laughed, "and probably still wet." Gertrude moved toward the back of the room. "And don't expect to see anyone you know. You remember what happened! The last time I posed Pablo rubbed my entire face out! I am without a head!"

I looked around the room.

"Alice!" Gertrude suddenly called out. "Here! Come here!"

I walked toward the back of the room.

There, in front of Gertrude, on an easel, stood the portrait of a woman, her body draped in a soft brown corduroy robe and turned slightly to the right, one hand folded gently over the other, the whole crowned with a head, completely and fully drawn in.

"Gertrude!" I said. "It's you! And he's finished it! You have a head!"

"More than that," Gertrude said, pointing. "A mouth, too! *I am smiling!*"

"Gertrude," I said, taking a deep breath. "You look just like the *Mona Lisa!*"

Gertrude turned to me. "It isn't pretty, Alice, I know. And whether or not Pablo painted it with love, because of his feelings for me, or to spite me, because he knows how I feel about that smile, I cannot say. But I *do* know one thing. The case feels right, at last! Pablo *is* the thief!"

II.

I cannot describe the next few days, Gertrude in the atelier, sitting in her chair by the fireplace, dejected as I have rarely seen her, saddened as if she had lost her best friend, which, in one sense, she had.

"Alice," she said, as I brought her a cup of tea. "When I started, I had no idea what it meant to be a detective. But now I do. Now I see that it means finding out things you'd rather not know. I don't know what Sherlock Holmes did about that. But I know what I'm going to do. Stop being a detective! I am through with the case!"

"But, Gertrude!" I said, handing her the cup of tea. "What will Pablo do without you?"

"What he did *with* me. Continue to cause trouble!"

"But he needs you!"

"What can I do, Alice? If I were to go to the police with what I know about Pablo, they would hang him for sure! And if I continue to probe into Pablo's life, no telling what else I will find!"

"Everyone has clay feet, Gertrude. It's to be expected."

"But not like this!" Gertrude looked at me. "I now know things about Pablo that no one should know—how he paints, and where he gets his pictures. I thought before it all came from within him, but I see now that it doesn't. It comes from the Louvre! He stole the *Demoiselles* from some African masks, and my portrait from Leonardo! That is what hurts! Not that he is the thief—I could forgive him that! But that he is not the genius I thought he was!"

"Gertrude, Pablo is still a genius."

"Then prove it!"

I, of course, could not, nor could I solve the case at hand. But I did find myself in the next few days thinking very hard about some things. Was Picasso really the thief, for example. Yes, I had seen Gertrude's portrait and yes, Picasso had copied her face from the *Mona Lisa*. But would he have to steal the painting in order to do that? Probably not. No, I thought, Gertrude was wrong. Picasso was not the thief. But if he wasn't, then who was? And where was the *Mona Lisa?*

It was at this point in the case, with Picasso in the dungeon of the Conciergerie, and everyone—Gertrude included—thinking that he was the thief, that I decided to go get help. And help, in those days, meant only one person—Max Jacob.

There was Picasso and Fernande Olivier and Braque and Matisse and Henri Rousseau and André Salmon and Guillaume Apollinaire, even Marie Laurencin. But of all the people in those early days in Paris, Max Jacob was the one I liked most. Although he did not have the gifts of some of the others, he still managed to hold his own in a company of geniuses. He did this in a number of ways. First, he was always polite, and kind. When Picasso and Fernande decided, for example, in a moment of misguided domesticity, to adopt a child, and then a week later decided to return her but could not, as the orphanage would not take her back, it was Max who found the little girl a home, even visiting her for months afterwards, always bringing candy and toys. There was also Max's absolute devotion to Picasso. "It is my duty on earth," he would say, "to keep Picasso happy," an enormous undertaking, as it turned out, because Picasso was so often sad.

But the thing I liked most about Max was his quiet confidence. Surrounded most of his life by geniuses, he never became envious, or thought himself less than he was. He kept his own counsel, and dignity. And if one were to have seen them coming down the street together—Max and Picasso—in those early days in Paris, Max standing tall and straight, obviously in control of himself, and Picasso short and hunched over, his eyes cast downwards, obviously in control of nothing, then one would have thought that it was Max, and not Picasso, who was the genius. And although Max, a Jew, would later die in a concentration camp, a victim of Hitler's Nazi Germany, life did not defeat him. Nothing ever defeated Max Jacob.

And so it was, on a day in early September, in the year 1911, that I went to see Max Jacob, and thus entered a significant new phase of my life.

Max lived at that time on the Quai des Fleurs, in Montmartre, in a small room that Picasso called "la salle perdue," a hovel. And while that word described the room's size, it did not describe either its warmth or charm. Too poor to buy furniture, Max had asked Picasso to paint some on his walls, which Picasso obligingly did, painting a large red velvet sofa with two matching chairs, and an antique oil lamp that hung down from the ceiling. There was also a large painted waiter, dressed in a black tuxedo, standing at attention, holding a tray of roasted potatoes, Max's favorite food. The rickety bed that Max slept on, however, was real, as was an old wooden desk and chair. A row of neatly arranged boxes, in which Max kept all his earthly possessions—a few clothes, a top hat, a walking stick with a gold handle, some books and piles of paper— completed the decor.

Max, of course, had been in on the case from the beginning. The only one of Picasso's friends to visit him in jail, Max had brought us news from prison. But once Picasso was placed in the dungeon of the Conciergerie, all visits stopped; Picasso could see no one. So we were now left to our own devices, to help Picasso as best we could.

"Max?" I began, as soon as I had settled on the bed that served as Max's second chair. "What do you think? Did Picasso steal the *Mona Lisa?*"

"I don't know, Miss Toklas. Pablo says no, he didn't do it. But that was before Géry told his story. Pablo *does* have a rather proprietary attitude toward things in the Louvre. I don't know what to believe!"

"Gertrude thinks that Picasso *did* do it. She has become a detective. She's working on the case."

"We live in troubled times, Miss Toklas. We are all going to have to become something, if we want to survive. Becoming a detective is one way, although I can think of better."

"Religion?" I asked, knowing of Max's interest in that subject.

"And astrology," he said.

I smiled. "I'll never forget the first thing you ever said to me, Max. We were at a party at Picasso's, in the Bateau-Lavoir. 'What is your Sun sign, Miss Toklas?' you asked me. 'Are you a Taurus, or a Pisces?' 'Taurus,' I answered, surprised that you had been able to guess. You smiled. 'Born to love,' you said. Gertrude, who was with me, laughed. 'What if Alice had said Pisces?' You smiled again. 'Then I would have said, born to love God.'"

Max, who was himself a Pisces, smiled. "It's the only thing to be. Pisces. The two fish seemingly swimming in opposite directions, but in reality forming a circle and moving upwards toward God. It's the most evolved of all the signs. If one wants to reach God, Miss Toklas, then one must be Pisces."

"We can't choose our birth, Max!"

"But we can! If one is not born a Pisces, then one can become one through meditation and prayer!"

I sighed. "Max, is there anything to it—astrology? Anything more than just superstition?"

"It is anything but that, Miss Toklas. Astrology is a carefully constructed system that organizes the universe, and that will, if we use it wisely, lead us to God. It is also a study of individuals. Our brains are imprinted at birth, with various influences and characteristics. This determines how we shall act."

"Is there no free will then?"

"We *always* have free will, Miss Toklas! Astrology just shows us what our choices are. It's up to us to make the right ones."

Max paused. Then, getting up from his chair, he went over to one of the boxes that lined his wall. Picking it up, he brought the box back to where I was sitting.

"Let me show you something," he said, as soon as he was seated again. He pulled out a long brown envelope from the box, and began to open it.

"Pablo's chart," he said, unfolding a large sheet of paper.

"Chart?"

"His horoscope. A map of the way the heavens looked at the moment of his birth, in October. Pablo is a Scorpio."

Max pointed to the chart, a large circle with spokes in it, the whole resembling a wheel. "It is, as you might suspect, an exceptional chart. It is characterized by trines. Most people don't even have one trine in their chart, but Pablo has four!"

"Trines?"

"Two planets 120° apart, in such a relationship as to form two points of a triangle. This allows energy to flow freely from point to point, without obstruction. Trines enable the native to express himself easily, and lead to great good fortune. There is also great energy here. Look! Pablo's Sun trines his Mars, setting up a condition whereby the energy of the sun can flow directly and without hindrance into his life and work. It gives him almost superhuman energy and will power. But there is something else. He has a Grand Cross. See!" Max said, tracing a large cross across Picasso's chart. "It's a configuration made when four planets oppose one another, and thus form a cross. It cuts across his whole chart, indicating that he will have some great difficulty to overcome. What that will be we will just have to wait and see."

Max laid down Picasso's chart. "I have another chart here," he said, reaching into the brown envelope again. "Your friend's, Miss Stein's."

"You've done Gertrude's?"

"She caught my eye at once."

Max opened up the large sheet of paper, upon which there was again a large wheel with many spokes. "It, too, is an exceptional chart. Like Pablo's, the chart of a genius."

"I knew that the first time I met her. I heard a little bell ring. But how can you tell?"

"There are several things. First, she has an extremely powerful aspect, a solar-powered brain."

"What?"

"Her Sun conjuncts Mercury. This means that at the moment of her birth, Mercury was in perfect alignment with the sun, in Miss Stein's case, at an exact orb of zero degrees. It's a position astrologers call 'Casimi,' the alignment of wave patterns so perfect that the energy of the sun can flow directly through Mercury, the planet of mental energy, straight into the native's mind. It creates great intelligence, genius even, especially when the conjunction is in one of the Air signs—Gemini, Libra, or Aquarius. Miss Stein is an Aquarius. Her Moon is in Virgo, another highly mental sign. Many writers have strong Virgo influences. All of this indicates a person who is ruled by her mind, and who is extremely gifted at expressing it."

"Does she have any trines?"

"Three, the most interesting of which is Uranus trine her Midheaven. This is an indication that she will achieve great fame, and that it will come quite suddenly."

"Can you tell when it will happen?"

"No, only that it will."

"Do you see anything bad in her chart?"

"There is nothing bad in anyone's chart, Miss Toklas. Only lessons to be learned. We all have difficulties. Our charts just show us what they are. Then we can work at overcoming them. If we cannot overcome them, then we can transcend them. That is when astrology becomes a spiritual guide, leading us straight to God, Who can free us of all burdens."

"Max," I said, once he had put the two charts back into the envelope. "Astrology. Do you think we could use it in any way? Not just for fun, but for a practical purpose? To help Picasso? Maybe even to find the *Mona Lisa?*"

"I have been thinking about that myself, for some time. There are some interesting things going on in the heavens now. Saturn, for instance."

"Saturn?"

"One of the great planets."

"How can it help?"

"Saturn can always help, if you ask the right questions. But let's not delude ourselves about the nature of our task, Miss Toklas. The real mystery about the *Mona Lisa* is not who stole her. They will find him soon enough. No one can hide such a painting for long. The *real* mystery is that such a painting was made at all. That a single finite being could paint something so beautiful, so infinite in meaning. Leonardo was obviously in touch with God when he painted it, with God speaking to us through Leonardo. That painting is but a piece of the mind of God. Think, then, Miss Toklas, how splendid it must be, the Whole! *The mind of God!*"

I will not here describe the next week, my getting up early while Gertrude was still asleep, and accomplishing my morning chores quickly, so that I would have time to stop off at Max's on the way home from Les Halles. I mentioned none of this to Gertrude, not out of fear that she would disapprove. I knew that she would. But I was not ready to tell her of my interest in astrology, suspecting that she might not find that subject as fascinating as I, and thus might try to interrupt what I had to learn.

The ancient art of astrology was, of course, a lifelong study, and could not be mastered in a short time. But I began to learn how to cast a horoscope, how to find the Ascendant and position the wheel, how to rectify a chart if the time of birth was not known, what the various aspects and houses meant. It was not long before I could converse quite easily with Max about the subject, he leading me gently and patiently through some of its finer points. And, after a great deal of hard work, we were finally able to shed much light on the case at hand.

I, however, was not a detective; that endeavor was the province of others. Although I had found out much, I did not know what to do next. I would have to go to Gertrude.

I found her sitting one afternoon in the atelier, seemingly at rest.

"Gertrude," I began. "I don't want to interrupt you if you are busy. But if you are not, could we talk? About the theft of the *Mona Lisa?*"

"Alice, I am no longer working on that case!"

"Gertrude, Max and I have found out something. About the thief."

"You've brought Max into this?"

"Yes."

"Alice, this is *my* case!"

"It still is, Gertrude. Only now you just have more information to work with."

"I don't need any more information. I know now more than I want to know."

"We started from scratch," I went on. "Max and I agreed that it had to be an inside job, and for the reasons you cited. But we wanted to include everyone. Not just Picasso and Piéret, but *all* of the suspects, everyone who was in the Louvre the day the *Mona Lisa* was stolen. Twelve men. Thirteen men. We also looked at the guard who was sick that day. Joseph Homolle."

"We have already discussed that. He's not a suspect!"

"We looked at the suspects from several different angles," I continued, "and began to eliminate some of them, and arrived, like you, at a list of seven men, the workmen who were in the Louvre on the day of the theft. I will refresh your memory as to who they were: Théophile Brion; Jacques Laclotte; Louis Bonnard; Justin Mantz; Vincenzo Peruggia; Roland Clement; and Maurice Béroud. And, while we were examining this list, Max and I found something curious. The suspects' names, to begin with."

"Alice, that's the first thing I checked. You know my theory about names—names claim, names blame, names determine. Take the name, Justin Mantz, for example, one of the suspects. Justin— 'upright, just one.' People rarely go against the grain of their names. It would have been hard, indeed, for Justin Mantz to be the thief!"

"You are right, Gertrude. Justin Mantz is not the thief." I looked at Gertrude. "What does the name 'Vincenzo' mean?" I asked.

"What?"

"Vincenzo Peruggia. He is also one of the suspects. What does his name mean?"

"It comes from 'Vincent.' 'One who conquers.'"

"Isn't that suspicious?"

"Not really."

"We think Vincenzo Peruggia's name *is* suspicious."

"Why?"

"It's Italian."

"What's suspicious about being an Italian?"

"Nothing, usually. But in this case, it might be something to think about."

"Why?"

"Don't you see, Gertrude? Peruggia's an Italian—the only one of the thirteen suspects who is not French. You know the recent history of the *Mona Lisa,* the trouble between the French and the Italians over it. The Italians think the painting belongs to them!"

"Alice, you can't accuse a man of being a thief because he's an Italian!"

"There's something else," I said. "Peruggia's a glazier. He's the one who recently put glass over the *Mona Lisa,* to protect it from vandals."

"Why is that important?"

"He would have been the last to touch it, the one most intimate with it."

"Alice, they were *all* intimate with it—Théophile Brion, who made its special frame; Roland Clement, who made the four iron pegs and wired it to the wall; Louis Bonnard, who cleaned it once a month. Intimacy is not argument!"

"Then I will tell you something that is! Peruggia's horoscope!"

"What?"

"I've done Peruggia's horoscope—with Max's help, of course. I am learning how to be an astrologer."

"That's nonsense, Alice! Nothing but superstition, a complete waste of time!"

"Listen to me for a moment, and I will prove it to you! Which of the last eleven years of your life, say since 1900, was the most difficult?"

Gertrude looked at me. "What are you asking?"

"Give me the date of the most difficult year of your life, so far."

Gertrude laughed. "I could name several!"

"Then do."

"Alice, what has this to do with the case?"

"Much," I answered.

Gertrude said nothing.

"All right, Gertrude. If you will not name it, then I will. I would say that the worst year of your life, to date, was 1903."

"What happened then?"

"Saturn was in your Sun sign."

"What?"

"You made a thorough mess of your life, Gertrude. You dropped out of medical school, just months short of getting your degree, and thus threw away four years of the most arduous work, to say nothing of a most promising career. There were other things

24

as well, equally unpleasant. You know what they were."

"Alice, *I will not have you talking to me this way!* That year *was* difficult. I will grant you that! But so have been many others. Many, *many* others. So what have you told me that I didn't already know?"

"I have told you why the *Mona Lisa* was stolen."

"Why?"

"The planet Saturn!"

"Alice, speak English!"

"Listen, and I will. Saturn is one of the eight planets, the most beautiful one of all. It is surrounded by many rings. Perhaps you studied it in school. I did. But it is also the most demanding. Saturn is the Great Teacher, the Celestial Task-Master. Approximately every thirty years, it passes through one's Sun sign."

"Alice, you are speaking nonsense!"

"Perhaps, but let me speak it! If one is living wisely when Saturn is in one's Sun sign, then this period can be one of great growth and new insights. But as most people do not live wisely, it can also be a painful time. Saturn asks great things of us. He sometimes tricks us, tempts us. He is always testing us. He demands perfection, and as most people are not perfect, they have a difficult time then. They do things they shouldn't."

"People are *always* doing things they shouldn't. Are you going to tell me they do this only once *every thirty years?*"

"I am saying that if you want to find out who stole the *Mona Lisa*, then look at the horoscopes of the suspects. Which man, potentially, had the greatest planetary pressures on him, and was therefore the most likely to give into his weaknesses? That man was Vincenzo Peruggia. He's a Taurus, and Saturn is now transiting that Sun sign."

Gertrude laughed. "Are only Tauruses having a difficult time now? It seems to me that a lot of people are unhappy. What about Pablo, to name one?"

"Picasso is a Scorpio."

"And Apollinaire and Marie Laurencin, both in prison? And Fernande, afraid to go out of her house for fear of being arrested? And me, who has just lost her best friend because he will never again be what I once thought he was, a genius? Aren't we *all* feeling Saturn?"

"There's a difference, Gertrude, between feeling sad, and feeling Saturn. It's a question of degree. Look at what Peruggia has done—stolen the most famous painting in the world and almost caused a war in the process! It *has* to be the work of Saturn, and Saturn is now in Taurus! *None* of the other suspects is a Taurus! Max and I did all their horoscopes!"

"Alice, I'm sorry to have to say this, in light of all your work. But you have convinced me of nothing. What you say is nonsense. No one in his right mind would believe it—not me, not the police."

"But we don't have to go to the police, Gertrude! We can go to Peruggia *himself!* He's still in Paris, still working at the Louvre, as if nothing had happened. I know his address. I know it might be risky, two lone women facing a criminal. But we could take Max with us. We could go and confront Peruggia with what we know!"

"And what is *that*, Alice? You haven't presented me with one shred of evidence that proves Peruggia's the thief. This is a criminal case. It must stand up in a court of law, before a judge and jury. We must deal with *facts*, not star lore and whimsy. I know you and Max were just trying to help. But you'd better leave the case to people who have a grasp of the real world!"

I sighed. "I know that I am not explaining it very well, Gertrude. This is all so new to me. And I know these aren't facts. But they are *truths*. After looking at many horoscopes, I am convinced of that. Sometimes the truth is different from facts—larger, intangible. But that doesn't take away from the fact that it is still there. Saturn is real, and does take its toll!"

"Alice, I did not know that you had become a philosopher, arguing about truth, as opposed to fact. It becomes you. But, as I said, we must deal with facts here. Anything else, however interesting, is just not helpful!"

Some weeks passed. And then, suddenly, the case began to pass out of Gertrude's hands.

A group of leading Frenchmen of arts and letters—Rodin, among them, I remember—indignant at the way the case was being handled, began to write letters to various newspapers. Joined by several well-known legal experts, the group managed to exert enough pressure on the authorities to force them to back down. Finally admitting that they did not have enough evidence to accuse either of the two suspects, Guillaume Apollinaire or Pablo Picasso, of the theft, the police reluctantly released them. Both men immediately fled France, Apollinaire to Italy, Picasso to some unknown

26

destination, not even staying in Paris long enough to leave word where he was going.

Weeks passed, and then months, the case gradually receding from our lives. Gertrude, involved in a new writing project, seemed no longer interested in the case. The Louvre returned to normal. A painting, Raphael's *Castiglione,* was hung in the place where the *Mona Lisa* had once been. And if the painting of a man with an ample beard, however handsome, could not really replace its predecessor, no one complained. France seemed at last resigned to its loss.

If France was resigned to its loss, I, however, was not. For I could not forget the case. It was not so much who the thief was that I wanted to know, but whether or not I had been right, about Saturn. So I continued to think about the case, seeing in it either a confirmation, or a negation, of my newfound astrological knowledge.

And then one day, about six months after the theft of the *Mona Lisa,* I finally had my answer, although it was to come in a way that I could never have foreseen.

I had developed, over the years, the hobby of collecting recipes, one begun out of sheer necessity, for if I didn't cook, Gertrude and I didn't eat. But as the years passed my hobby had also become something else, the means by which I had extended my eyes and ears over Paris. For to speak of food was to speak of many things. The best people, of course, with whom to speak of food were the cooks of our friends, and before it was over, I would know many cooks, and thus many things. And the first of my cooks was Fernande's and Picasso's, Dora.

On the day in question, on the day that I was finally to know about Saturn, I had been visiting Dora, talking to her about food, and thus learning that Picasso had come back to Paris, but that he was in hiding, afraid to return to the rue de Clichy, as his house was still being watched by the police. I expressed surprise at this. But, oh yes, Dora said, it was true. A policeman was there every day. I thanked Dora for her recipe—a particularly nice one for flan—and then left, noticing as I did that it was as she had said. Across the street, standing next to a lamp-post, twirling his billy club, was a policeman, watching Picasso's house.

I am not sure whether it was the sight of the policeman, or the story I had just heard about Picasso, still suspected of being the thief, that inspired me that day. Probably both. But I had not gone a dozen steps when the idea suddenly hit me. Of course, I thought, why not do it? Why not use the trouble that has been sent to you? It's the perfect plan!

My mind quickly began to take shape, plotting an itinerary. How was I going to get there? The obvious way would be to take the omnibus, going first down the rue La Fayette past St. Vincent de Paul's, then turning south onto the Magenta until I came to the Place de la Republique. And, with a bit of luck and some horses that were not too tired, I would be there in about half an hour. But that might be too soon, I suddenly realized. What time was it? I began listening for bells, but heard none, and then remembered that on my way over to Dora's, I had heard a clock chime four. It must now be close to five. I would have to kill some time, then. An hour should do it; that way I would arrive around six, when he was sure to be home. I would have to walk, then. I sighed, thinking ahead to where I was going, and not liking the prospect.

Discretion was the better part of valor, I had realized years before, while learning my way around the streets of Paris; there were some parts of town that were best left to themselves. Such was the one I was headed for now, a rundown section of Paris. Even in broad daylight, it was not a place to be. But it had to be done. Steadying myself, and looking over my shoulder to make sure of the policeman, I came to the corner of the street, turned, and began my journey.

I will not here describe the next hour, my walking down streets too numerous to name, until I had come to my objective, the district in question. The street itself, the rue de l'Hospital-Saint-Louis, was not hard to find, running alongside, as it did, the hospital itself. But the house, #5, was another matter. It was only after two turns up and down the street that I realized where it was, lodged between two houses, #3 and #9. Number 5 was as I had expected, a rundown rooming house, too poor even to have a concierge. Stopping before the house, I collected myself, knowing that from now on, whatever I did, for better or for worse, would be a part of history.

But first I must confront the policeman, for he, of course, was still with me. Seeing him on the corner, pretending not to notice me, although he had just followed me halfway across Paris, I decided to approach him directly. Going up to him, not even introducing myself, I wasted no time, telling him that I knew he was following me, but that that was part of the plan. I had led him here for a purpose. Then I spoke my mind. "I do not have time to argue with you," I said, "or even to explain. You will just have to take my word for it. But the great painting, the *Mona Lisa,* recently stolen from the Louvre, is in that building, #5. And if you want to go get it, I will help you. The thief is also in there!"

I will never forget the moment that followed, the policeman whose name I did not then know but who I would later find out was Pierre Chabert, looking at me as hard as I've ever been looked at, trying to tell from my eyes whether or not it was true, that the *Mona Lisa* was in a room not steps away. But he must have seen something, for he did not hesitate. Immediately taking charge, handing me his police whistle, he ordered me to go stand in the street, and to blow as hard as I could until more policemen came. Then, motioning me toward the street, he started toward the house.

It must be recorded that I did, that day, as I had been told, but I did not do so happily. For I had not just walked across the city of Paris in order to stand in the street and blow a whistle. Doing so just long enough to summon another policeman, to whom I hurriedly told the story, I then gave him the whistle and told *him* to blow hard. I had business elsewhere.

Moving toward the house, I quickly climbed the front steps, and entered the building. As my eyes began to adjust to the sudden darkness of the hall, I wondered which of the several rooms the thief was in. They I saw, at the end of the hall, an open door, with light streaming out into the corridor. The thief's room, I thought. Cautiously approaching, I crept along the hall, preparing myself for the worst. But if I had expected a fight, the thief overpowering the lone policeman Chabert, and then coming after me, that was not to be the case. For as I reached the open door, and looked into the room, I saw the sight of my life.

I had missed the opening moments of this scene, which I would later read about: the young man in the room—surprised by the sudden appearance of the policeman who he was sure had come for him—unable to do anything else but to reveal himself. Meekly, almost with relief, almost as if he were glad that it was finally over, the young man had motioned the policeman over to where he was standing, in the corner of the room, by his bed. It was then that I arrived, just in time to see something that would be forever fixed in my mind: the sight of a young man down on his knees, bent over a small trunk that he had just pulled from under his bed. Opening the trunk, almost apologetically, he began removing some articles of clothing—a pair of old shoes, some woolen underwear—and a bag of tools. Then lifting up a false bottom, he took out a painting. Before my eyes, what seemed to be the *Mona Lisa* suddenly appeared. When the policeman Chabert excitedly cried out, "Mon Dieu!"—and pointed to something on the back of the painting—the seal of the Louvre, I knew that it was true. The painting before us was, indeed, the *Mona Lisa!*

It was a sight to remember, the *Mona Lisa,* not six feet from where I was standing, its graceful form and face, with its inscrutable smile, imparting even to that shabby room a moment of rare beauty. But it was not to last. For suddenly the hall outside the room was filled with policemen, all wanting the thief. There were so many policemen that I was pushed aside, out into the hall, finally even out into the street. But that did not dampen my spirits, nor diminish my pleasure. For I had seen what I had come to see: the thief, and the *Mona Lisa!*

It would all be confirmed the next day, the identity of the thief, whose name was, in truth, Vincenzo Peruggia, and the fact that he had stolen the *Mona Lisa* from the Louvre. News of his arrest made headlines. Huge photographs of Chabert, Peruggia, and the trunk with its false bottom were suddenly on the front pages of newspapers throughout the world. There were celebrations everywhere, by the Italians, who wanted to honor one of their own, Vincenzo Peruggia, and by the French, who knew that their painting, the *Mona Lisa,* would soon be returned to them. On the day that occurred, 20,000 Frenchmen lined up outside the Louvre, hoping to be among the first to view once again their beloved painting.

Amidst all this celebration, there seemed to be only one unhappy person—Vincenzo Peruggia. Tried and found guilty of the theft, he was imprisoned in the Conciergerie. He did, however, seem to have one happy memory of his deed. Asked why he had stolen the *Mona Lisa,* Peruggia was quick to answer: because he felt that the painting had been unlawfully taken from Italy by the French. But he would never have stolen the painting had not he, a glazier in the Louvre, been asked to place protective glass over it. That was when it had happened. Holding the *Mona Lisa* in his hands, he had been overcome by its beauty. "I could not help myself," he said. *"She smiled at me!"*

Oddly enough, none of this had much impact on our household. Perhaps Gertrude remembered our earlier discussions about the case; perhaps she did not. But at any rate she seemed uninterested in its final outcome, or in the fact that the thief turned out to be one Vincenzo Peruggia. Deep into the writing of the book that would become her early masterpiece, *Tender Buttons,* she now seemed more interested in art than in crime. "The *Mona Lisa* is once again safe in the Louvre," she said. "What more needs to be said?"

I, of course, knew that much more could be said, especially about who the real thief had been, and about who had helped to find him. But I said nothing. For one does not have to get recognition for one's deeds, I also knew, in order to have the satisfaction of having done them. I was, however, curious about one thing.

"Gertrude?" I asked. "And Picasso? You haven't spoken to him since he returned to Paris. When are you going to forgive him?"

Gertrude looked at me, her dark eyes blazing. *"When he takes that smile off my face!"*

Murder by Snail

Nancy R. Herndon

EASING THE STRAP of her leather bag from one shoulder to the other, Detective Sergeant Elena Jarvis inventoried the improbable collection of people in the living room.

One patrolman who had put in the call and now wore a peculiar expression, almost as if he were about to burst out laughing. (If this was another joke cooked up by the boys in the squad room, she'd kill them.)

One good looking, dark-haired female Caucasian, about thirty-five, wearing a beautifully cut rose wool suit. (Elena would have traded a week on the day shift for a suit like that.)

One red-bearded Caucasian male wearing a sweatshirt that said, "Poets do it in iambic pentameter." (Obviously a total jerk—like Frank, Elena's ex-husband.)

One blonde airhead in Reeboks and an expensive jogging suit.

The poet and the airhead had greasy yellow spots on their clothes, as well as red marks and peeved expressions on their faces.

"What have we got, Officer Pollock?" Elena asked, not really wanting to know.

"Hard to say for sure, Detective. Attempted murder. Assault with a deadly weapon." The patrolman made an odd snorting sound.

"What weapon, Officer Pollock?" She didn't see any weapons.

"A snail, ma'am." Pollock then gave in to a series of undignified snickers.

Mr. Iambic Pentameter, flushed with indignation, shouted, "You think this is funny, do you? My ex-wife tried to murder me."

Elena sighed and asked sarcastically, "How? Did she hurl the snail at you?" This had to be a precinct joke.

"I don't like your attitude," snarled the poet.

Elena didn't care much for his either. "Let's start with your names."

The woman in the tailored suit, who had been looking amused, bestirred herself. "I'm Dr. Sarah Tolland, Chairman of the Electrical Engineering department at the University. That's Miss Kowolski, my ex-husband's fiance." She nodded toward the blonde in the jogging suit. "Miss Kowolski is, I'm told, an aerobics instructor, as well as a vegetarian."

"I didn't want to come here," complained Miss Kowolski. "I told Gussie I didn't. Everyone knows about people like engineers and atomic scientists and people like that; they eat absolutely poisonous things—red meat and eggs—you know—and they hate vegetables, and they. . . ."

Did she think she'd been poisoned? Elena wondered. With a snail? Neither one of them was gagging—or vomiting—or dead.

"The—ah—gentleman is my ex-husband, Angus McGlenlivie," concluded Dr. Tolland, finishing the introduction once Miss Kowolski had wound down. An ironic smile flitted across Sarah Tolland's face.

Elena was intrigued and found herself rather liking the electrical engineer, if that's what the woman really was.

"I'm sure you've heard of Gus." Sarah glanced benignly at her former husband. "He's the author of the well known poetry collection, *Erotica in Reeboks,* published by the Phallic Press of Casper, Wyoming."

Phallic Press? Now Elena knew they were putting her on.

"Phoenix Press," snapped Angus McGlenlivie, "and you needn't sneer, Sarah. I'm the only tenure-track poet the University's ever had, and *Erotica in Reeboks* is about to go into its third edition."

"A tribute to the taste of the poetry-reading public, I'm sure," said Dr. Tolland, and she turned back to Elena. "Be that as it may, Gus seems to feel that I attempted to injure him with a snail."

"That's right," said the poet. "She lured me over here promising snails in garlic butter and then exploded one in my face—and Bimmie's."

"Bimmie?" asked Elena, beginning to feel confused.

"That's me," said Miss Kowolski, pouting, "and this is a designer jogging suit. It cost almost a whole week's salary, and now it's got garlic butter all *over*."

"Soak it in cold water," Elena advised. An exploding snail? McGlenlivie had to be kidding. "How did your ex-wife cause this explosion?" she asked. Their little marital tiff had had an authentic ring to it, and hadn't she read a news report somewhere on exploding snails?

"She turned on the blender in the kitchen."

"You think the *blender* triggered the explosion?" This man was as crazy as he looked.

"Yes," said McGlenlivie. "She probably had it wired."

"And here I thought I was just making hollandaise sauce," murmured Sarah Tolland.

"You've never made hollandaise sauce in your life, Sarah," snapped McGlenlivie. "I couldn't believe it when you offered to make snails in garlic butter."

"So it was at Dr. Tolland's suggestion that you come here, you and Miss Kowolski?" Elena couldn't believe that she was asking these questions. What *was* that snail story she'd read?

"Well, I invited us," McGlenlivie admitted. "I wanted Sarah to meet my new fiance."

Now *that* had to take the prize for insensitivity, thought Elena. If Frank, her own ex-husband, had wanted to bring over a fiance, she might have exploded a snail in his face too.

"But it was *Sarah* who insisted we come to dinner."

"And then she exploded the snail with the blender? While making hollandaise sauce?" Elena dropped into a chair. Halfway through her shift, dead on her feet, and she was stuck with three lunatics and a giggling street cop—for Pollock was at it again. Elena gave him a hard look. She no longer believed that this was an elaborate practical joke, but only because her colleagues couldn't have come up with anything so weird. That bunch had all the ingenuity of secondhand bubble gum.

"So your contention is that your ex-wife exploded the snail by making hollandaise sauce? Is that right?" Elena took out a notebook. Maybe she could send this in to the *Reader's Digest*.

"How the hell do I know what she was making?" said McGlenlivie peevishly.

"Hollandaise," confirmed Sarah. "You can check that out if you like, Detective."

"She's an electrical engineer. Can you think of anyone better qualified to figure out how to make hollandaise sauce and kill me at the same time?"

"Do you have some reason to believe that your ex-wife would want to kill you, Mr. McGlenlivie?" Elena asked.

"Who can understand the nature of woman?" said the poet with a grand gesture. "Women are mysterious creatures."

And men are morons, thought Elena. How had Sarah Tolland, who seemed the most normal of the three, got herself married to this particular moron? "We usually hope for a more concrete motive, Mr. McGlenlivie, at least if the case goes to trial."

"Jealousy," said the poet. "She was always jealous. And she's probably still irritated about the divorce."

"You surprise me, Gus," said Sarah. "Didn't you tell me yourself that we had a friendly divorce?"

Elena noticed a certain dryness in Sarah's voice and glanced at her sharply. "Is that the way *you* view the divorce, Dr. Tolland?"

"She resented my coaching the girl's intramural volleyball team too," said Gus.

"How could I resent that," murmured Sarah, "when the team provided the inspiration for a book of poetry that went to three editions?"

"True," Gus agreed.

Erotica in Reeboks? Had he been fooling around with the whole team while Sarah was home making hollandaise? Elena could see that it might be tempting to explode a snail in the face of a man like McGlenlivie, but would a jury buy it?

"You definitely resented all my pretty little poetesses calling the house. Why else would you get us an unlisted number?"

"Just trying to protect your writing time, Gus. I'm sure Winnie—"

"Bimmie," corrected the vegetarian fiance.

"— Bimmie will want to do the same."

So he had been unfaithful with female students as well as female athletes, not to mention wanting to introduce his fiance to his ex-wife. Sarah Tolland certainly had a motive, and she had created the opportunity, which left the M.O. Could you kill a man with an exploding snail—or even injure him seriously? And how would you go about it?

Elena had been sprawled in one of the comfortable tobacco-brown silk chairs, resting her feet as she questioned McGlenlivie and his ex-wife. Now she rose and wandered through the dining room into the kitchen. According to the poet, Sarah had turned the blender on just before the explosion. Well, that must be the blender in question. It looked innocuous enough, didn't seem to have any suspicious attachments.

She glanced over her shoulder to make sure no one was in the dining room, then threw the blender switch. It burst into whirring life. No explosion followed. She turned the machine off, lifted the lid from the container, and sampled the contents. Hollandaise sauce, rather bad hollandaise. For one thing, it was too lemony. She replaced the lid and removed the container in order to examine the bottom of the base. It appeared to be innocent of any sinister tampering. Then she stared thoughtfully at the blender. Could it be rigged to explode a snail shell? If that were possible, a doctor of electrical engineering might well be the person to do it.

Elena abandoned the blender and returned to the dining room to examine the scene of the crime—or non crime. Nice teakwood dining set, she noted admiringly. Sarah Tolland had good taste—in clothes and furniture, if not in men. "Which shell exploded?"

"There—that one," cried McGlenlivie, jumping up to poke his finger at one of the twelve snail shell compartments in the round plate.

Elena studied the plate. Eleven shells were intact; one was in pieces. Eleven compartments were swimming in garlic butter; one was nearly empty, no doubt because its garlic butter was now spattered on the dinner guests. She leaned forward for a closer look. Half submerged in bits of shell and garlic butter lay a curl of purplish-brown stuff. She picked up a small fork and nudged it.

"Snail," said Sarah Tolland quickly.

Elena nodded.

"She turned on that blender and ka-boom—shell fragments flying all over the place," said McGlenlivie. "It was terrifying."

Ka-boom? Shell fragments? He made it sound like a Batman comic strip or a World War II movie on late night TV. Elena's ex-husband had been addicted to that *macho* garbage.

"Look here." Gus pointed to a small cut on his cheek. "Shell fragments. I'm lucky I didn't lose an eye."

"And I probably *will* lose my suit," added Bimmie, clearly still anguished over the damage to her lilac velour jogging outfit.

"We were both scalded by hot garlic butter."

Scalded by hot butter—that rang a bell.

"I offered you antiseptic burn cream," Sarah reminded him. Then she smiled at Elena, a tolerant adult dealing with hysterical children.

"Burn cream?" Bimmie whimpered. "What good will that do? What if I need plastic surgery? I'm only nineteen. I'm too young for plastic surgery."

Elena examined the three red splotches on the girl's face. "First degree," she judged.

"Is that bad?" asked Bimmie anxiously. "Will I be scarred?"

"You'll be as good as new in a week," Elena assured her.

"She will not. Whose side are you on anyway?" A frustrated Gus tugged wildly at his red beard. "An attempt has been made on my life. I'm a respected poet. My following. . . ."

Elena stopped listening because she had finally remembered about exploding snails. "Mr. McGlenlivie, are you aware that snails have been known to blow up on their own?" she asked. "There was a case reported in the papers. A restaurant patron received painful burns when an exploding snail spewed hot garlic butter in his face. What would cause that, Professor?" Elena asked, turning to Sarah Tolland. "Pressure building up while the snail was cooking?"

Sarah shrugged. "Quite possibly."

Had Sarah got the idea from the news report and manufactured her own exploding snail, Elena wondered, or was she just lucky? Either way, Elena didn't think the D.A. would want to prosecute. Howl with laughter, yes. Prosecute, no. Especially with a victim like Angus McGlenlivie in his "Poets do it in iambic pentameter" sweatshirt.

"You might have a civil case against your ex-wife, Mr. McGlenlivie, but—"

"What's that supposed to mean?"

"For damages. You could sue her."

"That's a good idea, Gussie," said the aerobics fiance. "I could at least get my jogging suit replaced."

"My life is at stake here. Who cares about your damned jogging suit?"

"You don't seem to have suffered serious injury," Elena

pointed out as she tucked her notebook into her heavy leather shoulder bag.

"You're not going to arrest her?" The poet was livid. "I warn you, I'll write a letter to the newspapers."

Elena nodded. "Sounds like a good outlet for a poet. Officer Pollock, maybe you could see Mr. McGlenlivie and Miss Kowolski to their car?"

"We jogged over," said Bimmie.

"That's it?" McGlenlivie's face was redder than his beard. "She tries to murder me, and all you do is see me to my car?"

"Well, no, Mr. McGlenlivie, not if you don't have one."

The poet slapped his chest and proclaimed, "Let us weep for civilization, which is, alas, in the final, tragic stages of decay."

Elena gaped at him.

"What could be more self-evident," he continued, arms waving dramatically, "when our very bards and prophets can be victimized by malicious technocrats?"

Sarah Tolland responded with a clear-eyed smile. Angus McGlenlivie dropped his arms and scowled at her. "You may expect to see yourself the subject of a satiric verse in my next volume, Sarah." With that threat, his fiance in tow, and Officer Pollock snickering along behind, Angus McGlenlivie stalked out.

Elena turned to Dr. Tolland. "How did you happen to marry him?" she asked curiously.

"Just one of those mistakes people make when civilization is in the final, tragic stages of decay," said Sarah.

"Uh huh." Elena grinned. "And how did you manage to explode that snail shell?" Although she knew she couldn't make a case against Sarah Tolland—unless, of course, Sarah confessed—Elena had the nagging suspicion that she had actually been investigating an attempted murder—or something. She'd like to know what. Dr. Tolland just laughed and relaxed into a chair, her long legs crossed comfortably at the ankle.

"Look, Dr. Tolland, maybe you ought to think about some therapy." If the woman had actually tried to blow up her ex-husband, then Elena felt an obligation to head off any further attempts. "Divorce can be traumatic. No one knows that better than I."

"Oh? Are you divorced, Detective?" For the first time that evening Sarah Tolland looked interested.

"Recently divorced. And I belong to a very good support

group." If she could get Sarah into the group, she could keep an eye on her, keep her from exploding any more snail shells in her idiot husband's vicinity, if that's what she had done. And get to know her, as well. Aside from having married an idiot, something that could happen to any woman, Professor Tolland seemed a likeable and interesting person. "I'd be glad to take you along to the next session."

"Thank you."

An ambiguous reply. Well, in for a penny— "We could have dinner together before the meeting."

"I'd like that." Sarah Tolland smiled.

Pleased, Elena smiled back. "I'll give you a call."

Once she saw through the window that Detective Jarvis had driven away, Sarah strolled over to the dining room table and stared thoughtfully at the purple-brown shred nestled among the snail shell fragments and congealed butter. How unusually astute of Gus to realize that his exploding snail had not been a natural phenomenon. It hadn't even been a snail—not that one. Fortunately, snails were much the same color as plastique, a fact that Detective Jarvis evidently did not know, although the lady had obviously guessed that something was amiss.

Of course, it hadn't been an attempted murder, just a little electronic hint to Gus, and it hadn't gone exactly according to plan. Sarah certainly hadn't planned to be visited by the police. On the other hand, a partial success was quite good enough. She had judged the amount of explosive nicely, no one had been hurt, and she'd accomplished her purpose. Gus was unlikely to suggest any more cozy evenings involving her and his fiances, his cow-eyed poetesses, or his nubile female volleyball players. Sarah had endured quite enough of that kind of thing during their marriage.

Then she smiled. Detective Jarvis might well turn out to be a new and interesting friend. Gathering up the snail platters, Sarah went into the kitchen to see if her hollandaise was salvageable. Maybe she should have invited the detective to share the rest of the dinner. No, she'd see her at the therapy group, and in the meantime, there was the pseudo snail to dispose of—carefully, very very carefully.

Mrs. Dunlop's First Case

Caroline Stafford

I WENT TO THE FUNERAL. It seemed like a good idea at the time, because I'd known Miss Wooten for seven years. Not well, you understand. She lived in the old house on the hill and was a recluse. The only people who crossed her threshold were her doctor, her three nephews, the handyman her niece sent when anything needed fixing, and the niece herself. Nobody else ever got Miss Wooten to open her door—except me. Sometimes she'd call up and ask me to pick up a few things at the store for her. Not often, because the nephews shopped for her once a month. But when the weather was bad and she was low on perishables, I'd take her what she needed. It had started not long after she'd inherited that old barn of a place from her brother Gerald. She only called me then because she had run out of eggs and we'd had such a storm that not even the snowplows could make it to Merton for almost a week, much less the nephews. We were used to that here in the mountains, like any Blue Ridge town. Maybe it was because I never pushed to know her better that she felt free to ask again. Being a widow myself, I know how easy it is to get set in your ways and not want to change them.

The whole town was upset when she died fiddling with a broken toaster that wasn't broken enough. Electrocuted herself. She lay dead in that house almost a week, according to the coroner, until a nephew came and found her.

So off to the funeral I went, like I said, wearing my best black straw hat. The three nephews and the niece were there, long horse-faces enough alike to show their Wooten blood, just like their aunt. The handyman didn't come, naturally, though he probably knew her better than her kin. Neither was the niece's husband present. In Pennsylvania, somebody said. He travelled on business. The nephews' wives were there, all in black and looking somber, though they were probably glad the old lady was dead before she got so feeble she had to move in with one of them. Not a lot of money in the family, though I'd heard tales that Gerald Wooten, Miss Wooten's brother, had once been rich. Going broke was the only reason anybody in Merton could think of for a man who had lived in California to come back here to die, a quiet little backwater like this with Charlottesville the nearest town of any size. The fact was that he'd had a real bad heart, but we didn't know that until it killed him, because he'd been a worse recluse than his sister was.

And do you know, not one member of that whole horse-faced family spoke a word to me at the services? Not that I'd done anything more than keeping a neighborly eye on Miss Wooten, but it would have been common courtesy for them to say afterwards, "Thank you for coming, Mrs. Dunlop." I'm no spring chicken, you know, and it's a long way from Merton to Charlottesville, where she was buried. Mad at myself for taking the trouble when it wasn't wanted, I stood by the grave and wished I was home scrubbing floors.

By the time I did get home, I was taking pleasure in making up nasty tales about the Wootens, excepting the old lady of course. Not that I'd spread such lies, no, it was just the satisfaction of blackening the character when I couldn't very well blacken those snooty eyes.

Instead of feeling better, by the time I'd had some coffee and homemade pound cake I was working around to having the family murdering the old lady. Before long, I decided that maybe they *had*—that's the worst part of living alone, there's nobody to tell you to stop being ridiculous. Tossing and turning in bed that night, I tried to think how to go about proving such a thing.

Well, who came to the house, besides the doctor? The nephews, George, Henry and Albert Wooten, but never their wives. The niece, Hazel MacRae, but never her husband Paul. And the handyman, Tom. No need to count myself, of course. Nor any strangers, because why should they walk in and kill an old lady with a toaster and then walk out again without touching anything in the house?

She even kept her purse in the hall, where I'd seen it every time she paid me for milk or eggs or bread.

George was the one that found her. And I know she was all right on the Tuesday before that, because I took her a quart of buttermilk and a box of soda crackers which she paid me for there and then. So Tom must have been the last to see her alive, when he fixed a rod in one of the clothes closets the very next day—a Wednesday, that was. I watched him carry the new one from his truck to the side door. Henry, Albert and Hazel hadn't been near her for three weeks. Unfortunately. If you've got a murder, you've got to have a murderer, and on the face of it, it seemed like I was fresh out of one.

So I got up and put on my robe and went down to my kitchen. I made sure the shades were down, because my neighbor Naomi was likely to come barging in to see if I was sick or something, with my lights on this late. Hauling out my old toaster, I set it on the cabinet and stared at it. I prefer oven toast, myself, but my late husband liked it brown on both sides. Putting in some bread, I remembered that one slot used to stick so that it wouldn't always come up before the toast burned. That brought back fond memories of my late husband picking the whole thing up and shaking out the bread before it was black. What if somebody had fixed Miss Wooten's toaster so that it jammed, and to keep her bread from burning, she tried to fish it out with a knife, woman-fashion? How was she to know, without a man there to yell at her, that she'd get electrocuted? I'd nearly done it once myself, before ours was fixed. Maybe not a certain way to murder somebody—unless you knew they liked toaster toast—but sure and untraceable. I sat there, nibbling the stack of toast I'd made, and thinking about it. That was how.

Now to the *why* and *who*. The only murderer we'd had around here was the Jacobs boy who shot a gas station attendant over in Ivy and robbed the till. A good fifteen years ago, that was. But Miss Wooten didn't have much money. Still, everybody used to think her brother did. What if he was a miser and had hidden the last of it somewhere in that old house? And somebody suspected it?

Then the question would be, who had time to look for it? The family when they visited, of course. Or Tom, while making repairs. But it wasn't likely that Miss Wooten would let *him* out of her sight long enough for him to go around searching, and he never stayed long anyway, just did the odd jobs and left. Besides, he'd be the first suspect if the police found a rigged toaster. But one of the family might have come across something and then decided to get rid of Miss Wooten so they could tear down a wall or uproot a floor, which she wouldn't allow if she was around.

But how to prove it? I thought about that awhile, and then went to the kitchen cabinet, got out a pencil and four sheets of paper, and began printing in large letters with my left hand. I HAVE PROOF— 9 PM TONIGHT. I KNOW HOW—10 PM TONIGHT. SHE TOLD ME—11 PM TONIGHT. I SAW YOU—12 PM TO-NIGHT. Folding the sheets, I put each one in an envelope. The next day I went into town, stopping first at the bank because it was closest. There I had to wait nearly fifteen minutes for the new girl to finish with my deposit, her whispering on the phone behind her hand most of the time and holding one old twenty I'd given her as if it had germs crawling all over it. That made me late, and I hurried down to the grocery store to borrow their Charlottesville telephone directory. The first letter I addressed to George, the second to Henry, the third to Hazel, and the last to Albert. Off they went on my way home, though before I got to the post office I ran into half of Merton, from Howie Jameson, our police chief, down to Eddie, the boy who brings my paper, all of them wanting to stand and talk and me fretting I'd miss the afternoon's mail collection.

The Wooten house was closed up, but I was certain everybody in the family had a key. All I had to do now was to sit in my front room with the lights off and the curtains open and my late husband's binoculars in my hand. When the one with the guilty conscience read my note, he or she would come to the Wooten place at the appointed time—and I'd watch them arrive. Then I'd telephone Howie Jameson, tell him the story, and let him do the rest.

That's how certain I was. You can be a big fool when you live alone and talk to nobody but yourself.

The letters would arrive on Tuesday. I'd paid enough bills by mail to Charlottesville to know how long it took if your letter was in Merton post office before three. But if nobody showed up, I'd simply watch on Wednesday night as well. It never occurred to me that nobody would even bother.

So there I sat in the dark all Tuesday night and didn't even see the Henderson cat, much less a Wooten. I had a headache all the next day. And Naomi came over to see why I'd gone to bed so early. I had to pretend I'd taken cold at the funeral and was trying to get some rest. I even coughed once or twice, so she wouldn't be won-

43

dering why the lights went off early again.

Wednesday night I saw the Henderson cat twice, and nothing else. Thursday night I watched again out of sheer cussedness while I tried to decide what I should do next to stir up the murderer.

Nine o'clock came. No George. Ten, and no sign of Henry. By eleven I wasn't expecting Hazel, and just as well. She didn't come. Maybe her husband was home and she couldn't get away. From where I sat I could see the house plain, front and sides. It began to look scary after awhile, and I thought about Miss Wooten laying there dead for days . . . alone. . . .

I jumped when the clock on the mantel struck midnight—and almost missed the sound of the china cabinet tinkling. I'd known that sound for thirty years. Somebody was in my kitchen and had stepped on the loose floor board by the cabinet.

"Naomi? That you?" I called, hoping she'd come over to see if I was in a raging fever or something. Nobody answered. I got up to fumble for the light switch, and before I could reach it a gloved hand clamped down over my mouth. My heart dropped into my shoes, and the next thing I knew I was being dragged down the hall in spite of all I could do. Somebody had turned off the stove light I'd left burning and the kitchen was as black as the rest of the house. There I was shoved to the floor and something brushed my hair before settling over my face. A rope? Shaking it off, I began to kick and fight all the harder, knocking over a chair before connecting with somebody's shin and breaking free long enough to yell as hard as I could. At the same time I rammed an elbow into something soft and scrambled across the floor to the back door, swinging it open and yelling again before I was caught. Back came the hand, and back across the kitchen I was yanked. This time the rope came over my head and stayed there, pulled tight enough around my neck to knock the rest of the fight out of me. Next thing I knew the stove light was back on and I was being hauled up on a chair, and before I could make sense of that, I felt the rope go taut above my head. Which meant it was being looped over that heavy hook my late husband had put up for me. It was there to hang a clothesline on in winter, and now it was to be *me* hanging from it, not the wash. The rope was too tight for me to scream, but I danced a tiptoe jig on that chair trying to get free and tore at the noose with my hands. He was back in a flash, the chair went over, and instead of tiptoes, I was dancing on air. The rope was cutting into my throat and what little breath I'd had was gone. There I was, swinging and flailing and already half dead of fright, a sudden red haze all around me and noise everywhere. Then I realized that somebody else was in the kitchen, and over all the shouts I could hear scuffling before the rope swung me enough to see Howie Jameson sitting on something. Just as that fact had registered, I blacked out.

I came to on the floor, Howie scowling down at me and Naomi holding my head, and Clem Farley, the other half of Merton's police force, trying to get some of my late husband's whiskey down my throat. Pushing him away, I sat up, felt sick, then dizzy, then forgot everything when I saw the huddled figure in handcuffs stretched out beside my stove.

A round, pale face looked up at me. Not George. Or Henry. Or Albert. Not even Hazel. The handyman, then? I'd only seen him at a distance. "But I didn't send *him* a letter," I managed to wheeze.

"What letter? What are you talking about?" Howie wanted to know. "How much mischief have you gotten yourself into?"

"Mischief my foot! I was trying to find out who killed old Miss Wooten, because you weren't doing anything about it!" I croaked hotly.

"*I* didn't kill her!" Howie's prisoner tried to sit up, wide-eyed and babbling. "She was already dead. It's true, I tell you!"

Howie nodded at Clem like an old know-it-all. "These two must be in on this together," he said. "Maybe he's come to launder the money, for a cut."

"Did he find it?" I demanded in a raw whisper, trying to get a word in edgewise. "I could have told you—"

But it was no use, Howie's prisoner was still gabbling like a turkey. "Aunt Betty called Hazel one morning to tell her she'd found old Gerald's money. Stuffed in a hollow pole he'd used for a clothes rod in the bedroom closet. One end fell out of the plaster, and rolls of bills came sliding out. Only, Hazel was at the hairdressers. So I told Aunt Betty to hide the rod and the money in the back hall and say nothing to anybody until I'd had a look. I said none of us wanted that old scandal raked up."

"What scandal?" Naomi asked. She likes scandals.

"Old Gerald served his time, but the money from the bank robbery was never recovered. Everybody thought one of his partners had hidden it, the ones who were killed," he was saying, paying no attention to her. "And Aunt Betty wanted no part of reporters and police coming around until we knew for sure who's money it was. So I sent Tom over to put up a new rod on Wednesday, then without telling Hazel what had happened, I pretended to leave that afternoon on my next trip, just as usual. Only I circled back and broke in to get the money. There was $63,000! I was ready to knock the old woman over the head if I had to, I'll admit that, but she was already—"

"You're Paul MacRae!" I broke in in astonishment, suddenly realizing I'd been wrong about who he was. He nodded, and I turned to Howie and told him my side of the story. Quickly revised, of course, leaving out any little mistakes I might have made.

I had to tell it twice because Howie didn't believe me at first, and there was a lot of confusion for awhile.

Seems that when I brought her those groceries on the Tuesday morning when she'd found the money, Miss Wooten had paid me with one of the old bank notes from the closet rod. (Tight-fisted as she was, it would have been just like her to spend Gerald's money instead of her own.) After the funeral, I'd put that money in the bank on my way to the post office. And the new girl noticed the old style bill, of a kind banks don't see these days, and trying to show off, she called Howie, whispering that maybe it ought to be looked into. And when he checked the serial number, Howie found it matched the loot from a robbery Gerald Wooten had been part of. So he decided I must have slipped into the Wooten place and found Gerald's cache after Miss Wooten's death. And he'd started watching me that very day, to see what I'd done with the rest of the money.

Then Hazel had gotten the "SHE TOLD ME" letter and while she thought I was just trying to rake up the old story about her late uncle being a robber, she talked about handing it over to the police. That put the fear of God into her husband, who guessed I must have sent it. He was afraid old Miss Wooten had told me about the money too, so he came to shut me up before I could spill the beans.

But Howie was already keeping an eye on me, parking his car in the woods behind my house every night, like they do on the television. That's how he'd heard my screams and gotten here in the nick of time. Merton hadn't ever needed a stakeout before, and I think the old fool was enjoying himself. No wonder it was left to me to solve Miss Wooten's murder.

"But I didn't kill her!" MacRae was repeating, quivering like a jelly.

"Take a closer look at that toaster," I said darkly, and was glad when they took Paul MacRae away so Naomi could help me up to bed. Being a detective was hard, tiring work. Dangerous, too. My late husband would have a fit if he'd known what I had been up to.

But Paul MacRae was right. There was nothing rigged in the toaster, and he hadn't killed Miss Wooten after all. Still, he'd broken into her house, taken the money without reporting it or the body, and he'd tried to kill me. They put my picture in the papers during the trial, and MacRae got thirty years. I bet his wife was wishing then that she'd been nicer to me at the funeral. Everybody in Merton came to talk to me about the case. But that was six months ago, and people forget quick. Still, I've gotten three letters in the mail already asking me to solve some crime somebody suspected had happened and the police won't believe them. I'm thinking about doing it, too. It beats loneliness any day, even at the risk of being murdered.

The Cherry on the Cake

Lea Cash-Domingo

I'M A PRIVATE EYE.

I work for a living. Not everybody does. Some work to keep busy, some to offer a helping hand or a sympathetic ear. I work because I have to work. That fact determines what liberties I take. For those cases paid by the hour I take my time, and for those paid by the job I cut as many corners as possible.

Some cases are more desirable than others. Some I know straight away I'm going to like. With others, I smell trouble from the moment the client says hello.

That's how it was with the Hall woman. She came into my office that afternoon looking like an entertainer without her act. She was about five feet ten, maybe thirty-five, with wavy brown hair and a pink Qiana dress beneath a white knee-length coat. I figured she was either a highly paid professional or married to money. The clothes were worth a good five hundred bucks.

"Can I help you?" I asked. "I'm Amando Russo."

"I want to see the person in charge of Search Incorporated."

"You're looking at her." It was more embarrassing for her than it was for me. I'm used to it.

She didn't disappear. Instead she sat. "I'm in trouble."

"Most people are when they walk through that door. What's your trouble called?"

"I need to find someone. Do you do that sort of thing?"

"It's what I do best. Are you trying to locate a husband or a boyfriend?"

"It isn't that sort of problem." She seemed reluctant to talk about it.

"Maybe you better tell me about it."

"Well," she hesitated. "I'm pretty sure you don't get many responses like mine."

"Let me be the judge."

"I'm trying to find out who I am."

She was right: I didn't get many requests like hers.

"There's more, though. I think I may have killed someone."

She had awakened that morning at The Lodge, a B-rated motel on University Avenue in Berkeley with no idea how she got there or how long she'd been there. She thought her name was Dani Hall because the name sounded familiar and she liked the ring of it.

Inside her purse was a wad of money, which was a good thing because it might be a few days before I discovered where she belonged. Besides the money, there was a Revlon lipstick, a pair of black sunglasses with silver sequins on the frames, a red scarf, and a pack of Kleenex. No wallet, credit cards, driver's license, checkbook, keys, or other items usually found in a woman's purse.

She didn't recall having a husband or boyfriend, but she was haunted by the idea that she had shot a man. She'd had a nightmare in which there was a gun. It was pointed at someone whose features she couldn't see, and the gun fired. The blast still rang inside her head.

When a queer assignment has the bad manners to land in my lap, I begin with what seems obvious. My task was to take what she said at face value. If she thought she had killed someone, chances were pretty good that she had. Or come close.

I called The Lodge and spoke with the manager, who told me a woman by the name of Dani Hall had registered Monday evening and paid a week's tab. Today was Wednesday. Next I called the Berkeley Police Department. I gave the clerk a description of my Jane Doe. The missing persons' file offered no match.

Sergeant Williams in Homicide had deposited a stiff at the morgue three days ago. He had also apprehended the killer. Was he sure he had the right suspect, I asked him. Yes, he was sure—he had an eyewitness.

I was on the phone most of two hours. After dialing Homicide in eight counties and countless cities, I made room for the near misses and began calling hospital emergency wards. At four o'clock I hit paydirt. Sunday evening, Kaiser emergency in Oakland and Mt. Diablo in Concord had admitted gunshot victims.

I didn't need to debate with myself over whether to make the trips. If the case could be solved quickly, I'd be able to pay the utilities, phone and janitorial bills with the three hundred dollars Hall had given me.

The gunshot victim at Oakland Kaiser turned out to be a false alarm. A man returning home from a weekend of hunting duck had accidentally shot himself in the leg while cleaning his rifle. The bullet had bruised his leg and after examination the physician had sent him home with an ice-pack and a prescription for codeine.

At Mt. Diablo, the nurse informed me I'd have to talk to the attending physician, who was scheduled to be on the ward the next morning, and no, I couldn't have his phone number. Nor could I give her my number to pass on to the doctor.

It was seven when I returned to my office. Before I called it a day, I looked up the Halls in the white pages of the Contra Costa and Alameda County directories. The surname Hall is like Smith. There were columns and columns of them. By eight-thirty, I'd called each. No Dani Hall.

I phoned my client at The Lodge. She'd awakened from a nap minutes earlier and was eager to talk about her dream. She'd seen a painted arrow wedged in the trunk of a genealogical tree. She wondered if it was significant. I told her I'd sleep on it, which is what I did. In the morning, I found it made as much sense to me as it had to her. I took my vitamins with scrambled eggs and the day's paper, then I drove to Concord to follow up on yesterday's lead.

Dr. Lewis, the attending physician at Mt. Diablo, was a reasonable man. He told me he'd patched up a victim of a gunshot wound who had lost a lot of blood, and after observing his progress for fourteen hours had sent him across the street to a psychiatrist named Weinstein.

Dr. Weinstein agreed to see me before his ten o'clock patient. He was a short, stocky man with a bald head and wire-rimmed glasses. "I remember the man, of course," he said. "I saw him Monday morning. I recommended counseling as soon as possible, but he wasn't interested."

I told him about my client.

"Funny thing, amnesia," he said, fiddling with a thick rubber band. "You might do well to have her looked at. These dissociative disorders can be tricky to diagnose, and until you've got an accurate diagnosis you can't be sure what you're dealing with."

I shifted uneasily in my chair and he continued. "Let's assume you're right. Let's suppose your client has psychogenic amnesia and her disturbance is simply limited to a sudden inability to recall important personal information. Then you're on the right track."

I didn't want to be mystified for the rest of the day. I wanted answers.

"I'd like to do the right thing," I said. "The immediate problem is that she thinks she may have killed someone. Dr. Lewis seemed to think there might be a connection between my client and the man he referred to you."

He let go of the rubber band and leaned across the desk. "The man's son is in the custody of the county juvenile authorities in Martinez. Nasty piece of business. The boy claims he shot his father to protect his mother. The man, on the other hand, denies the existence of a wife. That doesn't mean he doesn't have one. These rigid types are usually married."

"Can you tell me his name?"

By law he wasn't supposed to, but he did, anyway. "Pierce. Jack Pierce."

My client's image of an arrow piercing a tree came to mind. Maybe I was on the right track after all.

The traffic moved along like a herd of cattle on the way to a waterhole. I left behind an entanglement of freeways and high-rises and entered the color-coded zone of condominiums and fast-food chains.

George Bellows worked the day shift. He was a large man with a don't-mess-with-me manner—the kind of counselor overnight psychiatric facilities advertise for in the *Tribune*. When I introduced myself and told him the purpose of my visit, he led me through a locked door to a staff lounge where we could talk privately.

"I can't say if Daniel Pierce is the boy you're looking for," he said. "The boy's in a bad way. He's been inside a few times."

"What's his mother like?"

"I never met the lady, but I can tell you a thing or two about the father. He's the type who comes home after a rough day's work, gets plastered, then beats the daylights out of his son in the name of discipline."

I had come across men who raised their sons by the back of the belt. They came from all walks: some were cops, some were blue-collar foremen, some were Silicon Valley executives. Their method of discipline didn't cure teenagers of their wildness: it usually made them wilder.

Bellows lit a cigarette. "Daniel is a kid who grew up too fast. First time he was picked up it was for hot-wiring a car. Next time it was for pawning his old man's diamond-studded watch. Every time he's been brought in, he's had black eyes and bruises. The kid's fourteen and growing. I mean, this boy's big. Hell, I wouldn't wrestle with him if you paid me, but his dad isn't too smart. Anyone who keeps beating his kid has gotta figure that somewhere down the line the kid's going to bust him back. It's the law of nature."

"Did he shoot his father?"

"Your guess is as good as mine. The kid's clammed up about it. When the sheriff brought him in, he said he shot his dad to protect his mother. All I know is that there was a cake. The kid said there was real fruit on top of the icing. He wanted a piece with a cherry on it. His dad said no. His mom began cutting the cake, and started to give Danny a piece with a cherry on it and the old man went bonkers. He grabbed the knife from her and began waving it like a madman. My hunch is that she's the one who went for the gun."

"That'd be my guess, too," I said.

"Kids're funny when it comes to coughing up the real story. Danny's no exception. The last thing he's about to do, now that the crisis is over, is bad-rap his folks. Don't ask me why: it's what the shrinks call family dynamics."

It's what I call not rocking the boat. The children *don't* talk, but the poison comes out all the same.

"I mean, ain't that too much?" George said, stubbing out his cigarette. "All Dan wanted was a damned cherry on his cake. That's all any of them ever want. I have ten boys on my ward and they all want the best their lives have to offer."

It's sobering to tell a client she shot her husband and her son's willing to take the rap for her. I lost a day deciding whether or not to tell her. I heard Dr. Weinstein's voice echoing inside my head, warning me that my client might be one step from the brink.

It was Friday morning when I told her who she was.

"Lenore Pierce." She tasted the words. "Where do I live?"

"Pleasant Hill."

"Are you sure?"

"Positive."

"Have I lived there long?"

"Long enough. You had a fight with your husband."

"I'm married." She said it with the awe of one who realizes the fantastic. "Is he all right?"

"He isn't dead."

Relief flooded her face. "I'm so glad, I'm so glad. Oh, thank you."

"But you tried." I was surprised by the harshness in my tone.

"How?" The word caught in her throat.

I felt sorry for her, but not sorry enough to spare her the truth. I told her about the cherry on the cake. "You shot him when he brandished the knife," I said.

The eyes have a way of telling it all. The amnesia fell away like the useless defense it was. I could tell by the intense way she stared at me that she was reliving the horror of that night in her mind.

"Daniel's taking the rap in juvenile hall," I said. And as I did, I knew where her fictitious name had come from.

Death On
Fifty-Sixth Street

Naomi Strichartz

IT WAS WITH SOME SATISFACTION that Marya Cherkova, former ballerina of the Borsky Ballet and now a professional psychic, put away her Tarot cards for the day. Her last client had been a young woman who wanted to paint, or if not paint, write, or if not write, God help us, dance. Here was a young woman who was convinced she was an artiste, but who had not yet found her special niche. Marya wanted to tell her, "Go home, enjoy your life, make perhaps a tasty quiche," although, quite possibly, the poor woman had no cooking talent either. Oh, to see ourselves as others see us, Marya thought with a sigh. Then Marya caught sight of her own reflection in the mirror and smiled. No longer ballerina-thin, she was plump and attractive in her deep-red silk robe. Marya loved red in the winter when it added the feeling of roses and rich wine to the gray city landscape.

But enough: tonight Marya's good friend Zoya Akimova was coming to enjoy a delicious Russian dinner, replete with vodka, and together they would herald in the New Year. Zoya was the accompanist for the Borsky Ballet, where she played the piano for classes and for company rehearsals. Although sixty-two years old, two years older than Marya, she continued in her chosen work, while Marya had been forced to find a new career. When she was fifty, Marya's body was like over-stretched elastic that refused to spring back. She ached all over: "No more juice," was how she put it, as she packed up her pointe shoes for the last time. But no, she would not become an old woman who sits around counting her losses, no. Marya found great joy in utilizing her psychic gifts for her clients and occasionally for the police, for whom she had solved several crimes.

The jangled ring of the telephone interrupted her pleasant reverie. Marya's heart sank when she heard Inspector Cohen's voice on the line.

"Happy New Year, Marya," the Inspector said, only allowing a tiny portion of his crush to be heard.

"Gabe, Happy New Year to you, too. Unfortunately, for tonight I have made other plans."

"Madame, I would not presume. . . ." he trailed off. "Today I am calling you on business. Urgent business."

"Business, what kind?"

"Marya, did you know Madame Fedorova, the old woman who lived in her studio on West Fifty-Sixth Street?"

"Know her?" Marya asked anxiously. "Of course. A lovely woman of the old school. Gabe, what has happened?"

"She died yesterday, sometime after her morning class. A blood test shows a massive overdose of digitalis. We found bottles of digitalis and Tylenol capsules on her table."

"Digitalis? But Galina was eighty-five. I know she took digitalis for her heart."

"It is too big an overdose to be accidental if that's what you're suggesting. Her students discovered her this morning when she didn't appear to teach her class. They have been asked to remain at the studio for questioning. Will you come?"

Galina Fedorova, Marya thought, remembering. Galina was almost crippled with arthritis but she still managed to teach a daily class in her small studio, with the help of extra-strength Tylenol. Mainly, her students were hopeless, although a few professionals came to her for coaching when they were not on tour.

"Boje moy," Marya said, lapsing into her native tongue, "My God, for what?"

"Money, jewelry, a grudge? We don't know yet, but we will find out, especially if you help us."

"Of course, I must do this. I will call Zoya and tell her dinner will be late."

"Thank you Marya," Gabe said, trying not to sound pleased about the nature of her date. "Do you know the address?"

"I know the place," Marya said sadly. "I will be there within the hour."

Marya changed quickly into her everyday clothes: a pearly-gray sweater, a loosely fitting blue jumper and worn, fleece-lined snow boots. She wrapped herself in her luxurious woolen poncho that was a riot of red, blue and green; like winter flowers, she thought. Marya grabbed her canvas tote and rummaged in the pocket for a bus token after rejecting her first extravagant impulse to take a cab. Reluctantly, she left her cozy Greenwich Village apartment for the cold, dirty street. I am saving money, she thought as she boarded the Madison Avenue bus. Money was an ever-growing concern, and working with the police helped make ends meet. She had recently helped them solve a murder in the Borsky Ballet Company and now, it seemed, she was to be drawn backwards in time again to the ballet world she had left ten years before. Although sixty, Marya knew she looked younger. It was the years of dancing that kept her muscles strong and the roundness she allowed herself since retiring was quite becoming. No more diets, she thought jubilantly, remembering her years of deprivation. These days she indulged herself, particularly enjoying a weakness for Russian meat dumplings, good black bread and rich, tasty cinnamon buns. Her hair, which she kept long, was still mainly brown, attractively sprinkled with gray strands.

Marya got off the bus at Fifty-Sixth Street and Fifth Avenue and walked briskly across town, holding her poncho against herself to ward off the wind.

When she arrived at the studio she paused for a moment in front of the small wooden sign: Madame Galina Fedorova, School of Classical Ballet.

The hallway was filled with policemen. A short, dark-haired man came to greet Marya. Inspector Cohen kissed her hand, the only intimacy Marya would tolerate. For Russians, this is like shaking hands, she had told him.

Two rookies smiled knowingly at each other and Marya withered them with a scathing glance, as she and the Inspector went into the tiny office where Madame Fedorova had died. A class list was on her desk consisting of only four names, which wouldn't add up to many dollars, Marya knew. Marya sat down on the chair and picked up the piece of paper to see if she recognized any of the names. Gabe did not protest, since fingerprints had already been taken. It was clear that Madame Fedorova knew her students well, since the list consisted of first names only: Laura, Freddy, Davida and Pauline. An old black leather bag lay opened on the cluttered desk, vintage Macy's, and shaped like a doctor's satchel. There was no money in the bag.

"It looks like robbery at first glance but it's unusual to use poison if that's the case. We think the murderer may be someone Madame Fedorova knew well."

"Looks like this or that," Marya said, "but things are not always what they look like."

"Let's question the four students who are waiting for us in the studio," Inspector Cohen suggested.

They found them wearing stunned expressions, sitting in their practice clothes with their large over-stuffed bags on the floor beside them exploding with leotards, tights and pink pointe shoes. A short, dark woman, her hair pulled back in a classical hairdo as for the stage, was sewing ribbons on a new pair of shoes and sobbing quietly. She sat in a rickety chair, one arm of which was threatening to fall off. The only other chair, without arms but equally unstable, was occupied by a man of indeterminate age who was talking nervously. A slender, red-haired woman was sitting on the floor exercising her instep by pushing it against a thick band of elastic. The latest thing, Marya thought, smiling to herself. The woman wore a blue leotard, pink tights and had pinned pink plastic flowers around her bun. The fourth student was also sitting on the floor, sipping a cup of tea and looking distraught.

"I am Freddy Cooper," the man said, a bit too jauntily for the occasion. "I take care of the studio for Madame, do her grocery shopping and clean her apartment. I have known her for many years. I used to dance on Broadway but I'm retired," he said unnecessarily. "She was like a mother to me," and then, reality penetrating, Freddy began to cry. "I'm sorry," he blubbered. "This is Davida," he said pointing to the woman who sat sewing. Marya noticed she had unusually short legs and wondered how she was able to dance on them.

"And this is Laura." The redhead looked up from her stretching and nodded. She looked a little too nonchalant, Marya thought. "And Pauline." Pauline stood up and shook hands with Marya.

"Madame thought so well of you," she said. Marya smiled sadly.

Marya looked carefully at Madame Fedorova's pitiful clientele, not one of whom was younger than herself. She suspected none had ever really danced and that they were lost in a world of self delusion.

Laura looked up at Marya.

"I studied with Madame every day. She taught me everything I know. In the afternoon I go to Howard Thomas. I have no," she considered the effect of her words and plunged ahead anyway, "competition here. But it's so impersonal at Howard's."

Davida nodded in agreement. "I only study with the Russians," she said, "because I admire their carriage and port de bras so much. Madame was my favorite teacher. Oh my! You are *the* Marya Cherkova. I have seen you dance."

Marya nodded graciously and turned her attention to Pauline.

"Madame and I were old friends," she said. "I take class for the exercise, I'm too old for this, really." Marya noticed that Pauline, attractive in her blue sweatpants, was the only one who didn't dye her hair.

"You are just three years older than I am," Laura said, blushing. "If I get into a company the credit all goes to Madame," Laura added, as though a contract were just around the corner.

"Marya, shall we interview each of them separately?" Inspector Cohen asked, taking Marya aside for a moment.

"You know, Gabe, what I want to do first is this: I will give them class. I want to see them dance and this will tell me what I need to know."

"Dance! At a time like this! Marya, I stick up for you, you know I do, I believe in you, but dance?"

"Yes," Marya said firmly. "But before this I will look in the back room where Galina lived. Please prepare yourself for class," she said, turning towards the four of them. "We will do class in memory of your fine teacher. It will be a tribute to her," Marya said, mentally apologizing to Galina Fedorova.

Gabe and Marya walked together through the tiny office into Galina's private quarters. The main room was cluttered and dusty. Freddy was evidently not a good housekeeper. But through the dust, Marya saw glimpses of another world. Over the couch, that must have also served as Madame's bed, hung an icon, a holy picture painted on tin. The Holy Family was wearing rich robes in reds and blues. Against the dark background the baby Jesus seemed to glow in Mary's arms. What a trick of paint and technique, Marya thought. The furniture was made of oak: an old bureau, a cabinet and a round table with two chairs. An overstuffed chair sat in the corner, doilies unsuccessfully attempting to hide the places that were frayed. Statues and standing lamps were everywhere. The room looked like an inexpensive antique shop. On the bureau some marcacite jewelry glittered against a dark cloth, a beaded black bag hung on the doorknob, smelling vaguely of stale perfume.

Little scatter-rugs threatened to trip them as they carefully made their way through a hanging Indian bedspread which separated the living room from the miniscule kitchen. Madame's stove was an electric two burner, big enough to make soup and a pot of tea. It sat on a formica table that was covered with photographs and news clippings. One article caught Marya's eye and she quickly put it into her tote bag. Madame's sink was small and inconvenient and the refrigerator was no bigger than a hat box.

Pretending to need the bathroom, Marya excused herself. Walking back through the living room Marya saw the many photographs hanging on the wall. She recognized one of herself and her eyes misted over. Who would poison a lovely old woman, she asked herself angrily. But she knew that in this frightening world there were many capable of just such a thing.

Marya locked herself into the tiny closet of a bathroom Madame shared with her students and inspected the article she had taken. She was amazed to learn that Madame's son, Igor, had killed a man thirty years ago and had been sent to prison for it. Igor Fedorov was a man with a drinking and gambling problem and he had run into serious debt. After a violent argument in a bar, Igor stabbed and killed the man who was trying to collect money from him. There were many witnesses and Igor was sentenced to ten years in prison. Although the ballet world knew that Galina had a son who was a ne'er-do-well, this, a murder, she had somehow managed to keep secret for all these years. So why, then, did Galina have this article sitting on her table in plain view? Or did someone, wanting to incriminate Igor, place it there after her death? All will be clear soon, Marya told herself. She knew she must show the article to Gabe.

"We will find him and arrest him," Gabe said predictably.

"Wait, Gabe. First we find and then we talk to him. He may be innocent," Marya reminded him. "But before that, I am giving these four a class."

"We will certainly talk to Igor before arresting him," Gabe said, "but Marya, no class, there is no time for nonsense."

"You dare call my sacred art nonsense!" Marya exclaimed. "You go and find Igor yourself. Unless he is hiding you don't need me for that. I promised class and class I will give."

Gabe grudgingly agreed and Marya remained in Madame Fedorova's studio, with her four students. Gabe insisted on leaving one policeman behind as protection for her.

Marya turned on the old record player, put on a badly scratched record, and the class began their pliés with exalted expressions. It was as she had feared and worse. Laura was very skinny except for a protruding belly. Her legs were undeveloped and Marya thought she had probably begun to dance in her forties, when most dancers think of retiring. She worked very carefully and seriously, perhaps realizing that at her age an injury would last forever. In her blue practice clothes and with her bright red hair only Laura's stomach and deeply lined face revealed her age. Davida was no more than five feet tall and her short legs were simply ludicrous for a dancer, no matter what her age. She wore pink tights, pointe shoes and a long tunic that was unsuccessful in disguising her gnome-like appearance. Marya had to work hard to control her expression. Poor Galina, to see this everyday! "Good," Marya said, mentally offering apologies to a higher being. Davida is completely hopeless, she thought, but of course, they all are. Pauline was the only one to realize it, however. She smiled bashfully and kept up the best she could. She wore her gray hair short and covered herself tastefully in a black leotard and navy sweatpants. She didn't take on the affected poses of the others and seemed to possess both humor and intelligence. Freddy's dancing was unspeakable. He cavorted on bent legs like a demented gazelle. Clearly, he had never danced professionally, because something of the past always remains. Marya gave them a complete class, from barre work through large jumps at the end. During the last combination, full of the customary high leaps, Marya prayed no one would hurt themselves. Like most older people, the four had great difficulty jumping. Marya noticed Laura looking at herself sideways in the mirror, trying to suck in her stomach, and she patted her own Buddha-like stomach with fondness. How nice not to have to torture myself like this anymore, she thought. She was encouraging to all of them and was careful not to smile with amusement.

Marya knew there were many ways of discovering what she wanted to know. By the end of class she had the insights she needed to solve the case. Laura and Davida, she realized, were not sane and lived in a world of self delusion. Freddy was ludicrous and perhaps mad as well. Only Pauline seemed aware of reality and Marya was sure she and Galina had truly been friends. The students applauded politely at the end of class and, as Marya hoped, were more relaxed and eager to talk. Freddy made tea and brought it out on a tray. Marya was starving and wished there were something to go with it. But in imitation of the professional ballet world, these would-be dancers did not want to eat.

"Ballet is my whole life," Davida said. "My husband died fifteen years ago and I was left quite comfortable."

"Comfortable? You are rich," Laura said with anger. "I have to struggle for my art," she confided. "I work at Woolworth's in order to pay for my classes." Marya suspected she also collected Social Security but restrained herself from remarking on this.

"You know," Davida interrupted, "Madame always said it wasn't your body, but the illusion you created with it that was important. And the feeling, the artistry. The body was just a tool. She said that," Davida continued, "but she only paid attention to Laura and her long legs. Laura, Laura, Laura. Sometimes she even called her Laurencia. I think I was really her favorite and Madame teased me with Laura to make me work harder."

Marya tried not to show her skepticism.

"Madame cared about all of us," Pauline said. "But she worried because she knew we couldn't become dancers at our age and some of us thought we could."

"I can still become a dancer," Laura protested loudly. "I dream of it night and day. And everyone knows I am Madame's best student." She crossed herself, remembering Madame was no more.

"Girls, girls," Freddy said patronizingly, "we should be talking about Madame, not ourselves, at a time like this."

"Freddy, I'm sure Madame Fedorova would want her students to talk about whatever will make them feel better," Marya said piously, wanting to encourage the dialogue.

"Madame helped me all the time," Laura continued, like a broken record. "I sometimes felt sorry for the others, I mean . . . I was her pet." Marya stopped herself from laughing by crossing her legs hard and emitting a small cough. "I don't know what I'll do now, I'm afraid to face life without Madame." Laura was crying now and Davida flashed her a contemptuous look.

"Madame Cherkova," Davida said, "I wonder, since Madame Fedorova can no longer help us, if you would consider coaching us. I would love to develop your lovely port de bras. I remember your arms were so beautiful, and I think that is what is really stopping us from truly becoming dancers."

Freddy got up suddenly and began to waltz across the studio. Clearly it had been difficult for him to sit still for so long.

"Yes I have no bananas," he sang out. Freddy's eyes darted furtively and he interrupted his song. "I studied with Madame every day, I was her own true love, what an old gal. Seriously, I took care of her. Did you know I danced in vaudeville?"

He really isn't in his right mind, Marya thought, wondering if he were on something, perhaps drugs. "I can certainly help you with your port de bras," Marya responded to Davida's request, hoping fervently that she wouldn't have to. "But first I must catch a murderer. Do any of you have any idea who would want to kill Madame?"

They looked around at each other. Finally, Laura broke the silence. "Madame's son Igor was here on Wednesday morning. He asked her for money again and Madame seemed upset when he left. But then, he came back yesterday and they seem to have made up. They were having breakfast when I arrived for class."

The others nodded in confirmation.

"I came a few minutes early yesterday," Davida said, "and I'm not sure they made up completely. The walls are thin in the dressing room and I couldn't help overhearing a few words."

"A few words about what?" Marya asked.

"I'm fairly sure it was about money and Madame telling him she just didn't have even enough for herself."

"Well, so perhaps I go talk to Igor. And tomorrow, if you like, we will work on your port de bras."

Marya got up to leave but Davida stopped her at the door.

"If you would consider giving me private lessons I could pay you well for them. It would help ease my pain at losing Madame," she explained.

"Yes, well. I shall certainly think about," Marya said, lapsing into idiosyncratic English and thanking God for her psychic gift.

She would never have to teach the likes of Davida. She closed the door behind her with considerable relief.

Marya glanced at her watch. She would have to hurry. Zoya would arrive soon and she was absolutely starving. Igor would keep until tomorrow, that is if Gabe succeeded in finding him.

Zoya arrived fifteen minutes after Marya and helped put the finishing touches on their supper. Marya had prepared hot cabbage soup and little lamb dumplings. She had bought pickled herring and good black bread on Second Avenue. There was a large salad, hot tangy beets and salmon steaks from the hopefully clean waters off the shore of Norway. "Everything does not have to be Russian," Marya said, and to emphasize this point further she brought out a bottle of Beaujolais. "This for now, Russian Vodka for later," Marya said as she and Zoya sat down to their feast. Zoya was short and plump with curly red hair. She was a quick, nervous sort of person, cautious and often afraid. She begged Marya not to get involved with another crime. In between delicious bites Marya told her friend what had happened to Galina Fedorova.

"Ah, Galina, yes, I used to play for her," Zoya sighed. "Such a nice old woman, who would want to kill her?"

"The police suspect her son Igor," Marya said sadly. "I don't want them to jump to conclusions, although it does look bad for him," she admitted.

"Igor! Well I heard he was not such a nice boy, gambling and always trying to get poor Galina to pay his debts. A shame!"

"Yes," Marya agreed, "but you know, to kill a mother, this is something really bad, the mind refuses to accept it. And yet, of course, it does happen," she admitted. "I assume nothing until I talk to him myself," she added.

"Did he have the opportunity?" Zoya asked.

"Galina's students say he visited Wednesday morning before class and he and his mother argued, they think about money. But yesterday, the day she died, he came again and they seemed to have made up. They had tea together before Galina's morning class. But Igor may have asked for money again, is hard to hear clearly through the wall," Marya explained ruefully. "Galina taught her class and seemed okay. The police think she died sometime that afternoon."

"What did she die of?"

"An overdose of digitalis. A big overdose. And no, I don't think

Galina took by mistake. And worse, Zoya, Igor was once convicted of killing a man and has been to prison. But enough for now. It is time for dessert," Marya announced, bringing little chocolate cream cakes and strong coffee to the table. "And no more talk of murder, we must just enjoy."

It was almost midnight when the two friends finished eating and began sipping vodka.

"So Marya," Zoya asked teasingly, "now will you read my cards for the New Year?"

"I thought you don't like Tarot cards. You say they make you nervous," Marya reminded her. "Perhaps tonight, Zoyishka, you will do a reading for me?"

"I don't know how," Zoya said, laughing.

"First I tell you, Zoya, the cards are not a game, nor do they tell the future. But for the receptive, the ancient images remind us of what truth lurks in our own minds. A card can help me solve a problem by making me aware of what I don't realize I already know. It can even help me solve a crime. Let's see what the cards tell us about Galina's death."

Zoya shuddered slightly as Marya took her cards out of a cedar box and carefully unwrapped them. The cards were a gift from her grandmother who taught Marya always to keep them wrapped in silk. The two women went into the front room where Marya met with her clients, and sat down facing each other. Marya shut the lights and lit a tall red candle. She wrapped a large blue shawl around her shoulders. Then she shuffled the cards and carefully laid them on the table in the formation called a Celtic cross.

"What do they say?" Zoya asked quietly.

"It has to do with deception and violence," Marya answered, "and the final card is quite puzzling." Temperance, represented by an angel, poured something from one vessel to another. "I must sleep on this," Marya said thoughtfully. "Zoyishka, Boje moy," Marya said, glancing at her watch, "it is one o'clock. You must sleep here tonight, look I make the couch into bed for you."

Zoya, too tired to refuse, sleepily agreed.

At nine a.m. the telephone rang and Marya regarded it balefully.

"Good morning, Gabe," Marya said sleepily.

"How did you know who. . . . Oh, never mind. Happy New Year, Marya. I wonder if you would like to be present when we question Igor."

"So police will not take holiday?" Marya said.

"No, the police will not."

"Then I will not either. Where shall I meet you?"

"Igor lives on West Sixteenth Street, on the corner of Sixth Avenue. Apartment 8C. He is expecting us."

"Good, I will be able to walk there," Marya said.

Zoya was still sleeping so Marya wrote her a note and left the apartment quietly. The Village was like a ghost town. Only liquor bottles, strewn carelessly in the gutters, indicated the revelry of the night before. Marya walked briskly, looking at the rows of apartment houses, all straight up and down, and gave thanks for her charming Village brownstone. Arriving at Igor's building, she nodded to the doorman, gave her name, and was immediately admitted.

Igor lived on the eighth floor and Marya, who detested elevators, mentally steeled herself for the long climb. "I hate elevators and I hate blood. I am a fine investigator," she thought to herself, chuckling as she trudged up the stairs on her still powerful legs. She stood outside Igor's door for a few seconds, regaining her breath, before ringing the bell.

Inspector Cohen immediately opened the door and, without bothering to greet Marya, resumed questioning Igor. Marya stood in the open doorway. "Oh no, Gabe has already made up his mind," she thought with dismay. "The man simply has no patience."

Igor was short and heavy-set. His eyelids were slightly hooded and his gray hair was thick. Unruly eyebrows helped to create a sly look but Marya knew that appearances could be deceiving. Though probably not in this case, she admitted to herself. Igor wore a large diamond ring on his pinky finger and worse, he was smoking a cigar.

"I will not enter unless you put out that repulsive thing," she announced. Igor obliged with a nasty smile. Inspector Cohen held the incriminating newspaper clipping on his lap, along with his pad and pen.

"So, Mr. Fedorov," he asked insistently, "where were you on Thursday morning at nine o'clock?"

"I was with my mother at her house. She invited me for breakfast. We had had a disagreement the day before, and she wanted to apologize for her harsh words."

"Did you ask her for money again?"

"No! She had already refused me and I still have some pride left, Inspector. I didn't kill her."

"You have killed before, however," Inspector Cohen shouted, waving the article in front of Igor's face.

"The man I killed was not my mother. And besides, that was nearly thirty years ago. I have changed since then."

"You still gamble and you still drink, don't you," the Inspector said challengingly.

"Yes," he said softly.

"Was your mother upset about anything the last time you saw her?" Marya asked.

"Yes. She was upset about some of her students. She was thinking of retiring."

"Why?" Marya asked, leaning forward.

"They were starting to take themselves too seriously. You know they are all, well, older. Mother said they were living in a dream world. One of them actually planned to audition for American Ballet Theater. Another kept pestering her for private lessons. And Freddy, for some reason, actually wanted her to adopt him."

"Adopt! But he is sixty if he is a day! Why?"

"She had no idea, but he was getting quite insistent. They are all a bit crazy, you know. Mother said that instead of shattering their dreams she would just retire and go live on the Tolstoy Farm."

"Did anyone overhear your conversation?"

"I don't think so. It was early for class. I wasn't aware of anyone in the studio with us."

"But the door was open and someone might have arrived?"

"Yes, of course, that is true," Igor agreed. Then, deciding that Marya was sympathetic towards him, he had the nerve to wink. Slavic men are simply insufferable, Marya thought, looking at him with distaste.

Gabe who had been quietly pretending not to listen, suddenly sprung to life.

"Mr. Fedorov, you have no alibi," he said pointing an accusing finger. "You, along with your mother's students, were the last to see Galina Fedorova alive. I needn't tell you that you are a suspect and that you had better not leave town. Do not be surprised if I return with a warrant for your arrest."

Inspector Cohen was pleased to accompany Marya down the long flights of stairs.

"Gabe, I think I begin to see the light," Marya said, timing the remark with their emergence into the brightly lit lobby. "I will be ready for a meeting with you and Igor and Madame's four 'hopelesses' this afternoon at four o'clock. Let us meet at Madame's studio and in her memory I will solve this crime."

"Should I be prepared to arrest Igor?" Gabe asked.

"Just bring an open mind," she told him, "and be sure Igor is present along with the others."

When Marya returned to her apartment, Zoya was awake and agitated.

"Once again you plan to confront a dangerous killer."

"Zoya, come along with me if you are worried. Really, this will be quite simple."

"No, I refuse to be in a room with killers and policemen with guns."

"Zoya, don't worry so much. True, someone killed Madame Fedorova, but is not necessary they will kill again. True, some killers get hooked and repeat and repeat like an addiction. But the Inspector will be there, as you say, with his gun, and this, when you expose a murderer, is so useful."

"Marya, do you know who did it?"

"I am not sure, but I will be soon. The pieces of the puzzle are coming together. The cards told me something, especially three of them. The Tower, the Seven of Cups and most especially Temperance. Class told me something important, too. Now Igor tells me something very useful indeed. Just one more tiny piece, and yes, I will know the truth."

Promising to be careful, Marya left her apartment, and throwing caution to the wind, hailed a cab which got her uptown in a record ten minutes.

The suspects were all gathered in Madame's living room, seated comfortably on the sofa and chairs. Inspector Cohen, supported by another policeman, sat close to Igor, in anticipation of his imminent arrest.

Marya nodded graciously and sat herself on the only available chair, the upholstered one with doilies, which, despite its shabbiness, was quite comfortable.

"I always think, don't you," she began conversationally, "that is so much nicer when murderer is a man. Men are naturally more violent than women, and here in this room sits Igor, the son, the," she looked apologetically at Igor, "the ne'er-do-well. The one who has killed before, and so we assume will do again. Igor needs money and mother says no, so he kills her. This would please me so much."

Inspector Cohen knew Marya too well to take any action, but Igor looked terrified and the other policeman watched him carefully in case he made a move to escape.

Marya continued. "But he didn't do it, no impossible. Igor had tea with his mother at nine on Thursday morning. She died, we believe, in afternoon, between three and five, of a large amount of digitalis, which takes two or three hours to kill. Galina taught her morning class just as usual. So, someone gave Galina overdose sometime after class and someone is not Igor, but one of her students."

Igor took a deep breath. "I didn't kill her. I loved her."

"Yes, I know," Marya said. "But still, and it is so unprofessional of me," she said glancing at Gabe, "I want killer to be a man. Freddy has keys to studio and to Madame's private quarters. He came and went as he pleased. For some reason he was anxious to have Madame adopt him. Why?"

"I loved her," Freddy wailed.

"But still, you could have poisoned Madame after class, after the others left. You returned and offered her some tea, perhaps?"

"No."

The policeman looked inquiringly at Inspector Cohen, who shrugged.

"Why did you want to be adopted, at your age?" Marya demanded.

"I never knew my own mother, she ran away when I was a baby and I was raised by an aunt who didn't love me. Madame was like a mother to me."

"And so when she refused to adopt you, you felt rejected all over again, and you poisoned her!"

Freddy began to bawl like a baby.

"Who would have thought Freddy did it," Laura said, incredulously.

"He did not do it," Marya said. "So we come to Pauline. Pauline is not a suspect. Igor assured me she was a trusted friend of Madame's and this I could see was true."

Laura and Davida, realizing they were the only ones left, exchanged terrified glances.

"Laura is Madame's best student. She expects to join ballet company but when she talks to Madame she is not encouraged. She overhears Madame talking with Igor. Madame was worried about Laura, who of course had no chance to dance professionally. But Madame did not want to burst bubble. She would retire, instead. So you return to studio after class and you kill her!" Marya said, pointing a finger at Laura.

"What do you mean, I have no chance?" Laura shrieked. "I am an artist, I will dance professionally! I will show everyone. You are just jealous. I will be a better dancer than you ever were."

"Laura is upset," Marya said understandingly. "I will now show you how I solved this crime. First I must tell you, last night Zoya and I read the Tarot cards."

"Marya, is this necessary?" Inspector Cohen asked warningly.

"Of course, or I would not bring it up," Marya said, offended. "The layout was most interesting. Three cards especially got my attention. They were the Seven of Cups, the Tower and Temperance. Of course everything pointed to violence and death, but this I already knew. I thought and thought. Temperance is holding two vessels and is pouring liquid back and forth from one to the other, one to the other. So, now you know."

"Know what?" Inspector Cohen exploded.

"Control yourself, Gabe. You demonstrate the violence of the male. Unfortunately, this crime, a horrible crime, was committed by a woman. A woman who arrived for class early on Thursday, as was her habit, and heard Madame talking to her son. They weren't talking about money, not this time. Madame was talking about her students taking themselves too seriously. Afterwards, the killer took class, as usual, and left with the others. But she was heartbroken. She decided to return and have it out with Madame, who must have told her, quite honestly, that she would never become a dancer. But to make things better, Madame offers her some tea. She goes to make it, taking her time and thinking of the best things to say. Meanwhile, the killer poured out the contents of several capsules of Tylenol, substituting the small digitalis pills, which Madame had already taken. The killer knew Madame would take Tylenol with her tea, she always did. They drank their tea and the killer departed. Several hours later Madame died here alone. Her heart beat slower and slower until it stopped. As we know, she was not discovered until yesterday. It was the Temperance card that helped me see this," Marya explained.

Laura was still sobbing.

"You are not sobbing for Madame, you are sobbing for yourself," Marya said. "But you are not worried about being arrested, are you?"

Laura shook her head.

"That is because the murderer is Davida!" Marya exclaimed.

Davida made no attempt to move.

"Davida was the one who always arrived early for class, she herself told us that. She was the one to beg Madame for private lessons. She asked me to give her some as well. Davida left with the others when class was over but she returned to talk to Madame, to make sure she hadn't misunderstood. Madame tried to be nice, but was honest. Davida could not allow her dreams to be shattered. She was the one to substitute digitalis for Tylenol. Then she planned to look for another teacher, one who believed in her. Am I correct?" Marya asked politely.

Davida nodded.

"As an afterthought, after Galina died, Davida emptied her drawers and went through her newspaper clippings. When she found the incriminating one about Igor she of course put it on top. This she did yesterday, when she arrived, again very early for class, which she knew would not take place."

"What did the Tower card signify?" Inspector Cohen asked, irritation transformed into admiration.

"Destruction and violence," Marya answered. "Actually, it was Igor who helped me most to solve this crime. I realized Madame would never leave that clipping on her table in plain view. She had kept his crime a secret for all these years. And of course the conversation he had with his mother the day she died was most significant." Marya gathered up her poncho and prepared to leave.

"What does the Seven of Cups mean?" Inspector Cohen asked.

"False illusions," Marya said sadly, closing the door behind her.

Murder Is My Business

Lynette Prucha

MARRIAGE, LIKE DEATH, was big business in downtown Los
Angeles. The storefronts along Broadway's Latino thoroughfare
proved it. Behind the large window of Bridal City, lace-tiara'd
mannequins wearing dusty peach, petal rose or mint green gowns
lined up like snow cones in seasonal shades of popularity.

Sticking out in the midst of all this tacky pomp and circumstance was the Bradbury Building. In that historic edifice, built in
1893 and recently made earthquake-proof, for the bargain price of
fifteen hundred dollars a month in rent, was my one-woman
detective agency, MARINO INC.

The INC was stenciled by mistake, but I never bothered to have
it removed. It gave the business more authenticity. Business wasn't
exactly booming, but I managed to cover my overhead, pay rent on
a one bedroom condo in West Hollywood, eat at City restaurant at
least twice a month and work out with a trainer at a prissy health
club on Robertson. Not bad.

My office was done up in what I'd call minimalist chic. Not too
much furniture and a view of an adjacent building with a fifty foot
mural of Hidalgo Rodriquez, patron saint of the streets. Actually he
was the first capitalist to turn a peso into a million bucks. His image
was all the art I needed.

It was a Thursday evening, somewhere between five and six.
My part-time intern had gone home for the Christmas holidays, and
for two weeks I was winging it on my own. I had reservations for

dinner at Engine Company 28 and I was just finishing some paper work on my last case, when the door to the outer reception area slammed shut.

A meek little voice managed to make itself heard and I replied by shouting, "In here."

Heels clicked along the tiled floor and I had barely glanced up from an overdue account when my eyes did a ring-around-the-rosy at the looker standing no more than three feet in front of me.

She was younger than thirty, but old enough to know what she was doing. The two-piece lamb's wool suit smelled new and expensive. The glasnost hat had a faux cluster of jewels appliqued on it. The entire outfit was black, including the silk seamed stockings and the patent leather bag she clutched in her gloved hands.

"Ms. Marino?" she inquired as I pointed for her to have a seat.

"Angie." I pulled out a pack of cigarettes from my top drawer, offered her one, but she declined. I had just inhaled my first puff of the day when she dropped the next line on me.

"My husband murdered me."

I stopped chomping on my cigarette long enough to watch the flicker of melodrama dance in her sea green eyes. For a minute I almost drowned in the turbulence of that ocean.

"You mean tried to murder you?"

"No."

I took another drag of the cigarette to help clear my head. Then I laid the burning stick in a clean ashtray, pushed up the sleeves to my camel jacket; the one I'd purchased in Neiman Marcus two months ago, the one I still owed $314 on. I figured by now I probably owned both sleeves. The rest of the jacket, along with the pockets and snazzy buttons had a way to go.

She removed her gloves and laid them on my desk. "Let me explain. I don't have much time." She pulled out a handkerchief and clutched the embroidered talisman in her smooth hand. "My husband has been having this affair for three months. I was hoping it would peeter out, that Roger would get tired and come back home and behave. We've been married nearly five years. Men are apt to stray sometimes." Her smile contained the thinnest veneer of sarcasm as she crossed her legs and waited for my response.

"Before you go any further, it might help if I knew your name and you understood my fees."

She replied with hesitation. "Ramona Millicent Hunnicut and

72

I'm sure your fees are reasonable."

"Hunnicut Textiles?"

"Yes. I gather you realize I value discretion above all else. If word gets out, it would be quite embarrassing."

"Of course." I was attracted to Ramona Millicent Hunnicut more than I cared to admit. My therapist said I'd moved beyond my damsel-in-distress syndrome. Thank you. No recriminations. Just a healthy dose of curiosity and simple animal attraction operating here. I ground out the tasteless cigarette, thought about my liaison later this evening and wondered what Mrs. Hunnicut was wearing under the widow's weeds.

"A week ago I did something quite shameful."

I raised an eyebrow and hung on every word. I gestured for her to resume her tale.

"I hired someone to follow Roger. The detective took these pictures." She opened her purse and pulled out two photos. "I have more, but they are in my safe at home."

Roger was a handsome man, tall, with a soft fleece of hair on his muscular chest. The lady-in-waiting kneeling in front of Roger had divine curvature and curly brunette hair that fell on her naked shoulders in frenzied tendrils. The other photo was a little more of the same, only this time, Roger was the supplicant.

"Why did you come to me, Mrs. Hunnicut? Why not Thachter & Associates? I understand they were involved in the Hunnicut investigation about three years ago." I'd suddenly remembered the rumors that had gone around town. Old-monied Hunnicut had been blackmailed by a drug cartel. It appeared Hunnicut refused to use his cargo as a front for laundered dough. The Colombians didn't appreciate his resistance.

Mrs. Hunnicut shifted uncomfortably in her chair. Her lips were creamy smooth, the jaw strong, the nose proud enough.

"My father hired Thachter & Associates. He's dead. I'm in charge now."

"Fine, then why not the dick you hired to take the photos?"

"Mr. Fletcher? I didn't like him. He was beginning to get too familiar."

I started to raise my eyebrow again, but it felt like old hat. I wondered if she meant Ned Fletcher, an operative I'd run into more than once.

"How familiar?" The words spilled out of my mouth.

Mrs. Hunnicut unbuttoned the top of her jacket. "He was a handsome man who tried to take advantage of my shame."

She gave me enough details to convince me she'd done the right thing. I'd had my suspicions about Fletcher, but I never thought he'd go this far. Lousy son-of-a-bitch. He probably figured he'd capitalize on this delicate situation. It had been done before.

"Besides, a friend of mine recommended I work with a woman. At least I know where they stand." Mrs. Hunnicut leveled a look at me that made my toes curl.

"That's why I came to you. I simply checked the phone book. Before my father died, he tried to buy this building. I saw your name listed, with the Bradbury Building as an address, and I called. Sorry I can't say you came highly recommended, but in my rush to find someone I didn't have the time to make extensive inquiries."

I nodded waiting for more, but she didn't give it. Her perfume appeared to travel off her body first class and infiltrate my train of thought. I conjured a spring bouquet, the delicacy of thistles blowing in the wind, and a Brazilian rain forest.

"I have no one to turn to. My husband rigged my murder, never suspecting I knew about his infidelities. He had no idea I had gotten into the habit of . . . spying on him."

Nothing like a healthy dose of back-stabbing to spark a marriage, I thought. "That still doesn't explain the fact that you claim to have been murdered. The dead don't often get a chance to talk about it afterwards." Somewhere along the line, diplomacy had jumped overboard. Mrs. Hunnicut could be just another nut case looking for attention or drama in her life. But then again she could be telling the truth.

"Let me explain. The day before yesterday, I went sailing with my husband. I gave Roger *Siren's Kiss* as a wedding present. It's a fifty foot, full powered Trimaran. Anyway, that night he was in a very good mood. We'd just made love and he was preparing supper for me. Roger's an excellent cook. He insisted I go up on deck and make myself comfortable in this make-shift divan he'd built for my convenience. I often spend hours reading and sunbathing there."

Mrs. Hunnicut's pale face didn't look as though she'd spent too much time exposing herself to the harmful rays of the sun. I could picture her in a 1940s one-piece white bathing suit, though.

"We had been out sailing all day, so I'd imagine we were about two hours from shore. The sky was black and there didn't appear to be a ship in sight."

I opened my desk drawer, stared at the bottle of Remy, thought better of it and pulled out a pad instead. "Go ahead," I said, scratching a few notes on the yellow paper.

"Anyway, I felt for the first time in months that perhaps Roger *did* love me, that his affair was just a meaningless diversion. Even on the open sea, I could smell the delicious aroma of the fresh lobster fettucine he was preparing. We both love garlic and herbs."

My stomach did a flip-flop at the mention of food. I had promised myself I wouldn't order an appetizer at dinner, but mentally blew off my good intentions.

"I'd had several glasses of champagne—he'd seen to that. But it must have been something more than champagne because I started to feel as if I was slipping away, like I was becoming one with the sea. The ocean was a bit choppy and I felt the spray of sea salt on my face. I was preparing to get up off the divan when I heard a clicking noise. I opened my eyes and stared into the darkness, but no one was there. Then I heard music coming from down below and Roger's deep baritone voice as he attempted an aria from *Rigoletto*. I was just about to close my eyes again, I suddenly felt so weary, when something snapped underneath me—like a spring—and before I knew it the divan flipped over starboard. I felt my body slap the ice cold ocean." Mrs. Hunnicut shuddered and clutched her handkerchief in her hand.

I urged her to continue. She measured her breathing carefully before commencing.

"I screamed and flailed my arms—I'm a poor swimmer and I was absolutely paralyzed with fear. Fear and an almost crippling relief that it would soon be over."

Her eyes narrowed in pain. Mrs. Hunnicut's voice was chilled with the terror of her recollection. I wasn't quite sure I should believe her story, but something in her straightforward manner told me I'd already bought it.

"I caught sight of the ship receding. I felt myself giving up on it all, Ms. Marino—Angie—and then I succumbed." Mrs. Hunnicut paused, dropped the photos in her bag and then continued.

"When I came to, I was shivering, my teeth were chattering. In fact the gentlemen who found me thought I was having a seizure. It took several minutes for me to realize I wasn't dead, that I had miraculously been rescued. I had been fished out of the water by two men who were on their way back to shore in a small power boat. They saved my life."

Here Mrs. Hunnicut's voice cracked and she put her handkerchief to her eyes to dab at the tears. Then she coughed.

"What were these men doing out so late at night?"

Mrs. Hunnicut nodded her head. "Needless to say, I really didn't care, but once I had sufficiently calmed down, I was able to observe that they'd gone fishing and probably had a bit too much to eat and drink. I dare say, they didn't expect to fish me out of the Pacific. If it weren't for the light they had attached to the side of the boat, I wouldn't be here to tell you this story."

I knew a little about boats, enough to know that a flood light off side would illuminate the dark sea. "Are you sure your husband tried to kill you?"

"Positive. Once Roger returned to the dock, he took his time and thoroughly cleaned down the boat—it's an obsession of his. I borrowed my rescuer's binoculars and watched him from their boat. I could see that he was whistling as he left the dock." Her voice contained an undertone of acidity. She winced slightly and continued. "Then he walked over to his car and drove away."

"But surely the power boat didn't dock at the same time your husband's boat did?"

"No. We made it about a half an hour later. Both boats were motorized, but I'm sure Roger was traveling at a much faster speed."

"He didn't contact the coastguard? No one? Just pretended you disappeared into thin air."

"Yes." Her voice cracked.

Mrs. Hunnicut pulled out a cigarette, tapped it on the desk and waited for me to light it. I did. I looked at the clock and figured I still had a good forty-five minutes before my dinner engagement. I urged her to go on with her most remarkable tale. "But what about your rescuers? Weren't they suspicious? What did you tell them?"

"Of course they were quite alarmed. I think they thought I was rather mad, you know, off my rocker. I was incoherent for quite some time. They gave me a change of clothes so I'd keep warm and I asked to borrow a hat, so I wouldn't be recognized when I got to shore, just in case. You see I still didn't know what I was prepared to do."

I leaned back in my chair and listened to the growing stillness outside the window. The process of detailing this confession had a soothing effect on Mrs. Hunnicut. A dead calm.

"You may think this rather strange, but for the past few months Roger's solicitations have been growing in proportion to his infidelity. He'd always been attentive, but lately there didn't seem to be enough he could do for me. Now that he was . . . misbehaving."

Misbehaving? Mrs. Hunnicut had a way with words. I almost expected to hear she'd pulled down his pants and given him a good spanking.

"I think I hate him more for that . . . the false solicitations, the simulated display of his affection, than for what he did to me. He'd stop at nothing to get what he wanted."

"And what *did* he want, Mrs. Hunnicut?" She didn't flutter an eyelash. It never failed to amaze me, this business of murder. How nearly 35% of all homicides are caused by family members, a lover, or children. Someone close. Someone trustworthy.

She looked at me, surprised. "My money of course." Then she took a deep breath. "Before this nightmare happened, I had decided to spend a few days visiting a college friend to clear my mind."

I smiled without knowing it.

"Did I say something funny?"

"No, of course not, Mrs. Hunnicut. Excuse me. But I just got this flash."

"A flash?"

"I know a little about your family, in fact a great deal. You see, it just so happens that we both grew up in Northern California and while I didn't go to Stanford, as you did, I attended my fair share of wild sorority parties in my days. I have this hunch that you were one of the Delta Chi's? Class of '80. Am I right?"

Mrs. Hunnicut looked relieved. She blushed. She smiled broadly and nodded her head. "Please don't remind me of any war stories. I was quite a wild young lady."

There was a twinkle in her eyes, but I couldn't tell if she was laughing with me, or at me. "Please continue, Mrs. Hunnicut."

"Well, I'd only been away for a day when Roger called me. He was telephoning from a phone booth because as he said, he'd been walking down the street, realized that he missed me immensely and called—just like that—to tell me he loved me. Needless to say, I was delighted, especially when he said he was sending me a surprise. In less than half an hour, a chauffeured limo pulled up in front of my friend's house and I was whisked away. Mary was off at a conference all day so I left her a note and said I'd call and explain everything later."

"So the limo dropped you off at the Marina?"

"Precisely."

"Any witnesses?"

"No. Just the driver."

"Did you get the name of the limo service or the license plate number?"

"Of course not." She dashed out her half-smoked cigarette in the ashtray. "I hardly suspected foul play."

Mrs. Hunnicut got up from her seat and walked to the dusty window. I knew I shouldn't have fired the cleaning crew until I found a suitable replacement. Having a woman like Mrs. Hunnicut in my office suddenly made me realize how drab and undramatic my work space was. I made a mental note to do something about it. Trade in minimalism for a little Italian avant-garde. I fought off the urge to light up another cigarette, my quota being one a day, as I examined Mrs. Hunnicut's long legs. A low whistle involuntarily escaped my lips. She whipped around and looked me in the eye.

"But I was wrong. My husband murdered me. And now I need your help." She moved back over to the desk and leaned as close as decency would allow.

The entire story smelled as rotten as a Bonita left out in the sun. "Why didn't you go to the police?" I asked, pulling away from her. I got up out of my seat.

Mrs. Hunnicut found hers and sat down.

"It seems to me you have a pretty good case," I continued. "Even if it was an accident, your husband never reported you missing. You had the two fishermen as witnesses. And some pretty incriminating proof to support his motive. Why didn't you go to the hospital or your physician if you thought he slipped you a mickey? We could have used this as evidence in our investigation."

"I don't care to have him arrested." Her lips tightened and puckered slightly. "I want revenge."

I caught a glimpse of myself in the mirror. I didn't look as bad as I should have after twelve hours of work. Pushing back a few stray hairs that had fallen into my wide open eyes, I examined Mrs. Hunnicut's determined face. I wasn't in the line of business to avenge murderers. I just helped to put them behind bars, the old fashioned way. But I was curious, it comes with the territory, and Mrs. Hunnicut looked desperate. The calling of my trade whispered in my ears, you should know better. But the warning was drowned out by a suggestive bellowing in my head, go ahead, take that occasional walk on the wild side.

"I'll help you," I said. Sure she had a pretty face and a nice pocketbook to match, but I was a sucker for a woman in distress. And more than that, I was intrigued.

Mrs. Hunnicut looked relieved. She smiled. The whites of her perfectly shaped teeth glistened. She wet her lips with her tongue and then smoothed back her hair.

So I hadn't worked out all the kinks in therapy, and when I did, I somehow suspected I might be six feet under.

The restaurant was half-filled. Downtown on a Thursday night was like a ghost town. The Bunker Hill yuppies headed to Beverly Hills and Westwood for their recreation. That's why I liked it here. I was chasing down my double espresso with a Remy Martin at this rather pricy eaterie, when Katherine leaned across the table.

"You've been preoccupied all evening. Is it another case?"

Katherine knew me too well. I'd managed to focus on how beautiful she looked in that cobalt Lanvin dress. The string of pearls around her neck were the ones I'd given her nearly a year ago. When I'd handed her a black velour box she was surprised. It wasn't her birthday, Christmas or Valentine's Day.

"These," I had said softly, clasping the expensive trinket around her lovely neck, "are for taking my breath away every time I see or think of you."

"Hey you," Katherine teased, waving her hand across my face.

I returned from my reverie, looked into her warm playful eyes and smiled. I knew I shouldn't have ordered the lobster fettucine. Not only was it too rich for my troubled stomach, it kept reminding me of what could have been Mrs. Hunnicut's last supper. I downed the double espresso and took a deep breath. "I can't get this woman out of my mind."

Katherine sat at attention. "Oh?" she probed, drawing out the exclamation. "Is she pretty?"

Leave it to Katherine to worry about "pretty" in my line of work. "No." I sipped a glass of ice water with a sliver of lemon floating on the surface.

Katherine looked relieved.

"She's beautiful."

Katherine's face dropped slightly and she rallied her defenses. "Suppose you start from the beginning, darling. We've got all night."

"No we don't. I've got to get an early start tomorrow."

A cloud darkened Katherine's lovely face.

"Sorry, angel. But there's nothing to worry about. I wouldn't trade you in for anyone in the world."

"You'd be a fool to do so, my dear. I was just worried about you. Last time you were rather mysterious with me, I ended up racing down to Cedars Sinai in the middle of the night. You were so doped up with pain killers you called me 'Mommy.'"

I couldn't help but smile. The Camarino case. Pretty nasty stuff. A kiddy porn shop on Western and Sunset. A mother had hired me to find her four-year-old kid. The old man skipped out with his daughter. He was pimping the poor baby to feed his habit. Nice times. "Don't you think I can take care of myself?"

"Only too well, I suspect." Katherine leaned closer and clasped her hand over mine, then leaned back and finished her cappuccino.

Katherine was good at leaving me alone with my thoughts. I'd never before met a woman who could second guess all my moves, love me to death and give me plenty of rope to hang myself.

Mrs. Hunnicut and I met later the following day for tea at The Far East Cafe. To ensure our privacy, I had asked Mr. Lee to direct us to a curtained booth, the only one in the restaurant. The greasy spoon was a favorite of mine. Mrs. Hunnicut had never before set foot inside. Once settled, I began to interrogate her.

"Why didn't Roger just ask you for a divorce?"

Mrs. Hunnicut smiled. "Roger had signed a prenuptial agreement that stated he wouldn't be entitled to a dime if he filed for a divorce. With my death, he'd stand to inherit a million dollars, plus my Bel Air estate."

"And what if you filed for divorce?" I cracked open a fortune cookie and watched Mrs. Hunnicut sip her tea. She was wearing a creamy beige suede suit and her lips were pale tangerine. There was something different about her, a sense of determination in the way she stretched her jaw, in the way her eyes fire up every time she spoke. She appeared to be a woman driven by more than a desire to seek justice. I wondered what Mrs. Hunnicut was like in bed.

"If I filed, which I never thought I would, I had agreed to pay Roger eighty thousand a year for three years."

Eighty thousand sounded like a lot of money to me. I looked down at the slip of paper I'd just removed from my fortune cookie. Fool's gold tarnishes. Was there a moral to this scribble? Why did Hunnicut's yarn fascinate me? Was I attracted to the money or the power? Maybe a little bit of both. Was this some voyeuristic quest to go poking through the dirty lingerie of her marriage? To pick apart the ragged emotions and make sense of it all? Something wasn't adding up, though. Roger didn't have such a bad deal, but it was hardly a million bucks. And if Roger was capable of murder, had he ever attempted anything like that before? "Could there have been any other reason Roger may have wanted you . . . dead?"

Mrs. Hunnicut looked rather distressed. Had I hit a nerve?

"I've been a good wife to Roger."

"I'm sure you have, Mrs. Hunnicut. But could something have happened to trigger this diabolical scheme of his?"

"I'm not sure I know what you're getting at." Mrs. Hunnicut sipped her tea thoughtfully.

"Let's move on. Tell me, how do you manage to dress so well if you haven't gone home in several days?"

Mrs. Hunnicut paused before responding. "What are you insinuating?"

I watched her finger her fortune cookie. Her nails looked as if they'd just been done. They were the same color as her lips, only shinier. "I'm not insinuating anything, Mrs. Hunnicut. You're my client and I simply have the prerequisite questions to ask. It's necessary."

"Of course. I'm rather edgy today," she replied, apologetically. "As for my wardrobe, I have a special account. It isn't difficult to withdraw money without my husband knowing it. Anyway, I have no idea whether or not Roger has reported me missing. As far as anyone knows, I'm still visiting with a friend. I'm not due back until tonight."

"Is it possible your friend . . . in Laguna . . ."

"Mary?"

"Yes, Mary, could have phoned the house to see what happened to you?"

"It might be possible. However, she was getting ready to go off on a ski trip. If she *did* call, I suppose Roger would have to alert the police and report me missing."

As I watched Mrs. Hunnicut carefully, my thoughts drifted back to events that had preceded this meeting. I felt as if I'd been watching her all night long in my sleep. That beautiful face of hers had haunted me in more ways than one. The obvious I'll leave out. But then there had been the nightmare. I'd seen her face and body—actually it was the naked body of Roger's squeeze—all green and bloated, floating in the sea. I was helpless, unable to rescue her from a school of sharks that swam around and around in some sort of cultish circle. I screamed. A shark lunged for her, gripping the lifeless body in its huge jaws. The water turned vermilion. I screamed again, only that time Katherine was holding me in her arms. After that, I couldn't go back to sleep.

I'd driven around the city for half an hour before the world claimed the sidewalks. And at nine o'clock sharp I found myself at the Hall of Records. With the help of a double espresso, I was sufficiently fired up to plow through the tomes of statistics and facts, musty footprints of the past. After an hour's dig and several phone calls, I'd discovered—thanks to Stanford's yearbook—that her college sister, a Mary Wexler, did indeed live in Laguna. And I found out something else.

When I examined the one photo of Mary, with her hair pulled back in a ponytail and wearing hardly a trace of make-up, I instantly thought of the woman in the photos Mrs. Hunnicut had shown me. Of course I had only a profile to go on, but my hunch was that Mary Wexler was two-timing her old college chum. Maybe it had been the juxtaposition of Roger's paramour and Mrs. Hunnicut's face in my dream, but whatever it was—even a dose of good old-fashioned intuition—I'd had the odd sensation that Mary Wexler played a pretty important part in this mess.

I'd left the Hall of Records, hit the pavement, put on my Ray-Bans and walked along Spring toward the Biltmore Hotel. It was close enough to lunch time and I knew I could make a few calls from there.

Mary Wexler was listed in the phone book . . . and she just happened to be at home when I called. At first she denied having seen Mrs. Hunnicut.

"I haven't seen *her*," she said, with distinct distaste, "since the wedding."

"You mean, since she married Roger?"

She hesitated. "Yes. Look, who are you and what's this all about," she asked me again.

"My name is Angie Marino. I'm a private investigator and my client hired me to protect his interests and yours." The lie came easily enough.

There was a long pause and then a cough. "I don't know what you're talking about."

I blurted out what I could only guess was one of her favorite positions and told her that in case her memory was still vague, I could produce a few dozen photos. I guess she got the message because suddenly her memory came back.

"What is it you want?"

"Have Mr. or Mrs. Hunnicut, for that matter, called you in the last day or two?"

She hesitated again. I could practically hear the soft whir of cerebral machinery, a veritable slot machine as her thoughts ricocheted from left to right and back again.

"Mona called and said she wanted to speak to me in person. She said she had something very important to discuss with me. That it concerned Roger." She stopped.

"Go on."

"She said she wanted to . . . work things out. That my coming would be in Roger's best interest . . . as well as my own."

"So?"

"So . . . I agreed to meet her at the Santa Monica Pier this evening."

"What time?"

"Midnight." She sighed and took a deep breath. Mary sounded as if she'd been through the mill and back.

"Isn't that a rather strange place and hour for a sorority reunion?"

"Yes. I told her so myself. But she said, 'Indulge me. You owe me that much.' She also said she knew about our affair and that if I was cooperative, she would be reasonable about letting him go."

"Tell me something," I said, lighting up my first cigarette of the day. "Why'd you do it? Why'd you go sticking your pretty neck out where it didn't belong?"

"I love Roger. I've always loved Roger. *She* stole him from me and made him marry her."

"The man's a big boy," I said.

She sniveled. "Yeah. A big boy with big ideas about his future. Poor Roger's no match for Mona. She'll eat him alive."

"Lucky for him he's got you, then," I said. It seemed to make her feel a little bit better.

"I'm going to call Roger," she said suddenly.

"Look, Ms. Wexler. I'm in a pretty nasty war of the sheets right now and from this angle, it don't look so good for you and it don't look so good for Roger."

I heard her sniffle a bit. She was crying and my heart went out to her. "Can you meet me here in L.A. . . . . at my office . . . at seven o'clock tonight?"

She blew her nose. "Well, I suppose so."

"Good. Because when I tell you what I've got to tell you, I want to make sure you're sitting down." I gave her the address and told her that under no circumstance was she to call either Roger or Mona. It was a gamble, but I liked long shots and I figured fifty-to-one Mary Wexler wouldn't pick up the phone.

I forced my thoughts back to the present as the waiter brought us a fresh pot of tea and I watched Mrs. Hunnicut examine the bottom of her cup, where fragments of tea leaves had settled.

She smiled and looked up at me. "Someone once asked me: 'if a man's worth was measured in gold, how rich would he be?' I thought of Roger and said he'd be as rich as Croesus. Funny how time and circumstance can change all that," she said.

I got the feeling that Mrs. Hunnicut might be thinking Roger wasn't worth a plugged nickel. Maybe I was wrong. She reached across the table and cupped her hand over mine. The collar of my button-down Ralph Lauren seemed to stiffen. I loosened the button.

Mrs. Hunnicut's lower lip trembled. Her fingertips felt as if they were grazing my flesh. "I'm sorry. This all seems such a mess."

I pulled my hand out from under Mrs. Hunnicut's and poured myself some more tea. My hands felt warm and safe around the ceramic cup. I thought it best to keep them there.

"You see, the day Roger and I went sailing, we actually had an awful row. I said some unforgivable things, things I just can't repeat to you . . . but I felt helpless. Roger was slipping away from me every day and . . . I didn't know what to do. You see, all my life I've been used to getting attention. Roger only gives it when he's so inclined and I just can't put up with that." She tapped her fingers on the wood surface and fidgeted under the table.

"I'm still not quite sure what you want me to do, Mrs. Hunnicut."

"I'll pay you ten thousand dollars," she said, her voice low and her green eyes peering into mine. She snapped her fortune cookie and pulled out the slip of paper.

I nearly choked on my tea. I studied her face. She was damn serious and meant every dollar's worth. "Ten thousand dollars! To do what?"

"I'd like you to help me scare my husband to death."

It was nearly midnight. Bel Air, a swanky neighborhood tucked away in the foothills of the city, was a heavily patroled province, but tonight it didn't appear as though anyone was on the payroll.

I had no intention of pulling off Mrs. Hunnicut's ludicrous scheme and I had told her so, in no uncertain terms. Instead, I had agreed to secure certain things she couldn't get for herself. I didn't expect any trouble gaining entry into her estate. She had assured me there were no dogs, no alarms, and no bodyguards on the premises. She also assured me that Roger would be sound asleep. I knew it was some sort of set-up, but I wasn't quite sure how it would all wash out. I had to wonder, though: was it the case itself or was it Mrs. Hunnicut who lured me further into this domestic coronary meltdown? Mind you, I had no intention of putting the moves on this broken-hearted creature. I valued my life too much. And in spite of her trying to pull the wool over my eyes with the yarn about Mary, I still imagined she'd gotten the raw end of the deal, married to a bad egg like Roger. Sure, we've all had people walk out on us, but how many of us can say our loved ones wanted to murder us?

I parked my Volvo in front of the gated estate, darted between two thick bushes and found my way on the other side of the gate. A dog howled in the night. I checked my watch. It was ten minutes before twelve. I figured it would take me no longer than fifteen minutes to do what I had to do. Mrs. Hunnicut had instructed me to crack open the wall safe and remove her will, along with several thousands of dollars in cash and six rolls of undeveloped film which could be used as evidence against her husband.

The wood floor boards on the patio creaked slightly as I made my way inside the Hunnicut Estate. I wasn't sure what I'd find. I believed I had sufficiently calmed Mrs. Hunnicut, convincing her that the best recourse was to get what she needed to prove her accusations and leave her husband with little or no ammunition that he could use in court. With her testimony and my confirmation, I felt confident that Roger would soon be behind bars. As far as I was concerned, that was revenge enough.

I turned on my small flashlight and followed the makeshift map Mrs. Hunnicut had given me. I stopped long enough to examine the wedding photo on a coffee table in the study. The perfect couple. How happy they looked. How time and greed had changed all that. I was just about ready to tackle the safe when I heard a blood-curdling scream come from directly above me.

I don't know how I made it up the stairs so quickly. I pulled out my .38 and with gun and flashlight in hand I stopped to listen outside the door of the master bedroom. The door was half opened.

"My God," a man's voice moaned. "Oh my God, you're not dead."

"That's right, darling. You didn't do a very good job of killing me."

"I don't understand, I thought I'd gotten rid of you for good."

I inched closer to the door. It sounded as if Roger was foaming at the mouth. From where I stood I could see Mrs. Hunnicut, dressed to kill in a silver lamé nightgown, her face pale and determined in the shimmer of moonlight.

Roger lunged for her like a rabid wolf, half-starved and out of its mind. But she moved out of his reach. "Oh my God," he groaned, and I caught sight of the shiny glint of a butcher's knife in her outstretched hand.

Within a split second Mrs. Hunnicut lifted her arm and threw the knife like a javelin.

"Hold it, lady," I yelled as I kicked open the door. Luckily the blade landed in the wood paneling about two feet above Roger's head.

"Angie, look what the man's reduced me to," she said without taking her eyes off Roger. "I hope you've enjoyed what little freedom you've had these last few days."

Roger, at least what I could see of him, sat up trembling, his forehead drenched with sweat, his eyes bulging as he stared over at the haunting apparition of his dear departed wife.

Mrs. Hunnicut sneered at her husband. "Thought you'd gotten rid of me, did you? Well, your little plan didn't work and now I'm home, darling. Come here and show me how much you've missed me and maybe I'll forgive you."

I watched Roger's white face as the color slowly crept back into his cheeks. He moved like a slug toward his wife.

Mrs. Hunnicut held her cheek up toward Roger. He leaned down and kissed her, then buried his face in her neck as she stood there, petting his matted hair.

They seemed to have forgotten that I was in the room so I let out a cough to remind them. When Mrs. Hunnicut turned to me, she had an envelope in her outstretched hand.

"You've been an expert witness, Angie, but I won't be needing your services any longer. That is, unless Roger decides to be a bad little boy and misbehave again."

I gave Mrs. Hunnicut a hard look. She was smiling pretty. Her eyes appeared to relax now that she had Roger in her arms again. I finally realized that the black widow had hired me to do what Fletcher didn't have the stomach for. After all, he was a married man himself. A dick, even a shady one, has to draw the line somewhere. I decided that this was the time to throw a wrench into her plans.

"You can come in now," I called out, and Mary Wexler stepped through the open door.

Mrs. Hunnicut's face turned white as she looked at Mary and then over to Roger. Poor Mary stood there, probably wondering how it had all come to this.

Till death do us part, was ringing in my ears. Roger may have botched Mona Hunnicut's murder, but Mona hadn't done much better. I knew I'd never be able to prove it, but I was sure Mrs. Hunnicut had made plans to get rid of Mary. She must have thought she could rely on me as a witness, a convenient alibi, in case anyone ever made any inquiries, or Roger got out of control again and decided to blab to the police. She'd probably hired some third-rate henchman to do the job right there on the Santa Monica pier. My stomach was twisted in a knot. I suddenly had no appetite for my work. Mrs. Hunnicut slavishly urged me to take the envelope, but I walked out, empty-handed.

It was still dark when I crept into Katherine's bed. Her skin smelled of sleep and her naked body was the only antidote for the evening.

"Darling," she murmured, barely above a whisper. "Are you all right?"

I wasn't in the habit of showing up unannounced at my lover's doorstep at five in the morning. I had a key, but I'd never used it before tonight. I cupped Katherine's breasts in my cold hands and felt her body shiver, then return my embrace.

"Is she as beautiful by moonlight?" Katherine asked as she bit my ear lobe.

I answered with a long kiss that buried the sound of Roger's scream and wiped out the scent of Ramona Millicent Hunnicut.

Katherine and I made love with such passion that even I was surprised. And as the first yellow rays of dawn streamed through the levelors, I noticed as if for the first time, Katherine's fine blonde hair on the white lace pillowcase. She'd fallen into a light sleep in the crook of my arm. I was almost too exhausted to join her, but then the tide of her breathing lulled me.

Partners at the Pump

Judith Post

WORKING A GAS STATION, you hear a lot. Most of the time, it piques your interest. More often than not, you forget it the minute you stick your head under a hood. But sometimes, it raises your eyebrows and stays with you a while. Me, being a girl, I tend to be nosier than my old man. At least, that's what Dad says.

My Dad and I run the station together, as a team. When I was a kid and always underfoot, the old man called me his junior partner. Now that I'm nineteen and still underfoot, he says the station's half mine.

I was pumping gas and listening to Dad and Harvey Buchanan, owner of our town's finest eating establishment—which isn't saying much—talk about the hot little hussy who'd strutted in with a trucker the other night when Dad said, "Your ears should be burning by now, Charlie!" My real name's Charlotte, but ever since Ma split when I was almost eleven, I've been known as Charlie. Which is fine with me, because I think Charlotte's a wimpy name. Ma only picked it because she thought it sounded fancy. I don't match it much.

I think about Ma every once in a while. She was a real beauty, if I remember her right. The old man says I have her good looks— the coarse, black hair and dark, brown eyes, the high cheekbones and oval face—he gets all lyrical about it. Says I'd turn heads if I ever washed all the grease off me. Me—I don't care. No one lives in Green Clover who's worth the bother.

Besides, Ma turned heads, and look what happened to her. Jumped on the back of a Harley and ditched the old man, who loved her something awful, and a little girl who'd have given a lot for only a little of her time.

But Ma was always too restless to sit at home nights with the likes of us. And the old man, well, he always said that she needed to sow her wild oats, then maybe she could settle down.

Seems like it's not going to happen, though. Because news is that Ma went and got herself killed in some big city, and they're sending her body back to Green Clover to be buried.

Dad took it OK when Sheriff Willard came to tell him. After all, it's been eight years now. Ain't like we'd been expecting her to drop in sometime. But the idea of her being dead doesn't set too good, either. And murdered is even harder to swallow.

I heard Willard telling the old man the particulars. Wasn't supposed to, of course, but neither man knew I was under Jack Holston's old Dodge, checking the steering.

"Got mixed up with some bad people, so far as I can tell," Willard said, scratching the tight elastic of his jockey shorts like he always does. The man's big middle pulls those shorts up tight around his privates, and he always has to scratch. "Sex, drugs—you know how wild your Pepper was."

Pepper—the nickname Ma had picked for herself. She'd always hated her real name of Rosemary. Said it sounded like some herb that should sit on a shelf, while she was more like a spice to add zest to life.

"And they're shipping her body home?" Dad asked. "Didn't she make any roots where she lived?"

"Never did divorce you—legal," Willard said. "So she's still your property, so to speak. Leastways, you're the one who has to pay to bury her."

"That's all right by me," Dad said. "After all, she gave me Charlie. Ain't no one done anything finer for me—ever."

When I heard that, well, I have to tell you, a lump caught in my throat near to choke me. 'Cause the truth is, I feel the same about the old man. He keeps joking that I should start looking for a young guy to settle down with, start a family. But there aren't too many men in this world as good as my dad. I'm going to have a hard time finding one—but he wants me to. Says just because he and Ma couldn't make a go of it, that's no sign marriage isn't good. Besides, he doesn't fool me none. The old man wants to be a grandpa and bounce a baby on his knee.

"If you don't get at it, I'll be too old to bounce!" he told me. "I'm not so young, you know. I was no spring chicken when I married your ma. More of a father to her than a husband, but that's what she wanted at the time. She'd run away from home and was just a skinny, scrawny kid with no place to go. I took her in and she thought she fell in love with me. Hell, she was just grateful someone finally did something decent for her. No way it could have lasted, but it was good while it did. Might have made it, too, if the Harley man hadn't shown up and she'd have had a few more years to age."

The Harley man had been a stranger to Green Clover whose bike broke down and needed repairs. It took two weeks to get the parts, and by the time he'd roared out of town, he'd sweet-talked Ma into leaving with him.

"She needed more," Dad said, trying to explain before the body arrived on the afternoon train. "I was too old and poor for a girl like her, but I tried to keep track of her—in case she ever needed me. First she went to Fairmont and stayed a month with the Harley. Then she moved on with a trucker. Ended up in Wolcottville. He dumped her and she met a traveling salesman. I lost track of her somewhere in Tennessee."

"She shouldn't have left you," I said.

"She needed room."

The old man never had a bad word for Ma. Me—I couldn't forgive her quite so easy.

"You going with me to pick her up?" Dad asked.

"She's my mom, ain't she?"

We closed the shop and drove the battered old pick-up to the depot on the edge of town. It wasn't used much these days, and weeds grew between the tracks. But today, the train screeched to a halt, and the doors of a boxcar slid open. Sheriff Willard's cruiser pulled in behind our truck, and Willard and my dad helped unload my ma's pine coffin. The station hand carried a cardboard box to the truck and said, "They sent all of her personal belongings. Not much, I guess, but the police packed them up for you."

"Thanks." The old man put them next to the coffin on the flatbed. "Well, nothing to do but bury her, is there? I've already talked to the Reverend. He's gonna meet us at the cemetery."

Most of the townspeople came to Ma's last farewell. Not out of respect for my ma, but because most of them knew my dad. You have to understand that Green Clover isn't much but a small knot of houses and businesses clumped around a few intersections in the highway. My dad and I only go to church on Christmas and Easter, but we've helped a fair share of people when a tire goes flat or a battery goes dead—and in Green Clover, that's considered religious enough. The Ladies' Aide Society brought a baked ham, some potato salad, and a fresh-baked apple pie for us to take home. The church deacons acted as pall-bearers. All in all, it was a pretty nice funeral.

A few times, I found myself wanting to pry the lid off of Ma's pine box, but Sheriff Willard warned us that she didn't look like much, what with three gunshot wounds in the head and face. I figured my curiosity about how she'd aged wasn't worth looking at the scraps that were left of her head, so I listened to the Reverend's sermon about the caterpillar becoming a butterfly and went home only partially comforted. After all, a caterpillar might crawl into a cocoon and come out all pretty in the spring, but my ma was more like a no-good worm. They turned into pesky moths or worse. I didn't have much hope for Ma in the after-life.

Still, when the old man and I drove home with our home-cooked meal and our friends' good wishes, I couldn't stop thinking of Ma. "Can I look at her things?" I asked Dad when we'd unloaded the truck.

Without answering, Dad pried the top off of the cardboard carton. Some frilly lingerie and two fancy dresses lay on top. Jeans and shirts came next. A box of gaudy jewelry was stashed in a corner, and an 8 x 10 frame with an old picture of Dad and me lined the bottom.

"At least she remembered us," the old man said.

I stared at the meager belongings. "That's it?" I asked. "That's all she owned?"

"Willard said she stayed in a rented, furnished apartment. Never stayed one place long."

I shook my head. What a pitiful handful of nothing to leave behind. There was no clue to my mother's personality, nothing I could cherish as a last memento.

The old man could guess my disappointment and handed me the picture. "Keep this," he said. "In time, you'll see that it must have gone everywhere with her. We were still a part of her, Charlie.

She still cared."

I looked at the cheap gold frame and the faded photo. Big deal!
I thought, but I took it upstairs and put it on the night table beside
my bed.

My dad took the rest of Ma's things and put them on the work
bench in our garage. Then we ate the meal the church women sent,
and turned the sign in the gas station's window from Closed to
Open.

In a few hours, life was back to normal. Me. My dad. And the
station.

Two weeks had passed, and memories of Ma had gotten to be
just that—memories—just like before—passing thoughts, no more.
Not many new people came to Green Clover, and when they did,
you remembered them. So when the big, white Lincoln pulled up
to the pump and the driver said he was having car trouble, I looked
him over real good. Curiosity mostly. A man had to make a lot of
money to own a car like that Lincoln.

He stuck out from our townsfolk like a pedigreed dog from a
pack of mutts. I don't know a thing about clothes or fashion, but this
guy's suit looked like it had been molded to his body. A gold watch
glimmered at his wrist, and a chain hung about his neck. My dad
thought that if a man wore anything more than a wedding band, he
was pretty suspicious; but this guy just looked rich. Like he had
more money than he'd ever know what to do with—and he
obviously knew a lot.

"What's it been acting like?" Dad asked when I motioned him
to the pump.

"It runs with gushes of speed, and it's died a few times."

"Hmm," Dad rubbed his chin. "Pop the hood and let me take a
look."

While the old man played with the carburetor and checked the
spark plugs, I pumped gas and washed windows.

"Mind if I use a bathroom?" the guy asked, getting out of the
car.

"It's in the garage," Dad called, still fiddling.

By the time the guy came back, Dad said, "No problem. Your
choke was open. No big deal."

"What do I owe you?"

"Just twenty-three for the gas."

The guy handed me twenty-five bucks and said, "Keep the change." Then he started the engine and drove away.

When I took the money to the cash register in the office, I noticed the side door that led to our house was left open. Funny. It wasn't open before. When I went to close it, I saw that the garage attached to our house was open, too. I walked across the small lawn that separated the station from our home and peeked inside. The box that held Ma's things on the work bench had been rummaged through. Clothes that had been neatly folded were now dangling over the cardboard edges. I shuffled through them. The jewelry box was missing.

When I told Dad, he scratched his chin. "Didn't look like a common thief, did he?" the old man asked. "And we don't exactly look like we'd have much to steal, do we? Think I'll mention this to Willard and see what he says." He left the garage and ambled to the house to call the sheriff. When he got back, I was working on Mrs. Fitzwilliam's Cutlass Supreme. She hardly ever drove it and it was in beautiful shape, but just like a hypochondriac, Mrs. Fitzwilliam always heard the engine cough or a funny noise somewhere in the rear and asked us to check on it. Dad and I would look, fill it up with gas, and drive it back to her place. She'd be happy with it for another month or two, then she'd hear something new.

"What did Willard say?" I asked as Dad started a tune-up for the Reynold's kid.

"There's been a couple of corpses turn up in your ma's old circle of friends. A detective thinks they're all connected. Willard says he might stop by sometime to talk with us."

"What about?"

Dad shrugged. "Beats me. The guy must be grabbin' at straws."

The next day, a decrepit, ugly green, unmarked police car pulled into the service station. I haven't seen many cars that look like they've put in that many miles and been so abused. The guy who stepped out of it didn't look much better. Dark circles cratered his eyes and his suit was as wrinkled as his forehead. Real detectives don't look much like the hunks on TV, I guess. Then he smiled—and he had a smile that would charm a dead battery to life.

As I walked over to greet him, I did my best to look casual. I've watched a lot of cop shows on TV, and Sheriff Willard never quite fit the image. This guy looked like he might be a taller, overweight version of Columbo.

"Hi, what can I do for you?" I asked.

He flashed his badge. "I'm Detective Walt Daniels," he said. "I'd like to talk to you about your mother."

I shrugged. "I can't tell you much. I haven't seen her since I was eleven. Dad could probably tell you more." I turned to yell for the old man, but he interrupted.

"Would you mind just telling me what you know?"

Another shrug.

"She never got in touch with you after she left?" he asked.

"No."

He looked me over. "Was she as pretty as you?"

I blushed. Not many people come to the station and tell me how pretty I am. I glanced down at my baggy overalls and scuffed gym shoes. "Prettier," I said.

"That's hard to believe."

"So what do you want to know?" I asked him.

I'd had enough of the compliments. He could tell, and got down to business. "Your mom sent you some stuff when she died, didn't she? Could I look at it?"

"Sure." I led him to the cardboard box in our garage. "The guy who drove the Lincoln took a box of jewelry," I said.

He rummaged through Ma's things. "That's it?"

"Not much, is it?"

He shook his head.

"There was an old picture of Dad and me, too. She must have carried it with her."

"Can I see it?"

I invited him into the kitchen and ran upstairs to get the photo. He stared at it while I got him a glass of cold Pepsi.

"And she just ran off?" he asked, when I sat down opposite him.

"Yeah, a guy with a Harley came to town, and she left with him."

"And she's been moving around ever since?"

"I guess."

"It's hard to believe—a mother taking off like that and never coming back to see her daughter."

"It happens."

"Yeah." He sounded kind of sad. "Well, I don't have much to tell you, either, except that your mom was a real sharp-looking lady, and she and her two girlfriends used to get dressed up and hang out at the bars, if you know what I mean. We think they got in the middle of something by accident. They either overheard or saw something they shouldn't have; and to make matters worse, they tried to put the heat on the wrong people. All three of them are dead now."

"So that's what happened," I said.

"Not much to go on, is it? We've tried digging every place we can, but we always come up empty. No one's seen anything, heard anything, or knows anything. Always a blank wall."

I nodded.

"It doesn't seem to bother you much. Don't you want whoever killed your mother to be punished?"

"I don't know. It's kind of like reading about a stranger in the paper. It's hard to get too excited."

He frowned, studying me closer. "Either that, or you won't let yourself. Maybe it's safer that way."

"Doesn't matter. I can't help you. I don't know anything about her."

He sighed. "I talked to your dad earlier, met him at the barber shop on Main Street. He said pretty much the same thing."

"Eight years is a long time," I said.

"Yeah, guess it is. Well, can you tell me about the guy who stopped in here yesterday? Did you notice anything specific?"

I made a list. "Dark hair, dark skin—like he was Italian or something—expensive suit, lots of jewelry, and a scar under his chin and part way down his throat. He drove a white Lincoln—this year's model—but I don't know the license number."

"He'd have changed it by now anyway," Walt said. "A scar, huh? Would you recognize his picture if you saw it?"

"Yeah, I studied him real good."

"Observant, aren't you?" he asked.

"Part of the job. Besides, I was curious."

He smiled and looked at his watch. "It's getting kind of late, took me a while to drive here. When does your station close? Don't suppose you'd care to join me for dinner? I hate eating alone."

He sounded sort of lonely. It hit me then that being a detective might not be all that much fun. Nothing compared to tearing an engine apart and putting it all back together.

I hadn't sold a drop of gas in the last hour, and the only car I needed to work on was an overhaul that needed a day, not a few minutes. "Things have been slow lately," I said. "I can close now. Dad will be playing softball tonight with his buddies, so I'm on my own, anyway."

"Good, where do you want to eat?"

"There's one restaurant that's nice and there's a bar two blocks down. I like either."

"Are you twenty-one?"

"No."

"Then we'll hit the restaurant." Just like a cop. I decided not to tell him that Dad and me ate in the bar almost every day for lunch. In Green Clover, the letter of the law's not so important. It's intentions that count. "You going like that?" he asked, studying my grease-blotched overalls.

"'Course not." I unsnapped them and let them fall to the garage floor. I had a pair of old blue jeans and a T-shirt on underneath them.

"Oh, that's a lot better."

I didn't miss the sarcasm, but he didn't know Green Clover. Nobody dressed up to go to Harvey's place.

I told my dad my plans, and Detective Daniels and I drove to the restaurant.

"Hey, Charlie!" Harvey said when he saw me. "How come you're not playing shortstop?"

"This is Detective Walt Daniels," I said. "He's here to ask about Ma."

"Oh, sorry. What can I get you then?"

We both ordered the swiss steak special with mashed potatoes and peach pie à la mode for dessert.

I have to admit I don't know whether what Walt said was all that amusing, but there was something about the way he said it that held my attention. Old detectives know a lot of good stories. Over dinner, he trotted out quite a few of them.

I knew he was trying to get me to relax—to trust in him and maybe confide some deep, dark secret. Problem was, I didn't have any; and I didn't know my ma from any other hooker in his city.

When we'd finished our meal, he said, "I don't suppose you could drive into town with me and look at some mug shots? It might help me know who to tail."

"I could follow you in, then drive back."

"No, we don't do things that way. I'll drive you in. I'll drive you back." Now he sounded like the old man.

"Are you nuts?" Then I had the answer. "I'll take the bus. It comes right through Green Clover every night about midnight."

"We'll pay for the ticket."

That settled, we drove to the ball park to tell Dad. I thought he might be upset. Instead, he looked pretty pleased with himself. Guess he thought I was finally showing more emotion about Ma's death.

Settled in the front seat, Walt and I talked the entire distance to the police station. By the time he pulled into the police garage, I knew that he was divorced and hardly ever saw his two kids. I could be wrong, but I think after talking to me, he just might try to change that. He didn't much like the idea that a parent could die and it wouldn't change a thing in his kids' lives.

"Not very sentimental, are you?" he asked, as he led me past the desk sergeant.

"Maybe not, but I know what counts, and I appreciate that. My dad's always been there for me. We're happy together. Don't see any reason to cry about something I can't change."

I found the man's picture on the fifth page of mug shots. Marco Pescutti, it said under his photo. A long list of arrests and charges were under his name. A professional crook, it seemed. An errand boy for some even nastier people.

Walt thanked me and drove me to the bus station. He stayed until the bus pulled out of sight.

On the trip home, I studied the people around me. The bus went from one backwater town to another until it hit the state capital. Everyone, including me, looked like they lived at one of the small towns except for one man who looked out of place. I couldn't quite decide why, at first. He was dressed in jeans and a T-shirt, but he didn't look comfortable in them. His gym shoes were brand new. His hair was too perfect—he probably went to a stylist instead of a barber. And his hands didn't have one callous or grease stain on them.

When I got off at my stop, the man was still on the bus, but that didn't make me feel too much better. The next town was only twenty minutes away—an easy walk, even for a city slicker. If he came to Green Clover, though, he'd be noticed. And he wouldn't have an easy time leaving without a car, I reasoned. I was probably getting itchy. Not like me. I didn't believe in panic. Always keep a clear head, and think your way out of trouble. It had saved me from lots of spankings from the old man.

I stopped at the creek on the way home and sat on its banks, listening to crickets, giving myself time to think. As I lay on my back in the tall grass, staring at the stars, I heard an engine purring down the highway. I watched as a black Chevy passed. No car I'd ever worked on. Didn't belong to anyone around here. So where was it going? It stopped in the shadows not far from our house. A spy sent to keep an eye on us?

Well, I'd show him what we locals thought of people with bad manners. I crawled in the tall grass beside the road until I was even with his car. Then I slid underneath it and disconnected the radiator hose. Next, I played with the fuel line.

While I was still busy, his door opened and he stepped out. Just as I'd thought. Brand new gym shoes. So white they almost glowed in the dark. But then they headed toward our house.

All of a sudden, I got nervous. Walt had said these people were mean and hired mean people to do their dirty work. They'd shot Mom three times and killed both of her friends. Maybe they didn't care how many people they killed, and Dad was in the house alone.

Dad kept a shotgun in our garage for rabbit hunting. I'd learned how to shoot when Mom was still home. I slid out from under the car and crawled to the side door of the garage.

The man was silently lifting the kitchen window. Dad had left the small lamp on over the sink to greet me when I got home. The guy could see what he was doing and could make sure no one was around. At least, he *thought* no one was around.

I grabbed the shotgun from the garage and slid two shells into it. I'd always loved a double-barrel. If you missed the first time—which I rarely did—you wouldn't the second.

When I came around the side of the house, the man had his leg hoisted over the window sill and was halfway inside. I stayed in the shadows until I reached the kitchen door, and then I leaned on the doorbell.

The man's hand slid inside his open shirt, but I said, "I wouldn't do that if I were you," and stepped into the light, aiming the shotgun at his chest.

"Holy crap! Don't pull the trigger, lady." Both hands flew over his head.

I could hear Dad's footsteps so I yelled out "We have company,

Dad. Call Sheriff Willard." In a second, I could hear him dialing.

About ten minutes later, Willard's state cruiser flew into our driveway.

"Well, well, what you got here, Charlie?" Willard asked, taking out his handcuffs.

Just then the man lunged, but Willard's about as hard to move as a Mack truck. The guy bounced to the ground and Willard cuffed him.

"He wouldn't have gone far anyway," I said. "I was under his Chevy."

Chuckling, Willard tucked the man into the backseat of his cruiser. "Good work, Charlie, but you two had best take care. Looks like this affair isn't over. I'll call your detective and see if he wants this fella."

As Dad and I walked back into the house, I said, "What do you think he was after? The first guy looked through the box Mom sent."

"Beats me," Dad said. Then our eyes locked on the framed picture I'd brought down to show Detective Daniels.

"I wonder—" I went to the picture and slid off the back. Between the photo and the back of the frame was a hollow space filled with a small cache of snapshots and papers. The newest addition was a small sheet of paper. Cramped scribbles filled the small sheet. 23&4,2-18; 3&M,4-9; St.&5,5-3; E.7&5,5-9 . . . the list went on. There were four one-thousand dollar bills stashed there, too.

"Your Ma's handwriting," Dad said. "Always was all tiny and tight."

I called Detective Daniels to tell him what we'd found. When I turned back from the phone, Dad was fingering the picture. His eyes and mouth looked pinched.

"She used us," he said, "to hide her papers in. Knew no one would wonder about a run-away wife keeping a picture of her old man and kid."

There were other yellowed slips of paper with faded ink that must have been hidden for a long time. The snapshots showed Ma and two other women making love to different men.

Dad winced as he sorted quickly past them. The notes were all little bits of information that might damage someone's respectability. One said, 'Fred Cox skimmed eight grand from the steel mill.'

Another said, 'Alex Winters keeps a mistress in Highland Park apartments.'

"Blackmail," I murmured. Ma had gotten herself blown away by trying to milk the wrong person.

"I hate for you to have to see this," Dad said. "Sorry, Kid."

I shrugged. I'd given up feeling abandoned by Ma. As far as I was concerned, it was her loss, not ours.

"We were just too good for her," I said.

The old man looked at me and smiled. "You might be right."

Detective Daniels visited us the next morning. It was Sunday, and the gas station was closed. Dad and I had our feet up on the coffee table, a big pan of popcorn propped between us, watching the Chicago Cubs play the San Francisco Giants. One slice of leftover pizza rested in a cardboard box.

"I owe you dinner at the fanciest restaurant in town," Walt said as he slid his bulk onto the far side of the couch and eyed the pizza.

"Help yourself," the old man said, getting a can of pop from the refrigerator and handing him a paper towel.

"That's Harvey Buchanan's," I said.

"Not your town, my town," Walt told us. "That list you gave me—took me a while, but all of a sudden, it clicked. The first two numbers were the location of liquor stores that were robbed in the last few months. The next two numbers were the dates." He took a bite of pizza and washed it down with pop. "The city has a Crime Stoppers number. Seems the liquor chain put up a $5,000 reward for a tip that would lead to an arrest in the burglaries. The guy who pulled the heists got busted when someone made an anonymous call."

"Rosemary?" Dad asked.

He still always called Ma by her real name.

Walt nodded. "Trouble was the guy's brother, Ernie, was a regular customer of Rosemary's, too. When she had money all of a sudden, it wasn't too hard for him to figure out how she'd gotten it. We've already picked him up, and we found the gun he used, hidden in his sock drawer."

"But what about the other two women?" I asked.

"They might have guessed which one of your mother's customers shot her. Ernie just couldn't take a chance on that, so he killed them."

"So Ma was responsible for their deaths," I said.

Walt looked uncomfortable and he changed the subject. "About my offer—a meal at a fancy restaurant."

But I wasn't finished yet. "The guy in the white Lincoln?"

"Works with Ernie. So does the kid who tried to break into your house. Nobody was sure how much your ma knew and that made them real nervous." Walt grinned. "The young kid's singing like a bird, fingering Pescutti as the guy who sent him to your place—told him to shut you two up if you got in his way."

"Shut us up?" Dad asked.

"Pescutti isn't known for his nice manners." Walt finished his pop and pizza. "Now—I'll try again—about taking you to dinner. How about tomorrow night? And this is a dress-up affair. Can you manage that?"

Dad and I looked at each other. "Can't," I said. "I'm going fishing with Slade after he closes the hardware store."

"Friday night?" Walt asked.

"Slade's taking me to a stock car race."

"Who's this Slade?" Walt asked, intrigued.

"Lives two towns over," I said. "Been friends forever."

"No romance?" he asked, teasing.

I grimaced.

"Next Saturday, then? You could meet my kids. They're going to spend the weekend with me."

Dad and I nodded. "That sounds nice—but nothing fancy."

"Charlie hasn't got a dress," Dad explained. "Ain't about to buy one, either."

Laughing, Walt said, "What the heck? I'll bring the kids over here and we'll meet you at Harvey's."

That settled, he took his leave. Dad and I settled back in our chairs and finished the Cubs game.

An Unmourned Death

Jaqueline Girdner

IT WAS THE SMELL that Officer Brenda Jackson could never get used to. She had learned to harden her tall solid body to the occasional kicks and blows of those she arrested, and her mind to the insults hurled at her as a black woman in uniform. Even the infinite panorama of senseless cruelty and violence didn't get to her much anymore. But the smell of dead flesh that assaulted her when she opened the apartment door was too much.

She pulled out a handkerchief and held it tightly over her face, forcing her spasmodic breathing back into regular rhythms before turning to her partner, Andy Stott. Andy's freckles looked like mud spatters against his suddenly pale skin. He lit a cigarette with a hand-waving flourish. Not that he smoked. He lit it to mask the smell.

"Shall we?" he asked, stretching his face into a one cornered smile. He bowed formally towards the room from which the smell emanated.

"After you," Brenda murmured with a small smile of her own buried in her handkerchief. A smile of gratitude for the shield against despair which his cheerful absurdity provided.

Andy waved the cigarette in front of him as he led the way into the scrubbed white kitchen. The kitchen was clean to the point of fussiness, except for the old man's body.

The body was no surprise. The apartment manager had told them that she hadn't seen Joe McGivern for a week. Not that she cared for him as a person, but it was her duty to report it. "Nastier than a pit bull with a headache," was how she had described him. McGivern was no longer capable of any nastiness, except for his odor. He lay slumped over the kitchen table in a dried pool of whiskey and vomit.

"Phew! Let's check the place out fast and call the medical examiners," said Andy. He bounced impatiently on the balls of his feet.

"Right," agreed Brenda.

The beige and white living room was uncompromisingly bare. No pictures hung on the walls. No knickknacks sat on the mantlepiece. The only furnishings were a brown and white plaid sofa, a pine coffee table and a fat old console television set. But at least the smell wasn't so bad in there. Andy had already moved on to the bedroom when Brenda noticed the white envelope on the coffee table. Purple ink spelled out "To Whom It May Concern" in flowing rounded letters.

"Wait," she called to Andy and picked up the envelope by its edges. It wasn't sealed. She shook out the folded sheets of paper inside.

"Suicide note?" asked Andy.

"Maybe," said Brenda, unfolding the sheets carefully and beginning to read.

"Hey, don't be shy. Read it out loud."

"Okay, okay. It begins, 'My name is Josie. I killed the old man.'" Brenda looked up at Andy. His eyes widened. Was this a homicide?

"Keep reading," he said, his tone suddenly serious.

"'I poisoned his whiskey. He makes me so sick when he drinks. He's a mean drunk. He has stomped out every loving instinct I ever had. He has slashed my paintings, ripped up my drawings and forced me to live isolated in this drab prison. And it wasn't only me. He drove our oldest girl to suicide with his cruelty. I can never forgive him for that. Our youngest, Sharon, is always good to us, but he treats her like dirt. He's even mean to strangers. He bumps people with his cart at Safeway, and starts fights.'"

"Remind me not to bump anyone with my cart at Safeway," said Andy, rolling his eyes.

Brenda aimed a steady, cool glance at him before returning to the letter.

"'If you are reading this, it means he took me with him. It doesn't matter. We're old and sick anyway.' It's signed 'Josie,'" finished Brenda. "And there's a postscript, too, 'Dear Sharon: I hope you don't find us. If you do, remember I've always loved you very much.'"

"Well, you're reading the letter," Andy said. "That means he took her with him, right? So where the hell is she?"

They searched. No one was in the tiny pale green bathroom. No one was in the spartan bedroom either. Andy was sliding the bedroom closet door open when they heard a key in the front door.

"Dad?" sang out a clear voice. "Josie? What's that awful smell?"

They hustled into the kitchen where they were greeted by the sight of a woman's polyester blue back bent over the old man's body. The woman's arms dangled loosely, as did her wilted blond hair. The only solid thing about her was the bulky maroon purse that she wore slung over a thin drooping shoulder. Brenda wondered how she could stand the smell.

"Police officers, Ma'am," said Brenda softly.

The woman turned her head slowly toward them. Her eyes were hazel and blank in a colorless face.

"He's dead," said Andy. The woman's eyes didn't even flicker. He put his hand on her elbow to guide her out of the room. "Who are you?" he asked.

"I'm Sharon . . . his daughter." Her voice had gone flat. The singing tone of her entry was gone.

Andy led her to the living room and sat her down on a couch. Brenda followed them, fully alert to every movement of the woman who had identified herself as Joe McGivern's daughter.

"Sharon, does your mother live here?" Andy asked in a gentle tone.

"My mother? My mother's been dead for years."

"Your step-mother?"

Sharon focused her eyes on him, as if he had just landed in front of her. "What do you mean? I don't have a step-mother."

"Who is Josie then?" asked Brenda. Sharon turned toward her and gave a quick snort of laughter.

"Josie? I'll show you," Sharon said and got up from the couch. Andy moved towards her to sit her back down, but Brenda shook her head.

They followed her into the bedroom where she finished sliding open the closet door. She reached in past the worn beige trousers and white shirts and pulled out a rustling purple silk dress. Then she reached for the upper shelf and grabbed a blond wig. She held them out to Andy.

"This is Josie."

Andy looked at Brenda with raised eyebrows. Did they have a nut case on their hands?

Sharon saw the look. She stuffed her hand in her purse. Brenda tensed and moved her own hand quickly toward her gun. But Sharon only pulled out a battered wallet. She opened it to show them a picture of an ugly old woman smiling benignly into the camera.

"Josie. She . . . he. . . ." Sharon faltered. "Dad." Andy shot another look towards Brenda. But Brenda was busy puzzling out Sharon's words.

"Your father was Josie?" Brenda asked.

"Only sometimes," Sharon answered sadly.

"But . . . then Josie killed herself too," blurted Andy.

Recognition and pain filled the void in Sharon's blank eyes.

"Oh no, not Josie!" she wailed and then began to sob.

Small-Town Ingenuity

Wendy Hobday Haugh

AGGIE REINWALD SAT at her kitchen table, steeping English tea to acid as the kettle sang shrilly on the stove. The day's mail lay scattered across the table, bills mostly except for one brown package from her great-great niece. Seven-year-old Tammy wrote as often as her struggling penmanship allowed, each letter a labor of love and a cherished addition to Aggie's life. Her brown packages always brought something delightfully unexpected. A colorful eraser shaped like a cheeseburger, or a pair of fuschia sequined sunglasses. Aggie had few living relatives, and Tammy lived the closest—just three states away.

"It's hell to be old," Aggie murmured. "The world isn't kind at all. Rude behavior—that's all I see these days."

She'd given it her best shot. Driving was difficult for her, what with her arthritic hip and all, but that afternoon she'd eased herself into her rusted old Duster and driven the four miles to town, no easy feat considering the rutted, soggy, late-spring condition of the long dirt road on which she lived.

She'd told Sheriff Ed Burcher everything, starting with her bittersweet bushes last fall. "They were bursting with berries, Sheriff. I grow them just for the birds, so they can find food in the winter and I can save money on birdseed. I'd never had such a marvelous crop, then—BOOM! Every last branch was stripped."

"Maybe you had some overzealous hikers," the sheriff suggested.

"No, sir," Aggie replied firmly. "The boughs weren't clipped neatly, the way any sensible naturalist would do it. They were ripped from the bushes, purposefully damaging the plants." Seeing skepticism in the lawman's eyes, she continued fiercely, "What about my crocuses? Six weeks ago I counted forty-seven in full bloom. The next day, BOOM! Every single one, stomped to bits."

"Maybe some animal was hungry," the sheriff offered weakly.

"Or my daffodils!" Aggie declared. "Seventy-nine daffodils were blooming out front in my half-moon garden. One morning I opened my drapes . . ." She stopped to stifle a sob, tears filling her faded blue eyes. "Every last one was uprooted, Ed. All my bulbs lay scattered across the front lawn. I suppose you'll say a feisty animal did that, too."

Sheriff Burcher sighed heavily. "No, ma'am, I suppose you've made your point. But honestly, Aggie, what would you have me do? Patrol your house round the clock, living way out there in the woods like you do? I've got heftier crimes right here in town, and with just one patrol car. . . ."

Aggie's bony fists clenched tightly. "Sheriff, my twelve lilac bushes are on the verge of full-bloom. With all the rain we had earlier this week, and now with this humidity, they'll peak tomorrow, no doubt. And he'll target them next, I'm sure of it. In case you're interested," she added, "*I know who he is.*"

The sheriff's head jerked toward her. "Who is it, Aggie? Show me the proof, and I'll pick this guy up in a flash."

Silence. "That's the problem," Aggie admitted. "I *think* I know who he is—Billy Merrill—but I haven't any proof."

"BILLY MERRILL?" the Sheriff hooted. "The mayor's son?"

"One and the same," Aggie replied indignantly. "Ever since my arthritis set in, I've had to hire help to work in my gardens. Last summer the high school sent me a list of local boys looking for part-time jobs. Naturally, when I saw Billy's name, I assumed he'd be reputable and a hard worker." Aggie snorted. "But what I *thought* and what I *got* were two different things. He was lazy and unwilling to take direction. Took him all day just to rake out one tiny ditch! Slow as molasses in January. And my flower beds. . . ." Aggie groaned. "He couldn't tell a perennial from the common weed, Sheriff. When I found he'd yanked out most of my myrtle along with the weeds, I fired him on the spot. Refused to pay him, too, figuring he owed *me* for all the havoc he'd brought to my gardens."

"How'd he take being fired, Aggie?"

Her eyes flashed. "Said he'd get even, Sheriff. Called me a lot of disrespectful names, threw my garden tools all over the yard, and then stormed off in a huff."

"Did he ever follow through, though? In all the months since last summer, have you ever had any trouble?"

"No, sir," Aggie admitted. "After Billy, I hired Davey Brink, a hard-working young man who lives just a bit further out than my place. Since then, all's gone smoothly."

The sheriff drew a deep breath. "I'd like to help you, Aggie, but frankly, I'd be just as suspicious of your new fellow. After all these months without trouble, it's hard for me to believe that the mayor's son is finally getting even. He was steamed at the time, sure, and he said some nasty things. But saying and doing are two different things. Billy Merrill is pretty well-liked in this town. I can't imagine him pulling shenanigans like these."

"Maybe he's just a politician at heart," Aggie sniffed. "They've been known to smile while they stab."

Burcher shrugged. "Fact remains, we need proof."

"You'll have your proof," Aggie cried. "He strikes by night, so just drop by my place tomorrow morning, or maybe the next day. My lilacs will be ruined, I can feel it in these arthritic bones. I need police protection!"

"We're small-town, Aggie," Ed Burcher replied with a touch of irritation. "One squad car, one sheriff, one deputy, remember? Not to mention, there's bingo tonight at Blarney Hall. I always patrol through town on bingo night 'til the bars close down, just in case there's trouble. But afterwards I'll take a run out your way. If you're really worried, Aggie, why not keep watch tonight yourself? If you see first-hand who's playing these pranks, we'll have a completely different picture."

Aggie stared wearily at the man. "I'm eighty-nine-years-old, Ed, practically ninety," she amended, remembering her upcoming birthday. "I'm doing okay for my years, but my days of pulling all-nighters are done. I can barely stay awake past nine o'clock!

"Wait a minute, Ed," she added a moment later. "Since the ground's still damp, maybe you could check for footprints, tire tracks—even dust for fingerprints on my house!"

Sheriff Burcher laughed. "You read too many mystery novels, Aggie. Forensic work is for big cities and television shows. We're just a one-horse town. Go home and catch yourself a nap. You look beat."

"Beat, but not *beaten,*" Aggie muttered later as she plunked a teabag into her favorite bone china teacup. "There must be some way I can catch my night stalker."

Through every window she saw the brilliant blossoms of her prized lavender lilacs. The air was rich with their heady scent. It brought tears to Aggie's eyes just to imagine the heinous destruction of her beloved bushes. "There's got to be *something* I can do to protect them."

Just then she caught sight of Tammy's yet unopened package. "Bless you, child," Aggie murmured. "I need a little light in my life today." Eagerly she tore away the brown paper, then burst into hearty laughter. "What on earth? One, two . . . *six* packs of cola-flavored bubble gum, for an old lady who barely has the strength to chew a piece of red mcat!" Aggie reached for the note, written so painstakingly in the child's phonetic spelling.

"Dear Great-Great-Ant Aggie,

This is an early birthday present for you, just from me. It's my most faverit flaver. Tastes just like a bottal of cola. Happy birthday! I LOVE YOU, Tammy."

Aggie smiled, turning the six packages of gum over and over again in her wirey hands. "You make me feel almost young again, Tammy—able to chew gum and stay up past nine o'clock."

A flock of finches descended upon the lilacs just outside the kitchen window. "My goodness," Aggie chided herself. "With all the excitement today, I forgot to feed you dear things."

Grabbing a canister of mixed bird seed, Aggie opened the kitchen window and filled the two nearby feeders. The pungent scent of lilac was overwhelming. Tenderly, she touched the delicate blossoms, certain that their judgment day was near at hand. Her glance fell to the dampish ground beneath the bushes, covered with the shelled remains of months of heavy bird feeding.

Aggie's leathery brow wrinkled as a germ of an idea took root. "The sheriff said I needed proof, plain and simple—nothing fancy like on T.V."

Abruptly, Aggie turned from the window and set the seed can down on the kitchen table. Drinking her tea quickly, she reached for the hissing kettle and poured herself another cup. *Tonight,* she vowed silently, *I'll defy old age at every turn.* Sitting down, Aggie reached for her six packs of bubble gum and carefully tore away the paper. Thirty hard lumps of brownish-pink bubble gum stared up at her. "I swear," she sighed, "just *looking* at them makes my jaw ache." A slow smile spread across her weathered face as she reached for her first piece. "Here goes nothing," she whispered.

For the next forty-five minutes, Aggie Reinwald methodically chewed one piece of bubble gum after another, interrupted only by an occasional gulp of tea. After each piece was sufficiently mauled, Aggie gingerly removed the gooey glob from her mouth and placed it on the kitchen table. She chewed slowly, carefully, trying to avoid the pitfalls of chewing bubble gum with brittle teeth and ancient dental work. Finally, the last piece was finished.

"Any decent lab would find my saliva saturated throughout that stuff," Aggie snorted, "but in a one-horse town like ours, I'd better cover all bases." She grabbed a handful of birdseed from the can and sprinkled it liberally over the soft wads of gum, adding a bit of spit here and there as needed.

"I always thought gum-chewing was a disgusting habit," she muttered. "Now I'm *sure* of it!" She massaged her lower jaw, which had begun to throb painfully, while her tongue tentatively washed over a couple of left-side molars. She glanced at her watch and gasped. "Evening's a-coming and my work's just begun! The time has come *to plant*."

At ten p.m. Agatha Reinwald sat in her rocker in a pitch-black house, close enough to the window to peer out from behind the drapes now and then but safely out of sight from anyone looking in. The extra cups of tea had helped somewhat, but her eyelids were very, very heavy. "Hang in there, Aggie," she pepped herself. "Remember the lilacs!"

Two hours later Aggie awoke with a start. She heard a strange rustling outside, accompanied by an occasional grunt and curse. She froze, her heart beating furiously while a great lump formed in her throat. Slowly she reached forward, drawing the heavy drapes back ever so slightly. *There he was,* destroying her lilac bushes with great, heaving thrusts.

"Scream!" her mind whirled. "Stop him!" But no sound would come, scared to death as she was. Drawing a deep breath, knees shaking like rubber, Aggie crept slowly toward the light switches. With just two flicks, she could flood the entire downstairs and the front yard as well. One, two . . . *three!*

Whipping back the curtains, she could just make out the young man's back as he hurtled through the front yard like a racing greyhound. Shaking uncontrollably, Aggie burst into strange laughter, half giggles, half sobs. Fumbling with the telephone, she managed to reach Sheriff Burcher.

"Pick him up quickly, Ed—yes, I saw him firsthand! And above all, ge*t his shoes!* You needed small-town evidence? Well, I just may have gotten it for you. Check his soles for. . . ."

Two hours later Sheriff Burcher sat in Aggie's kitchen, drinking a cup of camomille tea. "I gotta hand it to you, Aggie, you outdid yourself tonight. Sure enough, the gum—cola bubble gum dowsed with birdseed—was all over the bottom of Billy Merrill's sneakers."

Aggie rubbed her by now pounding lower jaw. "I was lucky to save some of my lilacs, at least," she said ruefully, "but I'll have to pay for *today's* shenanigans with a trip to the dentist *tomorrow.*"

Sheriff Burcher smiled. "You missing something, Aggie? Anything in particular?" he asked casually, dipping a hand into his shirt pocket and plunking something down on the kitchen table. "You know, for an eighty-nine, almost ninety-year-old, you make one helluva detective."

Aggie's faded blue eyes widened with astonishment. "You found *that* in the gum, Sheriff?"

"Yes, ma'am, and something tells me that this little silver rock will match up *perfectly* with that aching hole in your molar."

Limited Partnership

Carol Costa

DANA READ THE FRONT PAGE article for the second time, then carefully folded the morning edition of *The Globe* and set it aside. She smiled as she imagined her editor calling to congratulate her on a job well done. She would pick up the phone and Sam would say, "Dana, the smartest thing I ever did was put you in charge of Globe Investigations. You and your staff are doing a bang-up job and your success in cases like these is making our newspaper one of the most respected in the country."

Her secretary's voice came through the intercom, interrupting Dana's fantasy. "Clark Donaldson is on line two." Marianne's crisp announcement brought Dana to her feet.

She ran a hand through her light brown curls, causing them to bounce in various directions as she quickly scanned her desk top, looking for the income tax packet she was suposed to have brought the accountant last month. She spotted it under a stack of file folders and pulled it towards her as she sat down again and reached for the phone. "Hi, Clark. I know what you're calling about and I apologize. I have it right here."

"This isn't about your taxes. I filed an extension." Clark's normally smooth voice was erupting with little gasps of panic. "Bonnie Jenkins has been arrested for attempted murder."

Dana dropped the tax folder and reached for a pencil, as a picture of Clark's young receptionist flashed through her mind. "The wide-eyed blonde with the pony tail?" Dana asked. "She's barely out of high school, and not big enough to hurt a fly. Who was the victim?"

"One of my clients." Clark whispered the information and Dana strained to hear the rest. "A man named Montana King. He comes to Crescent Hills once a month to drop off his accounting work. Apparently, he and Bonnie have been having a . . . a . . . oh . . . you know. Anyway, it happened in the Parkview Hotel. Bonnie's brothers were waiting for me when I got to the office this morning. They're blaming me for her involvement with King, and they threatened to squash me like an insect if I didn't do something to help her."

"Hold on, Clark," Dana interrupted. "Are these guys gangsters or what?"

"The Jenkins Brothers are professional wrestlers, big as bulls and twice as mean. You've got to help me, Dana. These guys could kill me with one blow. I promised to help Bonnie, but I don't know . . . " Clark suddenly stopped talking as if he had run out of breath.

"All right, Clark," Dana said in what she hoped was a soothing tone. "Let me call Bruno and see what the story is and I'll get back to you."

Clark hung up without saying good-bye and Dana quickly dialed the police station and asked for Detective Al Bruno.

Bruno and Dana had what some people might call a relationship. Dana liked to think of it as a convenient friendship for an investigative reporter. She seldom admitted her true affection for the homicide cop whose personality was as large and overpowering as his linebacker's physique.

"Detective Bruno." His tone was impatient.

Dana grinned. "Hi. Did I catch you at a bad time?"

"The way this day started out, there isn't going to be a good time." His voice had softened considerably. "How about lunch? I need some cheering up."

"And I need some information. Are you involved in the Jenkins' case?"

"Unfortunately. Are you buying?"

Dana hurried off to meet Bruno. It was a little early for lunch, but since both of them usually skipped breakfast, it didn't matter. They settled into a back booth at the coffee shop across from the police station. Bruno was disheveled. His thick black curls needed a barber's touch, and despite his attractive features, his unshaven face made him look sinister.

"Must have been an early call," Dana said, running a finger across the stubble on his chin.

"Five a.m. This little girl wakes up in a hotel room, finds the bed next to her covered with blood, and starts screaming her head off. You know her?"

"Yes. She works for my accountant. Clark called me in a panic over her arrest. The victim is one of his clients."

"*Alleged* victim. We haven't found him yet, only the hysterical girlfriend, bloody bed sheets and a big knife wrapped in a blood-stained towel and stuffed in the wastebasket. The reporters are eating this up. All the details will be in your afternoon edition."

"So what do you think happened to the victim?"

Bruno shrugged his massive shoulders. "He got the hell out of there before his berserk girlfriend could finish him off. Craziness runs in her family. Her brothers are that maniacal wrestling tag team. We're checking all the hospitals and clinics in the area. With all the blood, the victim had to seek emergency treatment. So what do you know about the guy?"

"Nothing except we have the same accountant. I thought I'd go over there after lunch and talk to Clark. Do you want to come along?"

"Whoa." Bruno held up his hands. "I'm assigned to this case and I'm questioning Mr. Donaldson *alone*."

"He's very nervous. Bonnie's brothers paid him a visit this morning. You'll get a lot farther if I'm with you." Dana smiled sweetly, and took a bite of the egg salad sandwich she had ordered. Bruno sighed. "I know," she said sympathetically. "You hate it when I butt into your cases, but Clark is a friend. He asked for my help."

"If he's worried about the girl, I can tell you she'll probably get off lightly. Our description of King says he's over six feet tall and weighs about two hundred pounds. Bonnie Jenkins doesn't weigh a hundred pounds soaking wet. It's hard to believe she could inflict any harm on a guy that size, unless she had help from her brothers."

"Is that a possibility?"

"No. They were on the road with a dozen other wrestlers. Just got back to town this morning after little sister had already been booked and fingerprinted."

As they finished their meal, Dana pried a few more details out of the detective. Bonnie claimed that she and Montana King spent the night together whenever he was in Crescent Hills on business. The desk clerk at the Parkview Hotel verified the fact that Mr. King and Bonnie showed up there once a month. He also said that King always paid cash in advance and was very generous with the staff.

Bruno and Dana arrived at Clark Donaldson's office hoping he could give them more information about Montana King. They found the accountant hunched over his desk staring at his uneaten lunch. Clark was a small man, with a bald head and pale green eyes distorted by the thick lenses on his steel rimmed glasses. Dana was always tempted to buy him one of those green visors that were worn by accountants in old movies.

"Montana King came to me about a year ago," Clark explained. "He had formed a limited partnership with a number of people in this area and needed an accountant to prepare monthly reports for his investors." Clark gave them the information in his slow methodical way, consulting papers that were neatly secured in a manila folder.

"What kind of business was he in?" Bruno asked.

"Cattle. He had a huge ranch in Montana. I have the location right here. Anyway, he claimed he found a new way to feed the cows which would make their beef lower in fat and cholesterol. The investors bought a certain number of these animals as newborn calves and over the months, they contributed to their care and feeding. They were to reap a huge profit from the animals when they went to slaughter. Here, I've got a profile on the whole thing."

Clark removed a pamphlet from King's file and handed it to Dana. It contained pictures of the animals in various stages of growth along with a graph that showed how their value increased along with their size.

"Why would someone who lives in Montana come to the Midwest for investors?" Dana wondered out loud.

"He owns the ranch there," Clark replied. "But other people actually run it for him. Monte lives in this area, and since his friends here wanted in on the investment, he decided to set up this special partnership."

Clark supplied Bruno with King's home address and Dana convinced the detective to let her come along to check it out. The house was located in a rural area off the main highway. It was nothing more than a one room shack with a bathroom the size of a phone booth. The furnishings consisted of a bed, a table and a single chair. There was running water but no electricity or telephone. Except for a few empty beer cans and some fast food containers, there was no evidence that Montana King lived there.

"Something is very wrong with this picture." Dana said as she and Bruno drove back to town. "People say King was a rich rancher, a generous man. Clark says he paid his accounting fees up front and never had to be invoiced. Yet he lived in the middle of nowhere in that broken down place with no conveniences."

"Maybe all the money he collected from his investors went straight to the ranch," Bruno said. However, when they returned to Bruno's office the detective only had to make one phone call to learn that the people who lived on the cattle ranch were the legal owners, and they never heard of a man named Montana King.

To add to the mystery, another detective reported that none of the hospitals or clinics in the area had treated anyone for knife wounds in the past twenty-four hours.

"Well," Bruno said with no trace of compassion. "Maybe he bled to death in some alley."

A different theory was taking shape in Dana's mind. "Can you arrange for me to see Bonnie Jenkins?" she asked Bruno. "I want to talk to her."

Bruno made the arrangements and then left the station. He intended to complete his investigation by questioning some of the investors in King's partnership.

Dana was ushered into a cramped conference room to wait for Bonnie. A policewoman delivered the young suspect and then left the room, locking the two of them inside. Bonnie's hair was pulled back in its usual pony tail. Her face had been scrubbed clean of make-up but her eyes and nose were red and puffy, a bright contrast to the chalky whiteness of her skin.

"Hi, Miss Sloan," Bonnie mumbled. She kept her eyes averted as she slumped into a chair.

"Bonnie, I'm here to help you. Will you answer some questions for me?"

Bonnie nodded.

"I'd like you to tell me about your involvement with Monte King. I understand he was considerably older than you are. How did this relationship get started?"

"I really don't know. It just sort of happened. I mean, I liked him from the first time he came into the office. He was so tall and handsome like he stepped right off a movie screen. Anyway, when he asked me out, I was so surprised I could hardly talk. The first few times, we just went to dinner and he was a perfect gentleman. He only came into town once a month to deliver his journals to Mr. Donaldson, but in between he'd call me up, and sometimes he'd send me flowers. I never had a man pay attention to me like that before. Anyway, one thing led to another and we started going to the Parkview Hotel together." Bonnie paused as tears began to run down her cheeks.

Dana opened her purse, took out a tissue, and handed it to the girl. "The Parkview is a pretty expensive hotel."

Bonnie blew her nose. "Everything we did was first class. I never knew anyone who spent money like Monte does . . . or did. . . . God, Miss Sloan, do you think he's dead?"

"No, I don't," Dana replied firmly. "Can you tell me about last night?" she asked in a gentler tone. "Try to remember every detail. It's very important."

Bonnie took a deep breath and told her story. "We went to dinner as usual. Nothing special happened. Then we went to our room at the Parkview, the same one we had last month. Monte usually ordered drinks from room service, but last night he didn't because he had brought a bottle of wine. He said it was a gift from one of his investors. I went into the bathroom and got ready for bed. When I came out, Monte turned the lights down and we drank some wine. I didn't like the wine. It had a bitter taste, but I didn't want to hurt Monte's feeling so I drank it all down. Anyway, after that I started feeling really sleepy. I could hardly keep my eyes open and Monte said I should just lie down and rest for awhile because we had the whole night to be together."

Dana made a few notes. "What happened then?"

"I fell asleep. When I woke up, it was still dark in the room. I reached out for Monte and felt something wet and sticky on the bed. I turned on the light and Monte was gone and the bed was full of...." Bonnie was trembling, unable to finish the sentence.

"It's all right," Dana said. "I know the rest." She placed a comforting hand on the girl's shoulder.

Bonnie tried to smile but only succeeded in twisting her mouth into a thin pink line. "I love Monte. I could never hurt him."

"Bonnie, did you invest in Monte's partnership?"

Bonnie started to cry again. "Please don't tell Mr. Donaldson. I used a phony name so he wouldn't know. He wouldn't approve of me mixing in a client's business."

"How much?" Dana asked.

"Two thousand dollars. I would have invested more, but that's all I could scrape together without my brothers finding out. Monte said when the cattle went to market, I'd earn enough extra money to go back to college on a full-time basis."

After Bonnie was taken back to her cell, Dana went to Bruno's office to wait for his return. More pieces were fitting into the puzzle she was trying to solve and they were forming an intricate, ugly picture.

"I can't believe these partners King rounded up," Bruno told Dana when he returned. "Not one of them knows squat about livestock, yet they handed over thousands of dollars to this guy. And they all said what a great guy he was, open and honest."

Dana left the station as Bruno was preparing his final report on the Montana King case. She was anxious to tell Clark Donaldson that the charges against his secretary were going to be dropped.

Clark greeted her at the door with a relieved look on his face. He had already heard the news. "One of the Jenkins brothers just called and apologized for this morning. Bonnie is going to be released. He said the police are closing the investigation."

"Since they can't locate a victim, they have no choice," Dana said. "Of course the news reporters have already convinced the public that Montana King is dead, so his partners won't be expecting any quick returns on their investments. They'll be angry when they find out Montana King is a con artist who doesn't own a ranch or cattle, but there won't be much they can do about it."

Clark stared at Dana. "Are you saying this whole thing has been a scam?"

"From the beginning, and that's why I'm not closing my investigation. I think Montana King has pulled this before in other towns, and if we don't warn people about him, he'll do it again. Tell me, Clark, do you accountants have a newsletter or some other way to communicate with one another?"

Clark supplied Dana with information on the national CPA journal he received every month.

Back at her office, Marianne typed up Dana's brief but informative article on Montana King and his Limited Partnership. A copy of Dana's article was sent to the editor of the CPA journal, who agreed to do a special mailing to all his subscribers.

Two weeks later, Montana King, who was now going by the name of Dallas Underwood, was apprehended in a small town just outside of Cincinnati.

"Mr. Cattle Rancher is going to be behind bars for a long time," Dana told Bruno after dinner that evening. "It seems he's pulled this same scam in a number of states. And with the documented proof held by all the accountants he'll be tried and convicted on all counts."

"I understand why King got the accountants involved," Bruno said. "It added credibility to his phony partnerships. But I don't understand the need for that bloody scene in the hotel room. Why did he go to all that trouble when he was leaving town anyway?"

"Didn't you see *The Globe*'s evening edition?" Dana teased. "They had the whole story, an exclusive."

"I hear it was written by a reporter who is always bugging me for inside information," Bruno said pointedly.

"Right. Well, it seems that Montana staged the hotel scene because of Bonnie. Remember her brothers, the maniacal wrestlers? They'd threatened to beat King to a pulp if he ever did anything to hurt their little sister. So, Montana, being a resourceful fellow, went to the Red Cross and offered to donate a pint of blood. While it was dripping from his arm into the bottle, he simply waltzed out, taking the bottle with him. That night, he ground up some sleeping pills and stirred them into Bonnie's wine. After she fell asleep, he spread the blood around and left town. He figured all the commotion about his alleged death, and Bonnie's involvement, would keep her brothers too busy to come after him."

Bruno nodded. "Having met the Jenkins Brothers face to face, I'd say King was smart to buy enough time to get far away from them. I just wish he'd done it in somebody else's district."

"Not me," Dana replied with mock sincerity. "It made a great story. Even my editor called to congratulate me on it."

"So how is Clark Donaldson taking all of this? Did he fire Bonnie? Has he had a nervous breakdown yet?"

Dana laughed. "Bonnie quit. She's gone back to college and her brothers are paying for it. Clark has hired a mature, *married* woman to take her place. As for the nervous breakdown, he told me he's saving that for August 15th."

"August 15th? What's that?"

"The day my extension expires. I still haven't turned in my tax packet."

Business as Usual

Elizabeth Pincus

I WAS HANGING UPSIDE DOWN from one of those wacky inversion boot devices when the shapeliest ankles west of the Mississippi came sliding across my field of vision. Actually, all kinds of ankles have been known to turn my head, so maybe it was my odd vantage point that rendered this pair so irresistible. They came to a rest right before my eyes; taut, mahogany-hued flesh poured into crinkly clean gym socks and a couple of beat-up Nikes.

I swung my arms in an arc, what you're supposed to do to return to the world of the upright. Only I did it a little too rapidly, causing the inversion contraption to fling me around with a loud, jolting thud. I felt blood whooshing southward. I shook my head to get the disheveled mop of hair out of my eyes.

The Nike-wearer chuckled. "Are you Nell?"

"Yeah," I replied, blinking. The rest of her was as splendid as her ankles. I glanced around the uncrowded expanse of the gym. "Who's asking?"

"I'm Johnnie Blue. That's J-O-H-double N-I-E. Short for Johnella. I was told to look for the redhead who, you know, *hangs* around here a lot." A smile played around her mouth.

"Hey, you're a card," I said, rolling my eyes as I bent down to unclasp the inversion boots. Stepping onto solid ground, I gave my bra strap a quick adjustment before reaching out to shake her hand.

"Okay. I'm Nell Fury. Now what can I do for you, Ms. Blue?"

"Pleased to meet you. Johnnie'll do. So—" She paused, searching. "You use all this stuff?"

She was nodding toward the room full of gym equipment: Nautilus, free weights, mats, a couple of stair-climbing torture machines. Mirrors rose up from almost every wall, bouncing back reflections of shiny metal and bright carpet. This spartan place was a training center for women only, attracting both serious weight-lifters and serious dyke-watchers. I was neither. Well, at least not since my wrenching failure to seduce a voluptuous bodybuilder left me convinced romance was for the birds.

I glanced at Johnnie Blue's halo of stubby dreadlocks and decided I could always change my mind.

"I just use the inversion boots," I explained to her. "They're great for stretching out your back, all your muscles. And it's kind of meditative to hang, it clears out your head. . . ."

God, Fury, cool it. You sound like some New Age twerp.

Johnnie was laughing. "I like you. You're funny." She looked toward the back hallway. "How about the sauna? You ever use that?"

"You bet. It's the other reason I come here."

"Great. They said I could try it out, on the house. Maybe we can talk in there?"

I gulped. "Sure thing."

Johnnie Blue headed for the locker room, a tiny spring in each of her graceful steps. I followed behind, wondering why my hips didn't do that when I walked. Maybe I could practice on the stair-climbing machine. But I knew I never would.

Johnnie Blue sweated as prettily as she walked. By the time we'd toughed out half an hour in the tiny wooden box, I had a new client. Also a new pal. Somehow talking business in the nude made for quick intimacies. I'd even agreed to defer payment at the outset, something they tell you never to do in the "How to Become a Successful Private Eye" instruction manual. But Johnnie Blue was a struggling stand-up comic with no idea of what it cost to buy a little rental heat. So I made a grudging exception.

Anyway, maybe Johnnie's problem would turn up nothing more than a heartsick fellow beaten down by too much grief. I told her I'd feel around for a day or two. If it turned into a real case, we'd have to renegotiate terms. Meanwhile, I had an invitation to see Johnnie perform the following evening at her favorite local nightspot, the Club Valencia.

Johnnie also told me she was a bonafide heterosexual. I never would've guessed it.

"I hope you don't mind," she said, almost sheepish.

"Nah." I fixed her with a half-cocked smile. "Besides, you're young yet."

I made my way down Market Street and stopped at the Hot 'n Hunky for a large fries, smothered in Heinz. Chewing the salty gems, I continued down the main drag that chops a wide diagonal slash through downtown San Francisco. It was a brilliant April day; I felt myself sweating up all over again as I trudged past an incongruous strip of fancy restaurants and decrepit furniture outlets.

Coming to a halt outside the Red Desert cactus store, I dumped my Hot 'n Hunky sack in a trash can. A stark saguaro cactus tipped precariously forward from its sandy perch on the city sidewalk.

I was on my way to the Strand Theater to look for a guy who had lost his will to fight. At least that's how Johnnie Blue had put it. Her friend Zeke Capron was assistant manager at the Club Valencia and also, until a few weeks ago, a key agitator at the AIDS Treatment Clearing House. ATCH, as it was known, was a community-based organization that worked to speed up drug trials and get treatments to people with AIDS. After intense involvement with the group, Capron had suddenly disappeared from ATCH. He told Johnnie he was spending his time at the movies.

"Maybe he just needed a break," I had said to Johnnie. I'd passed a few afternoons at the Strand myself.

"No." Johnnie was firm. "Sure, maybe he's burned out, but there's something else he's not saying."

As I approached the movie house, I wondered how in hell I was going to get him to say it to *me*. I practiced a sincere smile. Hopeless, Fury. This detective business suddenly seemed like more of a crapshoot than usual.

I glanced up at the movie marquee. The day's double feature was *The Screaming Skull* and *The Beast with 1,000,000 Eyes*. Goody. I'd missed them the first time around. I handed over a few bucks and passed through the lobby which reeked of cooking grease, urine, and patchouli. I could do without the latter.

Through the hazy darkness in the theater, I only saw a few Black men. I was told Zeke Capron wore tortoise-shell glasses and a trademark San Francisco Giants cap. Shouldn't be too hard. I spotted a likely candidate slouched midway down on the right. I slid into a seat one over from him.

Capron jumped.

"That part always gets me too," I whispered.

He looked at me blankly.

"Too bad about the baseball stalemate," I said, with a nod to his cap. "The Cubs deserve another shot at the Giants. This is going to be their year, I can tell."

Capron continued to stare at me. Not annoyed, just puzzled. "Do I know you?"

"No." I waited a beat. "Johnnie Blue sent me."

"Oh shit!" he blurted. A chorus of angry "ssshhes" spilled out from a few rows back. I hunkered down in my seat. I could sense Zeke Capron glowering.

"Listen," I whispered back. "You're not going to believe this, but I'm a private investigator. Johnnie cared enough to seek my help. You want to give me a few minutes in the lobby?"

Capron shot me another look, this time more weary than angry. He stood abruptly and pointed a lanky finger toward the back exit. I followed him out. Over my shoulder, a platoon of bobbing skeletons loomed ominously from the silver screen.

Our few minutes in the lobby turned into an extended chat down the street at the Starlight Room. I guess Capron was tired of being bugged by his friends—in the case of Johnnie Blue, his ex-lover. Or maybe he'd never met a private eye before. Sometimes the novelty just opens people right up. That is, if it doesn't scare 'em off.

Over cokes and Beer Nuts, Capron told me he was fine, really, and just wanted to cool out for awhile.

"Too many people have died," he said, a small twitch playing at the corner of his mouth. "Hell, Johnnie knows that. I'm tired, is all."

"But she said ATCH gave you hope." Even as I said it, I knew it sounded corny as all get out.

"Hope, no. It gave me work to do, that's all. Now other people are doing it."

We were quiet for a moment, listening to the clink of glasses behind the old-fashioned bar. I popped a few Beer Nuts. And thought about what Johnnie Blue had told me.

"Okay. So nothing scared you, right?"

"Wrong. Everything scares me! Watching the evening news. Walking down the street. All the desperation. I've even started on AZT—that's *really* frightening. But did something scare me away from ATCH, like Johnnie thinks? No way."

I didn't believe him. He went on.

"She thinks I was spooked by Gayle's death, hell, or that Newley kid's. Just a drop in the bucket. The goddamn bucket." He swilled the rest of his coke, fighting back his agitation.

"Who's Gayle?" I asked.

Capron told me that Gayle Letournier had been ATCH's executive director and the first Black woman to work with the group. She'd encouraged the involvement of a number of people of color. Her death last month after a bout with pneumocystis had been a major blow to ATCH. Then her replacement, a white guy named Bradley Myer, was trying to pick up the pieces when an anguished volunteer killed himself in the ATCH office.

"I remember that," I said. "He was gay, right, kind of a hot-shot activist?"

"Yeah. Sebastian Newley." He shook his head. "It's a nightmare. That's all there is to it. But like I said, Johnnie knows that already. So you're wasting your time Miss Private Eye."

"That's Nell to you, buddy." My tone was as kind as his. We parted that way, friendly-like, but I could tell neither of us was satisfied. Capron walked back toward the Strand. I headed the other way, homeward, but first I made a quick detour to the Hayes Valley office of a local gay newspaper.

The phone was ringing when I finally got back to my apartment at seven o'clock. I snagged it in the middle of a ring. "Yeah?"

"Hiya Nell."

"Phoebes!" Perfect. Phoebe Grahame was my best friend. She was also a voracious reader, which came in handy from time to time. I'm not so shabby, either, but I didn't cover the range from *People* to *The Racing Form* to *Tikkun* quite as thoroughly as she did. If there was dirt, Phoebe usually knew about it. Or how to find it.

"Are you working, babe?" she asked.

"Like a dog. Tell me, what do you know about the AIDS

Treatment Clearing House?"

"ATCH. Hmm." I smiled, imagining her cropped head tilted in thought. "Well, it was started a couple of years ago to counter the government's negligent response to the AIDS epidemic—"

I swear. Sometimes you can just picture Phoebe standing on a stump somewhere, mobilizing the People.

"—and they focus almost solely on treatment issues. I think they work both above and underground. I mean, they put pressure on hospitals and the state, but they also work with buyer's clubs and try to get drugs to people who need them, even if they aren't legal yet."

"So does the group clash with the more mainstream AIDS organizations in town?"

"ATCH is known as a fringy crowd. . . . But they do such different work. The groups seem to cooperate, for the most part. At least they keep up a facade. The pharmaceutical companies, though, like the makers of AZT? They probably have a gripe with ATCH. A threat to profits, you know."

"Yeah." I wondered if Zeke Capron got into hot water through his work at ATCH. Hmm. Maybe Sebastian Newley did, too, and Capron knew about it. "Phoebe, do you remember that guy who killed himself last month at ATCH?"

"Uh huh. Stuart, or Steven. . . . What was it?"

"Sebastian. Sebastian Newley."

"That's right. Right after the director died, too." Phoebe sighed. "That's the other thing I was going to tell you. There was a big staff shake-up and they hired some straight-arrow type to take over the head job at ATCH. Apparently he was handpicked by a few power players on the Board of Directors—"

"This new director. You mean—" I searched my memory. "Bradley Myer?"

"That's him. Clean cut, fundraiser background. Apolitical. There was a rumor that a couple of Board members had ties to pharmaceutical interests and they wanted someone like Myer in there to make ATCH, ah, less confrontational. If you ask me, less effective."

I kicked my chair leg, scuffing the heel of my oxford even further. Capron had said Myer was doing a decent job. Hadn't he? I asked Phoebe why there hadn't been a ruckus if what she said was true.

"Oh, there was. Remember that demo over on Divisidero? In front of the ATCH office? There were a few wimpy articles in the bar rags, too. But Gayle Letournier's death really hit people hard. I guess they just wanted to keep ATCH alive, and decided a fundraising pro might be worth a little political compromise. And I hear Myer's done some decent stuff, like beefing up a new program to assist homeless people with AIDS."

"Phoebe, can you hang on a second?"

"Sure, kid."

I heard her break into a Paula Abdul tune while I rifled through my trusty white pages. There it was: Bradley Myer, only one listing, address given. Sometimes investigations were so easy I was amazed I got paid for them. Then I remembered I *wasn't* getting paid for this one. Geez. Well, I was hooked now. Shady dealings at ATCH or business as usual? I'd scope out Mr. Myer tonight, if I could find him, and visit ATCH tomorrow.

Phoebe had called to invite me out for drinks. I declined. But she agreed to lend me her ancient Duster. I changed into my black hightops and pulled on a ragged sweatshirt to cover up the new catsup stains. Stylish.

Phoebe came tooling up some twenty minutes later, armed with egg salad on sourdough wheat and a couple of A & Ws. We polished off the sandwiches out on my stoop on Ramona Avenue as the sky deepened to cobalt blue.

I told her a little about the case.

". . . so I read about Sebastian Newley's suicide in a couple of old gay papers. Made me wonder. Why would such a gung-ho activist kill himself? Who knows. But maybe that's why Zeke Capron's so depressed. In fact, maybe Newley was his lover—"

"I thought you said this Zeke guy was straight?"

"Yeah. But—" I shrugged.

Phoebe laughed. "I know. You can never tell anymore."

Before we parted, Phoebe lit into me about taking on a client for free. "How are you supposed to pay the rent, Nellie? Shit. This Johnnie Blue must be something special."

I blushed. "I like to do a little pro bono work now and then."

"Oh yeah? I just thought you were pro-Chastity Bono." She chuckled. "See you sweetheart."

•

I aimed the car toward Market, crossing over at Church Street.

Myer lived on Sacramento at an address that must fall near the ritzy shopping zone of upper Fillmore. Heading northward, I wondered what I could accomplish at his residence. Hopefully I'd catch a glimpse of him and do a little eavesdropping.

Traffic was clogged near Haight Street. I inched along, taking in the gentrified sights that gave way to a flat expanse of housing projects. I crossed Geary. Stopped at a light, I noticed a surgical supply house on the corner with macabre metal instruments leering out from its grimy display window. I hung a left at California, cruised up to Sacramento, and found a parking spot a few doors away from Myer's number.

I sauntered down the street, casual-like, just out for a stroll. Myer's front door was well lit, but I couldn't make out any noise from within. Checking furtively for witnesses and seeing none, I scurried along the side of the house and plopped myself down below an open window. I was partially shielded by a leafy outgrowth, but I didn't know how long I'd be secure in this spot. All I could hear through the window was canned laughter from a sitcom. I waited.

An hour later my knees were throbbing; wetness from the mucky ground had soaked the seat of my pants. I still hadn't seen anything, though I'd heard footsteps moving through the front rooms. Suddenly a telephone rang right inside the window. I crouched lower. A ruddy face crowned with dirt-blond fringe moved into view. The fellow loosened his tie with one hand and picked up the phone with the other. TV still blabbed on in the background. I strained to hear.

"Myer here. . . . Yeah, hi Leland. . . . goddammit! That's all I've got for tonight. . . . okay, okay. . . . Right. Tens and twenties. And don't ring the bell, I'll be waiting at the door. . . . Give me a minute, Leland! . . . okay, fifteen." Bradley Myer slammed down the receiver and stomped away.

I let out a nervous breath. Moving to the corner of the house, I tried to stay in the shadows and keep an eye on the front door. Sure enough, a Honda Civic showed up in fifteen minutes, and a tiny man swimming in a baggy old army jacket left it idling at the curb as he hustled up the front walk. Leland, no doubt. He exchanged a brusque word or two with Bradley Myer, but I couldn't hear what they were saying.

Myer passed Leland what looked like a manila envelope and

slammed the door on his retreating back. As Leland buried the stash in the folds of his voluminous coat and hopped into his car, I made a dash for the Duster. Leland was too preoccupied to notice me, I hoped. Panting and flushed, I sidled up behind the Honda as Leland waited at a red light. We were off.

By the time I finished tailing Leland through miles of San Francisco roads and back alleys, I must have seen him pass out a grand of cold cash, in tens and twenties, to dozens of street people who thanked him with hugs, or nothing. His last stop: the Twin Peaks bar at Castro and Market. I watched through the wide front window as he greeted a handful of gay friends and bought the gang a round of drinks.

I caught up with Zeke Capron at the Strand the next day at noon. It was just a guess he'd be there; I hoped to talk to him again before heading over to ATCH. Sure enough, he was in the same row, Giants cap tilted rakishly back. He was watching Steve McQueen bomb up and down city streets as the Golden Gate Bridge glinted majestically in the distance. I sat a little behind him and waited until a scene with the young Jacqueline Bisset was over.

I leaned forward and tapped Capron's shoulder. "Hi there."

"Oh god," he said, swiveling around to frown at me.

"So Leland's blackmailing Bradley Myer. Can you tell me why?"

"What?! Leland?"

"Uh huh." I nodded back toward the exit. This time it was Capron who followed *me* to the lobby. The patchouli aroma had faded. Lucky day. We staked out a private corner and fell into harried conversation.

"Leland?" Capron repeated, incredulous. "Little short guy? Light brown skin?"

"Yup." I told him about my exploits of the night before. "I figured you knew about the blackmail and were nervous about it. I heard ATCH was helping homeless PWAs, but I didn't suppose coercion was involved." I ended on a questioning note.

"No, neither did I, Nell. I thought Leland was just another volunteer." A giant cloud of despair seemed to weigh down his eyelids. He tugged off his glasses and rubbed vigorously for a moment. I could tell he was trying to make up his mind about something.

130

"Look Nell," Capron continued, "what ATCH does is essential. Nobody else is worried about those people on the street. Or about speeding up drug trials. Unless they can make a profit, of course. So when Bradley Myer got hired, I didn't protest too hard. I figured he was bringing more money to ATCH because AZT manufacturers were buying him off."

I stared at Capron.

"Yeah, wild, huh? I think they're giving him funds for new programs as long as he'll push AZT. You know, along with other treatments. I used to help ATCH with bookkeeping. The budget for the program for the homeless seemed too small for what we were providing—emergency shelter, hospital visits, food. I think Myer is paying cash off the top. Dirty money."

I thought for a moment. "So you haven't said anything about it because you don't want to jeopardize the program for homeless PWAs?"

"That's right." Capron replaced his glasses. "But what I told you yesterday is true. The corruption was eating at me. I had to get away for awhile."

Just then a trio of kids with matching blue mohawks traipsed into the lobby. After an extended commotion at the food stand, they headed back to the theater leaving a trail of mottled orange popcorn kernels. I was tempted to grind a few into the dank carpet.

"Maybe Leland—" I stopped. I still didn't know his last name. "Maybe Leland also found out that Myer was taking bribes. And decided to squeeze him for a little more money. For a righteous cause."

"Maybe."

But something else was going on behind Capron's sad eyes. I had a queasy feeling we were both groping for an obvious truth that lay just out of reach. Capron was fidgeting, though I doubted it was in eagerness to get back to the movie. We stepped outside together, blinking against the startling midday sun. A heap of shiny litter lay scattered before us in the gutter, like so much discarded costume jewelry.

I decided not to tell Zeke I was headed for ATCH. I didn't want him to think I'd screw up the blackmail scheme. In fact, I could've called it quits at that point. I could've given Johnnie an edited account of corporate influence peddling at ATCH—business as usual. But I was playing a hunch and wanted to know a little more about Myer's affairs. Zeke must have had a hunch, too. When we said goodbye, he didn't mention his destination either.

I found out later that Zeke Capron knew it was Leland who discovered Sebastian Newley's body. If I'd known, I might have approached ATCH with a touch more circumspection. Instead, I strode through the office door with a pretext all honed in my head. I was a nursing student interested in learning more about alternative treatments for people with AIDS and HIV-disease. I'd see if Myer came off as a PR man for AZT. Or if anything else seemed off-kilter about the operation.

ATCH occupied a small refurbished storefront on the outer edge of the Western Addition. The office had a slapdash feel to it, though I noticed a fresh coat of mint green paint on the window frame abutting the sidewalk. A rack stuffed with informational packets crowded the left wall. Every surface was cluttered, too, with notebooks, newspapers, a couple of clunky old-style telephones.

A computer monitor hummed away, unattended, on a desk against the far wall. But the room was void of humans. Odd.

I slowed my step as I neared a flimsy partition leading to another room out back. Peeking through the passageway, I caught sight of a young woman recoiling in terror as she tried to dodge a kick aimed squarely at her kidneys. All I could think was to keep her away from the nasty force of those boots. I dove, knocking us both against the partition.

It gave way with a splintering crash, plywood tumbling around our bodies. The woman started sobbing. She gulped desperately for air. I grabbed a jagged bit of wood to use as a shield. Ignoring a jolt of pain that zipped across my left shoulder, I thrust out the wood in time to deflect a follow-up kick veering straight for her head.

"Goddammit," came a hollow voice from above our frightened huddle. I glanced up sharply. Bradley Myer stood poised, strangely serene, his suede Timberlands a tasteful match to his well-creased khakis. His crown of dishwater hair poked out in little groomed spikes. Only the 6-inch hunting knife in his right hand seemed out of place.

"Who the fuck are you?" he asked in the same low-key monotone. He didn't seem to care about the answer. In fact, he seemed totally zonked.

I tried to draw a steady breath, then gasped. Leland No-Last-Name lay sprawled on the floor not ten feet away.

Next to me, the young woman struggled to regain her composure. "I think he's okay," she said to me softly. "Just knocked out from a punch."

"Oh, he's okay," Myer said. He took a step toward Leland, toying all the while with his knife. "But not for long."

"What's going on?" I mouthed to the woman, weighing my options. Bradley Myer started rocking on his heels, fixated on Leland.

The woman ventured a hushed explanation. "He said he'd kill Leland, just like he killed the other guy." Her moist eyes widened. "We all thought he killed himself. . . ."

"Sebastian Newley?"

"Yeah."

I gasped again, stunned. Bradley Myer had murdered Newley and made it look like a suicide. The activist must have demanded an end to Myer's acceptance of corporate hush money. And Leland must have witnessed the murder and started blackmailing Myer in turn.

I asked the young woman how she ended up in the middle of the current fracas.

"I was answering phones up front and I just stepped back to give Bradley a message. Bradley was yelling at Leland, saying he wouldn't pay him off anymore. When they saw me, Bradley pulled out the knife and flipped out . . . he started kicking me. . . ."

"Shut up!" bellowed Myer, suddenly turning on us in a frenzy.

I moved fast. I sprang off my haunches and plowed full force into Myer's knees. I heard a satisfying little crunch as he went over sideways and cracked an elbow against the hardwood floor. He groped frantically to recover his knife. It had clattered just a few inches away. With a sweep of my throbbing left arm, I sent the blade skittering across the room where it lodged between a couple of rusty old file cabinets.

I realized I'd split the flesh along the side of my forearm, but it didn't stop me from moving in on Myer. I grabbed another piece of splintered wood and thwacked him hard across the temple. He collapsed with a grunt. That'd do it.

I saw the young woman scrambling for a phone, so I rushed over to check on Leland. Just then, the ATCH front door clicked open. Zeke Capron and a couple of the city's finest came charging through, shouting, hands on their holsters, like this was just another day in the wild, wild west.

Later that night I was sitting at a table near the front of the Club Valencia. An elaborate bandage was wound tightly from my wrist to shoulder, holding my left arm immobilized. It didn't hurt so badly after a double scotch.

Phoebe was with me. We were watching Johnnie Blue finish up her set. She looked adorable in powder blue shorts, an oversized white cotton shirt, and the beat-up Nikes that caught my eye in the first place. She ended with an atrocious joke about Chastity Bono.

"Did you feed her that lousy pun?" I asked Phoebe.

"Yeah! I think it's a riot." She was laughing.

I groaned.

Johnnie joined us a few minutes later, Bud in hand. "Nellie! Are you okay? Zeke told me everything." She gazed mournfully at my wretched arm.

I shrugged. Little beads of moisture glistened from Johnnie's hairline. I swear, this woman looked great in sweat. "You were really funny," I said shyly.

Phoebe asked me about Zeke's timely arrival at ATCH.

"After I told him about Leland's blackmail scheme, he remembered Leland had been the one to find Sebastian Newley's body—and Bradley Myer had been on the scene too. Zeke began to wonder if Leland had witnessed a murder, and if that was his basis for blackmailing Myer. Zeke didn't know for sure about the murder, but he was suspicious enough to go to the police. They agreed to visit Myer with a few follow-up questions."

"So now Myer's under arrest?" Johnnie asked.

"Yeah," I said, "with a wicked headache."

I'd spent most of the afternoon at the cop house. Leland had come around okay, but was being charged with blackmail. He'd probably get off easy in exchange for testifying against Myer. I hoped he would. Zeke was in pretty good spirits. He planned to organize a community response to the atrocities at ATCH and demand an inquiry into misuse of power on the Board of Directors. Hopefully he'd help get the organization back on track and keep its crucial services alive.

As I finished my explanation, comic Marga Gomez bounded to

the stage and began her routine. She launched into a scathing bit about the Nicaraguan election: ". . . the most democratic election money could buy." If I wasn't already swooning over Johnnie Blue, I'd be dying over Marga's knockout gap-toothed smile.

"So are you going to start bringing home the bacon now, Nell?" Phoebe was ribbing me.

"Nah," I said. "I thought I'd retire, play the ponies every day, maybe write my memoirs."

"Oh sure. That'd be an instant bestseller."

I sighed. Actually, I got a message that afternoon from a pal at Continent West Investigations asking me to help with a complicated background check. Dull work, but I needed the cash. Pinky would be here soon.

Phoebe must have been reading my mind. "Is Pinky still coming?"

"Yeah," I said, smiling. I explained to Johnnie Blue that my daughter Pinky went to school in London, but was planning to spend the summer with me in San Francisco. "Except she's been all nervous about it since the big earthquake."

"Sounds like a smart kid," Johnnie said.

Yes, indeed.

Your Keys or Mine?

Gail Giles

"SO, JERRY, YOU LOOK LIKE the cat's breakfast. Having a bad day?"

"Bugs, you silver-tongued devil, my day was ruined at two a.m. Yours is about to be ruined even as we speak."

Bugs sat down on the chipped and scarred wooden chair and rolled up to her desk. "Can't happen, Detective. My day is unruinable!"

"You've been assigned to help me on the Playgirl Robberies. There was another one last night."

"O.K., I lied. It is ruinable. Why me? Why you? Why the Playgirls? Good grief, I'd rather go to a Tupperware party."

"I figured that was your idea of a good time. Since I am wise and wonderful I can give you answers. Why you? Because we need a woman's viewpoint. Why me? Because I'm the smartest beast in captivity. Why the Playgirls? Because rich women being ripped off tend to be very verbal and our eminent chief does not want their pretty faces in the newspaper saying bad things about our city's finest. There, does that satisfy even nosy little you?"

"Look Jerry, I became a cop to protect the innocent, the poor, the oppressed. You know, the huddled masses? I was promised life among the lower element. I don't care to retrieve expensive baubles for the pampered and the petulant."

"Face it, Dudley Do Right, the rich get robbed more often than the poor. And that's a fact, Jack!" Jerry pushed himself up from his

136

desk and thumped Bugs' head with his pencil. "We are due to make our esteemed appearance at a briefing in ten minutes with the chief. Look ambitious."

"Come on, Jer. Only a fool would fall for that."

"You got it. That's who we're gonna see."

The chief was handing out packets as Bugs and Jerry walked in. He addressed the other officers. "Men, these are the detectives who will be handling this case. Detective Barnes has been on the case since the first robbery and we have now added Detective Buglasko. You men will provide the support the detectives need. Detective Barnes, would you like to take over?"

Jerry rose and straightened his tie. He smoothed it over his bulging stomach and hoisted his permanently wrinkled brown pants. "This is the seventh robbery in eight weeks. The take is jewelry, furs and valuables, small collectables, silver, Steuben glass, you guys know the drill. There is no sign of forced entry in any of the robberies. The victims are all between twenty-five and forty, pretty, single and rich. None of the victims have been present at the time of the robbery. We can find very little that the victims have in common. Only two know each other and that is only through overlapping social contacts. A friend of a friend type of thing. We can find no motive for any of the robberies other than pure and simple theft. None of the women use the same hairdresser, chauffeur, maid service, etc.—any of the places you look for access to keys. Nothing."

One officer raised his hand. "Have you checked their ex-husbands or lovers?"

Jerry grunted. "That's a very good question, but a dead end. We got a mixed bag. Some have never married, some are divorced amicably, some not so amicably, but the ex's have been cleared one way or another. There are no exclusive boyfriends in the bunch, although a couple of the women do say that they see one man more regularly than others. None of them seem to be very romantically involved, hence the name, Playgirl Robberies."

Bugs raised her hand. "So, who do they date? Does any name crop up there for more than one woman?"

"No cigar, Bugs. We checked on all female and male visitors to their homes in the last three months. No cross connections."

Bugs picked up a strand of her shoulder length hair and twisted it around and around her index finger as she listened half heartedly to the other questions. She started making notes on her legal pad. She pulled the strand of hair out, then made a loop and tied a knot; she pulled it tight then let it go. The hair instantly uncoiled and straightened. Bugs snapped the tablet shut. She had the connection.

"Jerry, hang on a minute. I've got an idea." Bugs stopped Jerry as the other officers were filing out and he was about to leave with the chief.

"Yeah Bugs, I know. That hair knotting thing is a dead give away, you know."

"Hair knotting?" Bugs looked puzzled. She shrugged. "Whatever that cryptic remark means—anyway, you're right, you do need a woman. I need to talk to our bevy of bejeweled beauties. I think they all have a secret and they aren't going to tell it to a male cop."

"O.K. Sherlock. What's up?"

"They are all rich, right?" Barnes nodded. Bugs continued, "O.K., they can afford it. A good one, too. Veddy, veddy discreet. Good clientele."

"Bugs, are we going to finish this or are we just doing laps?"

"A video dating service, Barnes. Think about it. The women are rich, attractive and single. Every last one of them. Meeting men is tough. I read in an article that you have a better chance of being killed by a terrorist than getting married, if you are female and over thirty. These women aren't going to tell *you* that they pay for a dating service, so why not let me talk to them?"

"Go for it, but be cool, Bugs."

"Corpses are cool, Barnes."

"Jerry, you are now the second smartest beast in captivity. I have snatched your crown from your balding pate!" Bugs jazzed in the door and planted a kiss on Barnes's forehead.

"You look like a bulldog in a porkchop factory."

"Cherries in all the slots, Bucko. All seven women use Discreet Dating Decisions, and all seven matched on a good-looking psychologist named Lawrence. The service demands that there be no last names given out unless both parties agree, no addresses are disclosed by the service, and the couple must meet at an agreed upon public place for the initial date."

"So, we're zero again. This guy doesn't know her name or address and how does he get in without a key. Come on, Bugs, give me a break."

"I think I can if we set up a sting and find out."

"A sting?"

"You betcha. Call the boss man and get me a ritzy address to come and go from. I'll set it up with the video service and we shall see what we shall see."

"So what if it's a coincidence and he's not our guy?"

"Well, I get a freebie date. Who knows, maybe I'll like him. I am terrorist bait, after all."

The bar was elegant and quiet, complete with circular booths, waiters as icy as penguins, flickering candles, glittering crystal. And there sat Lawrence, all business suit and quiet East Coast class as opposed to West Coast flash.

A heart thumper, Bugs thought with a silent whistle as a waiter escorted her to the table.

Lawrence thanked the waiter and smiled. "Emily? If you're not Emily, lie to me because after I've seen you I won't want to trade."

"Then Emily it is. You *are* Lawrence?"

"Definitely. Sit down. I've taken the liberty of ordering a white wine."

"Lovely."

The moment hung. Then stalled.

Lawrence rescued it. "Here, let's break the ice." He pulled out his keys and handed them to Emily. "Take my keys and give me yours. All you have, any kind, house, car, diary, jewelry box, gate, refrigerator, wine cellar, anything. Even the key to your heart."

"I don't think I understand. Why do you want to change keys?"

"It's a game of perception. You look at my keys and tell me all you know about me, then I'll do the same."

"But you'll win. You're a psychologist."

"That's why I like to play. Why impress you with what I don't know?" His laugh was like champagne. "Here, you start with mine." He winked as he took her keys and slid them into his jacket pocket.

Bingo!

Bugs leaned back in her chair and studied the keys. "All I see are keys. I can't figure anything out from these." She produced what she imagined to be a vaguely sexy pout.

Lawrence flashed a Tom Cruise mega watt smile.

Orthodontia, Bugs mused, darkly. No one can be born with teeth that belong in a Crest ad.

"You can find all sorts of things once you get the hang of it. Notice my car keys. Are they American or foreign?"

"I don't see a car key." Bugs responded.

"What does that tell you?" Lawrence asked.

"Oh no! You're too young to drive! I was afraid there had to be some significant flaw."

His laughter was easy with a hint of vibrato. "Not quite. But you *are* delightful. Would you care for more wine?"

"By all means. I'm doubly delightful with more wine."

Bugs scanned the room as Lawrence turned to signal the waiter. She saw the typical array of wealthy patrons, businessmen, late cocktail drinkers, and early dinner dates. The dimmed lights caught the twinkle of tasteful diamonds, carefully barbered heads bent to look at the time on whisper-thin watches. Conversations were kept low, the faces were slightly bored but pleasant. There was only one woman at the bar, sipping a glass of wine. Bugs noted that she glanced away quickly when they made eye contact.

Looking for love in all the best places, Bugs thought. You might as well cruise the classy restaurants. I think terrorists stick to airports.

Lawrence returned his attention to Bugs when the wine was poured. "Now *your* keys are a give away."

"How so?"

"No car ignition key, but a glove box key, so you must have used a valet parking, but you keep the keys separate. That shows a cautious, careful nature. You also keep your house key on a separate ring and this is the key to a security system, also showing a cautious nature."

"Maybe I'm a cynical, suspicious old bat."

"I think I need another date to find out. I'm terribly intrigued. You insisted we meet only for cocktails tonight. Have I charmed you enough for you to consider dinner tomorrow? If I haven't, all those years of social tutoring and learning to use the proper fork will have been for naught and I shall have to drink a Clorox cocktail and throw myself in front of an oncoming train." He handed Bugs her keys, folding her fingers around them, then patting her hand. "I have convinced you that I'm not a masked marauder, a fractious fiend, a lascivious letch, haven't I?"

Bugs smiled. "That was my enigmatic Mona Lisa smile. Dinner sounds wonderful. We can't have you leaping out in front of Amtrak or committing social suicide by using the wrong fork. But, I think I'll hold on to my air of mystery a while longer. My careful, cautious nature insists that I meet you again at the restaurant. You understand, don't you?"

"Of course, tomorrow night, same time, same place?"

"Fine, same time, same place, different socks."

Lawrence was taken aback. "How does one politely respond to that? Do my socks offend your artistic sensibilities or do I need Odor Eaters?"

"Neither, but Aunt Bertha always insisted on fresh socks in case you should ever be in a car accident."

"I always thought that was underwear?"

Bugs rose and flicked her hair. "It is, but I don't know you well enough to chat about your skivvies." She sashayed out and handed her parking receipt to the valet. As she waited for the borrowed Mercedes, she ran one thumbnail along a groove in the apartment key. A thin sliver of wax curled up, then blew away in the evening breeze.

The woman from the bar was being handed into her car just ahead of Bugs. As the woman drove away, Bugs wondered if she would go home now, or move on to the next elite restaurant.

Bugs drove back to the borrowed apartment slowly, pondering how the hit was made. Lawrence had made no effort to find out her address or her last name, not even her phone number. If he was the thief, how could he use the keys? She mentally sorted the pieces of the puzzle as she pulled into the circular driveway of the borrowed condo. She got out of the car and handed the key to the apartment's valet. As she turned to go in, a car passed under the streetlamp, and Bugs saw the woman from the restaurant in the driver's seat.

Reaching up, Bugs separated a lock of her hair and began twisting it, then nodded at another car that came down the street. Jerry Barnes flashed a thumbs up sign to Bugs as he drove past and rounded the corner.

The apartment was dim and silent. A key scraped in the lock and the door swung open. A small key was inserted into a pad on the foyer wall, disarming the alarm. A woman, dressed in exercise clothes and carrying a large tote bag, closed the door carefully.

She pulled a flashlight from the bag and searched for the bedroom. Finding it, she opened a large armoire and groped in drawers until she came up with a jewelry box. She slid it into the tote then yanked a fox jacket from the cedar hanger and stuffed that in as well. She headed for the dining room. Pulling velvet bags from the tote, she loaded them with silverware. She unrolled a long padded runner and began bundling crystal accent pieces into its folds.

"No scratches, no breaks. This is a great haul," she whispered to herself.

The overhead lights flashed on.

"Put the tote down and raise your dainty little hands, sweet knees." Jerry Barnes stood in the kitchen doorway, gun in hand. He flipped his badge open as two uniformed officers came in the front door.

"I'm several years of hard time lookin' at you. Pleased to make your acquaintance, ma'am."

The woman's shoulder slumped. "Do you mind if I make a phone call?"

"Well, I'm supposed to make you wait until we get you processed at the station, but I'm an easy kind of guy." Barnes hitched up his double knit slacks, then gestured toward the telephone. "Be my guest, fair maiden."

The woman grimaced then began dialing. As soon as she completed punching in the last number, Barnes snagged the receiver and listened.

"Just as I thought." He grinned happily and spoke into the mouth piece. "I'd like to speak to Detective Buglasko, please."

Bugs returned to the table, smiling invitingly at Lawrence. "What do you think about skipping dessert and going someplace where we can talk more privately?"

Lawrence touched his starched white napkin to his lips. "Where did you have in mind?"

"The police station, my little bunny fluff. You're under arrest." She flipped a badge onto the table. "Why don't we break the ice. You can look at that and play your game of perception."

Three hours later Lawrence and his wife were in custody, jewels, furs and other valuables were being cataloged as evidence and Barnes and Bugs took time out from congratulating themselves to explain their case to their chief.

"Let me tell you how it happened, Chief," Bugs said, leaning back in her chair. "It was all sort of a double reverse play. The way it works is that Lawrence makes the video for the dating service and when it pays off he makes an arrangement to meet the woman. He neglects to tell his new-found friend that he has a wife who is also in the bar, or restaurant. He plays this break-the-ice game and takes the woman's keys. While she tries to tell the story of his life with his keys he is pressing her keys into a wax mold in his pocket. The wife gets a sign when Lawrence is ready and leaves first, getting in position to follow the woman when she goes home. This way, she finds out the address without Lawrence having to ask. They make a set of duplicate keys from the mold and when Lawrence goes on the second date, his wife goes to the victim's home and cleans the place out. Barnes tailed the wife after she followed me to the swanky apartment I was using. Then I met Lawrence for the second date, and Barnes met up with the wife—catching her red-handed. She asked to make a phone call, which Barnes interrupted, discovering that she called the very same restaurant where yours truly and Lawrence were having a romantic dinner. Barnes had the waiter call me to the phone, I brought Lawrence back to the station, and everybody is happy. Except for Lawrence, of course. The only keys he wants to see now are the ones to his cell."

Bugs stretched her arms high over her head and smiled. "It's great being the smartest beast in captivity."

Barnes chortled. "Just until the terrorist gets you, Bugs."

"I'll get you for that one, Barnes, you wait and see."

Clear as Glass

Helen and Lorri Carpenter

TAMARA ARNOLD'S EYES widened behind her designer glasses. "Nathan will be arrested if he comes out of hiding!"

Emma Twiggs, seated on the velvet sofa to the left of Galveston Investigation's anxious client, shifted her gaze to her handsome nephew's cheerless face, and waited for his reaction. It wasn't long in coming.

"Okay, fill me in on the details," James Galveston said, in a voice that held more than a trace of reluctance.

"Yesterday Nathan went to see Harold Symthefield," Tamara Arnold replied hurriedly, as if she were afraid of being interrupted. "Harold represented my husband the last time he was in trouble with the law."

While Tamara talked, Emma jotted down what she considered pertinent impressions. Before her vacation, her nephew, with his clients' consent, had begun filming his interviews. The camcorder, concealed inside a custom-designed cabinet, was now recording their conversation, leaving Emma free to observe body language and listen for nuances which could only be gleaned by a trained sleuth during a live session. She was delighted with the new equipment, and with the fact that Jim had taken the time to train her in handling it.

"Who accused Nathan?"

Emma recognized the inflection in her nephew's staccato query and wondered why he seemed so tense.

"Harold Smythefield's wife, Ginger, and his legal assistant, Patricia Ryan," Tamara answered timorously.

"Did either of the women actually see your husband commit the murder?"

"Ginger Smythefield says she saw Nathan kill Harold, but she couldn't have, because he didn't."

"Let's assume your husband is innocent," Jim said. "Based on that belief, we need to know the rest of the circumstances."

Tamara removed her glasses and dabbed at a tear that had spilled onto her cheek. "Nathan had an appointment at Harold's office before noon on Sunday. The two of them discussed Nathan's upcoming trial. Late last night we heard on the radio that Harold Smythefield had been murdered. His wife told the police she saw Nathan commit the crime."

As the tears began to flow unchecked, Tamara lowered her lashes and added, "My husband assured me Harold was alive at the end of their meeting."

Emma, bothered by the young woman's obvious distress, said, "Tell Nathan we'll take the case."

Tamara's nervousness eased, and as her facial muscles relaxed, her features became almost pretty. When she spoke, the thistle-haired sleuth heard the heartfelt sincerity in her words. "Thanks, Emma. You too, Jim."

Moments like this made Emma glad she'd become a P.I. She looked at Jim to see if he was enjoying Tamara's pat-on-the-back as much as she was, but even the goodbye he offered the young woman as she left his office was said through lips set in a down-turned line.

"What's bothering you, Jimbo?" Emma asked, when they were once again alone and her nephew had re-seated himself behind his desk.

Jim's taut expression faded into the semblance of a smile. "I didn't want to take this case because I assisted the police, behind the scenes of course, in nabbing Tamara's husband for his last crime."

He paused, then his mouth twitched in amusement at her disbelieving look. "You don't know everything that goes on around here, Aunty. While you were on vacation, Galveston Investigations—meaning me—was not idle."

"Therefore, it's fortunate Galveston Investigations' Special Assistant—meaning me—is back," she informed him. Closing her notepad, she tapped the cover with her pencil. "I can hardly wait to start working on our newest caper."

"Good, since it was your idea to take this assignment in the first place," Jim said wryly. Then, as if to show her he wasn't displeased with what she'd done, he crossed the room and gave her a helping hand as she struggled to escape from the depths of the soft sofa.

In the reception area, Nancy Barnes, Jim's invaluable secretary and Emma's strongest supporter, set down the detective magazine she was perusing. "You two going somewhere?"

"Aunt Emma and I are headed for Harold Smythefield's office," Jim answered, in an unusually cordial tone. "There's a video in the camera that's ready for transcription and filing, whenever you have time."

Nancy snapped her chewing gum in acknowledgement.

Something very strange is going on around here, Emma thought, as she followed Jim to the waiting elevator.

Just before the double panels slid shut, the sleuth took another look at Nancy. Her friend, coffee cup in hand, feet propped on desk, reclined in her chair, talking on the phone as if she were at home instead of at the office.

Emma was making a mental note to ferret out exactly what had transpired during her two week vacation when the elevator halted its downward motion and the doors swished open.

As they stepped into the lobby, Jim said, "It's strange that Harold Smythefield met with Nathan on Sunday. Could the two of them have been discussing more than Nathan's upcoming court appearance?"

"What else would a shady character like Nathan and a lawyer have in common?" she asked, temporarily relegating the unusual behavior of her two favorite people to the back burner.

"Nathan Arnold is an accomplished art thief, Aunty." Jim held the heavy glass portal that served as the main entrance of the Galveston Building, and let his aunt pass through to the sidewalk. "Many lawyers have wealthy clients looking for what you might call 'tax free' ways to invest their money."

Emma pondered Jim's explanation while he summoned a taxi. When they were seated, she wondered aloud if Harold Smythefield was acting as a go-between.

Her nephew shrugged. "At this point, I couldn't say, but the mere fact that Nathan has convinced Tamara of his innocence doesn't mean anything. He's a persuasive con. I brought up the point because I want you to go into this case with your mind open to all possibilities."

Emma was gratified by his display of fraternization, and could only marvel at how far their working relationship had come since her first assignment over three years ago. In those days, her nephew wouldn't have dreamed of sharing his thoughts about a case-in-progress. She opened her mouth to tell him how pleased she was, then decided it was better not to let him know, lest he go back to his old ways. Instead she quipped, "A good investigator is always empty-headed."

Ignoring Jim's dark look, she smiled into the rear view mirror at the cabby, who was chuckling in appreciation of her humor. Suddenly, in the middle of a wink, he stomped on the brakes, cut across the road and pulled to a halt in the side parking lot of a brick office building that proudly bore the gilded sign 'Harold Smythefield, Attorney at Law.'

Standing on the pavement waiting for Jim to pay the fare, she saw a tall woman, visible through the large picture window on the first floor of the building.

"I wonder if that's Ginger Smythefield or Patricia Ryan," Jim remarked, when the cab pulled away.

As Emma stared at the span of glass which exposed a clear view of a well-appointed office, the executive-suited blonde inside pulled the cord on the Venetian blinds.

"I'd like to handle the questioning, if you don't mind, Aunty," her nephew requested as they walked to the entrance.

Jim was doing it again. Emma halted in mid-stride, not sure if she'd heard correctly. She turned to her nephew, saw he was waiting for her reply, and realized her ears hadn't been playing tricks.

"What's going on?" she asked, immensely relieved her senses were in working order. "You've never been this nice to me on a case before."

When he hesitated, she pressed her advantage. "Spill it."

"Actually there *is* something. While you were on vacation, Nancy and I. . . ."

The sound of briskly approaching high heels halted him in mid-sentence. Emma turned her gaze to the broad-shouldered blonde bearing down on them, and realized it was the woman they'd seen in the window. With quick scrutiny, the sleuth noted how well the tailored cut of the blonde's navy suit complemented the platinum color of her hair. A heavy gold chain fell between twin mounds of cleavage, and matching adornments graced both wrists and ear-lobes.

Without mincing words, the Amazon addressed Emma. "You're in a private parking lot. Do you have a reason to be here?"

Emma, lost in fascinated study of the lustrous silver-blonde curls, didn't answer. Not a strand out of place, the sleuth thought. How extraordinary. I wonder if it's a wig?

She was pulled from her contemplation by the sound of her nephew's brisk introduction.

"I'm James Galveston." His tone was low-pitched and firm with authority. "This is my associate, Emma Twiggs. We're here to investigate the murder of Harold Smythefield."

The woman warmed up as she accepted the business card Jim extended, and said, "I'm Patricia Ryan, Harold's paralegal assistant. If you're working with the police to convict Nathan Arnold, I'll be glad to help in any way I can."

Emma opened her mouth to clarify their position, but Jim nudged her with a discreetly placed elbow. "Thank you, Patricia," he said, flashing his best Clark Gable grin. "May we inspect the murder scene?"

A friendly glint softened Patricia's sea-green eyes, and Emma, reminded of her nephew's unabashed ability to charm reluctant females, smiled to herself.

"Of course." Patricia gestured toward the picture window, still covered by the drawn blinds. "You can see it from here. Ginger was in the parking lot, exactly where we are now, when Harold was murdered. The blinds were up, of course, so she could look into the room. She saw the whole thing."

"Were you in the building at the time?" Jim's tone was mild.

Patricia affirmed his statement with a nod, then said, "Come inside."

Harold Smythefield's inner office was the last room at the end of a long, carpeted hallway. Patricia opened the door, then stepped aside so they could enter.

"Tell us what happened," Jim said, as he looked around the large room.

"I was sitting over there," she indicated a barrel chair against the far wall, "taking notes. When the argument began, Nathan was standing here." She tapped her foot on the carpet in front of the wide desk. "On this very spot."

"And where was your boss?" Emma asked.

"Harold was seated at his desk with his back toward Nathan. I could tell by his posture he was very angry. He barely looked up, just asked me to please leave them alone."

"What happened next?"

"I returned to my own office and shut the door to block out the shouting. It went on for a long time. Then there was silence, until Ginger ran into the building with a police officer in tow. When we entered Harold's office, he was on the floor, the bloodied ashtray lay beside him, and Nathan was gone. The officer said Harold was dead."

"Was it Harold's usual practice to schedule appointments on Sunday afternoon?" Jim wanted to know.

"Oh, yes," Patricia replied. "In fact, he used to say Sunday was the best day for getting work done. He always came into the office at eight in the morning, and worked until one, when he and Ginger had a standing lunch date."

"Thank you," Jim said. "We'd like to look around for a few minutes, if you don't mind."

Patricia shrugged. "Feel free. I'll be across the hall. I have to weed out the files and see what can be delegated to other attorneys before we close the office."

After Patricia left the room, Emma pointed to a chalked X on the corner of Harold Smythefield's desk. "The murder weapon must have been here," she said to Jim, who had seated himself in Harold's chair. "If Harold was turned away from Nathan, he wouldn't have seen the blow coming."

She twisted, studying the rest of the room. The still-shuttered picture window caught her attention.

"Nathan's back would have been to the window. I wonder if Ginger Smythefield is absolutely certain the man she saw in the office with Harold was Nathan Arnold. Had she seen Nathan before?"

"I'll ask Patricia."

Jim was about to push himself out of Harold's chair when, as if in response to her name, Patricia appeared in the doorway.

Directly behind her stood a reed-thin woman dressed in an expensive dark brown pantsuit. Almost before her feet crossed the threshold, she spoke in a tone cold enough to freeze mercury.

"I'm Ginger Smythefield, and I demand to know exactly what you're doing in my husband's office!"

Jim stood and moved toward Harold's widow with the confidence of a man experienced at soothing highstrung women. "Hello, Ginger. I'm James Galveston."

"Patricia told me *who* you are," Ginger Smythefield replied, obviously not impressed by his friendly stance. "I want to know what business you have here."

Jim sidestepped the interrogation with a query of his own. "Can you tell us what you saw through the window, Ginger?"

"I gave my story to the police," the trim woman said stubbornly. "I won't repeat myself."

Emma recognized a resolute sadness behind the widow's tough exterior. Stepping forward, the sleuth put a hand on Ginger Smythefield's arm. "I understand how recalling those details might be difficult, and we're sorry to put you through the pain all over again," she said, "but we must know if you're positive Nathan Arnold murdered your husband."

Tears filled Ginger's eyes. Moving to the window, she pulled open the blinds. Sunlight flooded the room. For a long, silent moment, she looked through the glass at the world outside. When she turned back into the room, she seemed more composed.

"Nathan Arnold was a difficult client. Patricia told me how enraged the man was about the possibility of serving jail time for his latest offense.

"I'd just pulled into the parking lot for my usual Sunday afternoon lunch date with my husband. I was still sitting in my car when I looked through the window and saw Harold and Nathan. They were shouting at each other." She closed her eyes momentarily, as if reliving the scene in her mind, then with great effort continued in a quiet voice.

"As I watched, Nathan grew more agitated. When Harold turned away—I think he went to answer the phone or something, I'm not sure, I lost sight of him for a moment—Nathan picked up the marble ashtray. I saw him raise it in the air, then strike a blow at the back of Harold's head."

A look of helplessness filled her eyes. "I was paralyzed. I

should have screamed, but I couldn't. All I could think to do was call the police. . . ." Ginger stopped speaking, and drew a deep, shuddering breath.

"Had you ever met Nathan Arnold?" Emma's tone was genuinely sympathetic.

Ginger shook her head. "No. The police asked the same question, except they phrased it differently. 'How can you be sure it was Nathan Arnold you saw?' Well, I'm positive. Harold told me Nathan was his only appointment for the day. Besides, Patricia was here, and she knows when Nathan left. No one else was in the office."

As more tears crowded Ginger's eyes, Patricia stepped forward. "Enough questions," the paralegal assistant said in a firm voice. "Let's go across the hall to the staff kitchen for a cup of coffee."

Emma feigned an interest in Harold's law books as the others filed out. Her attention was actually riveted on a specially-designed cabinet sitting unobtrusively in the far corner of the room. At the door, Jim paused and glanced over his shoulder. His eyes followed her gaze, then with a nod he indicated he would keep Patricia and Ginger busy while Emma pursued the lead she'd found. Barely a second passed before he stepped into the hallway behind the two ladies.

The sleuth could hardly believe he'd given her the okay. I'd better hurry, she thought, afraid he might change his mind before she could complete her mission.

The cabinet had the same fast-release catch as the one in Jim's office, and the door opened easily when Emma touched the spring, revealing a small camcorder.

Pressing the buttons for instant review and high-speed reverse, the sleuth bent over the viewfinder, scrutinizing the taped picture as it unfolded before her eyes.

Nathan Arnold, tall and dark-haired, stood before the camera, apparently oblivious to its presence, toying with the ashtray and gesticulating angrily at Harold. The attorney, a mocking smile playing around the corners of his mouth, was ordering his troublesome client from the office. The tape ended as Nathan left.

Emma frowned. Since the time and date had not been superimposed on the tape, the visual record did not conclusively prove Nathan's innocence. He could have come back later. But why bother, she reasoned. He didn't appear to know the camera was running. If he'd wanted to kill Harold, he would have committed the crime before he left.

Emma's fingers toyed with the buttons on the machine, and the tape once again began to rewind. The puzzled sleuth backed the film to the beginning of the reel, then re-started it. The movie that played before her eyes made her blood run cold. She watched until the film blanked out and the scene with Nathan came back on. She was filled with such revulsion her hands shook as she snapped off the recorder.

Ejecting the tape, the sleuth slid the cartridge into her voluminous handbag. She drew a deep breath to calm herself, then opened the door and stepped across the hall into the kitchen. The room's three occupants looked up at her arrival.

"Did you get lost in the hallway?" Patricia Ryan's tone sounded abrasive.

"No. I was soaking up the ambience at the scene of the crime."

Emma, trying to restrain her feelings, seated herself at the narrow table and lowered her handbag to the floor beside the chair. Pointing to a framed photograph gracing the shelf over the coffee maker, she turned to Ginger, and in what she thought was a remarkably calm voice, said, "I'm sure Harold's death will be hard on your young son, too."

Ginger, still drying her eyes with a tissue, paused to stare at the picture. "That's Patricia's child, Teddy. He's four. Harold adored the boy. In fact, he planned to sent Teddy to Yale. Since we had no children of our own, Harold often asked Patricia to bring Teddy to the office. My husband loved to babysit." She sighed. "That was Harold. Taking time from his busy schedule for a boy with no other father figure in his life."

Changing the subject, Emma asked, "Did Harold use a camcorder to film his interviews?"

Ginger raised splayed fingers to her lips. "Of course," she said. "I completely forgot to mention the recorder to the police. I'll bet there's a tape that will show. . . ." Her voice broke and she couldn't go on.

"There, there." Patricia's tone was soothing. "Harold told me he wasn't using the camcorder Sunday. That's why I was in the office taking notes."

Emma arched an eyebrow at Jim. "Maybe Ginger's right.

There could be a tape in the machine. One that proves Nathan Arnold's innocence."

Patricia's green eyes darkened. "That's impossible!"

A sad-faced Ginger backed her up. "I saw Nathan hit my husband with the ashtray."

Jim furrowed his brow. "Could we hear my aunt . . . ah . . . my associate out. She may have uncovered some pertinent information."

Emma thanked him with a grateful glance, and repeated her words. "There could be a tape in the camcorder that proves Nathan didn't murder Harold Smythefield."

"Ridiculous!" As Patricia shouted the word, she leaped to her feet, upsetting her full cup of coffee.

The scalding liquid shot across the table toward Ginger's lap. As the slim widow jumped up to escape the hot coffee, Emma pushed herself to a standing position. Then, pretending to stumble over the straps of her purse, the sleuth fell against Patricia.

In the midst of all the confusion, a perfectly coiffed platinum wig landed in a heap on the floor, revealing Patricia's own short, dark hair, cut in the smooth, curved line beauticians once referred to as a d.a.

"Why, from the back she looks just like Nathan Arnold," Ginger exclaimed, astonishment edging her voice.

"So Patricia Ryan murdered Harold," Emma said, wrapping up her summation an hour later as Jim and Nancy stood in her office at Galveston Investigations.

"From her vantage point outside the picture window, Ginger thought she saw Nathan clobber Harold. But actually it was Patricia, without her wig. She knew the Smythefield's had a lunch date every Sunday, and that Nathan would be in the office just prior to Ginger's arrival. Unfortunately for her, she didn't think to check the tape in the camcorder, which showed Harold very much alive when Nathan left."

Nancy fixed her friend with a look of admiration. "Emma, you're truly a professional. I have one question though. Why did Patricia want Harold dead when he was such a wonderful employer, and so nice to her son?"

"Harold wasn't at all nice to her son," Emma said, knowing the details of what she'd seen on the camcorder would be forever seared in her memory. "The tape revealed the true motive for murder. When I replayed the entire reel, I found a scene so vile. . . ."

The sleuth shuddered, and forced herself to continue. "Harold was never babysitting Teddy. He was sexually abusing the little boy . . . and filming his actions. When I found out that Teddy was Patricia Ryan's son I realized her motive for killing her boss."

Jim and Nancy were silent for a long moment. Then Jim stirred. "Aunty, you amaze me."

"Thanks," Emma replied modestly. "But actually, your advice to me to go into this case with an open mind was what did the trick. Sometimes things aren't what they seem, even when viewed through a clear pane of glass."

"I have to give you this one, Aunty." Jim patted her hand as if a fellowship had been established between them. "You've become an expert detective."

"I agree." Nancy smiled and snapped her gum.

"Thank you again." Emma accepted the accolades with pleasure.

"In fact," Jim remarked, straightening his muscular frame, "I think I should take the two sweetest ladies I know out for a celebration."

"Your treat?" Emma queried. At his acknowledgment, she asked, "Would someone please tell me what happened around this office while I was on vacation? Did aliens come in and replace my favorite people with look-a-likes?"

"No. Something worse." Jim glanced at Nancy. "I guess we should tell her."

Emma sank into her chair, her matchmaker's heart hammering with trepidation at their solemn faces. "What?"

"While you were gone, Nancy and I went on a date . . ."

". . . and," Nancy interrupted, "I decided it was something we should never do again."

"In order to achieve her objective," Jim explained, "Nancy has become the epitome of everything I dislike in a woman."

"Did my plan work?" Nancy asked, gazing coolly at her boss. Jim nodded. "Almost too well."

"Then I can stop being obnoxious and get back to business as usual . . . after I refuse to have lunch with you, of course."

Emma felt as if she'd missed the ferry. "Let me get this straight," she said. "The date was a flop?"

Nancy laughed. "The date proved you were right all these years, Emma. Jim and I *are* made for each other."

This is the strangest conversation I've ever had, Emma thought. Aloud she said, "My investigative prowess appears to be on the blink. Please enlighten me—in English."

Her nephew leaned across her desk, and in a tone that lacked its usual brashness, said, "Nancy believes a personal relationship would jeopardize our professional one."

At his words, Emma finally understood why Jim had been so nice throughout this case. Her nephew wanted her help for more than one reason.

Before she could tell him she'd figured out his ploy, Nancy spoke to Jim. "I'm sorry if I hurt your male ego, but some things just aren't meant to be. Now, if you'll excuse me, I have work to finish."

Jim threw his hands up in the classic gesture of defeat as the door closed behind his secretary. "Women," he said, to no one in particular. "Who can understand them?"

Recognizing his words as the time-honored lament of a man whose charisma had finally failed him, Emma came around her desk, raised herself on tiptoe and bestowed an affectionate kiss on his cheek. Silently she was thinking that Nancy's indirect strategy might actually work better than any direct approach she herself could have contrived.

"You can't win them all, Jimbo," she said aloud. "Now stop sulking and take me to lunch."

Don't Shoot,
I'm on Vacation

K.T. Anders

"IS THIS SEAT TAKEN?"

I looked up from the pitiful wad of lettuce that passed for a salad at the airport coffee shop and met the bland grey eyes that were focused on me. I felt a thud in the pit of my stomach. Under the table, I involuntarily slipped my feet back into my black high-heeled pumps.

"I'm on vacation, damn it."

The eyes flickered with what might have been sympathy. "I know," he said.

"It's Saturday. As of six p.m. last night I'm incommunicado. You do not exist for me. Go away."

He sat down opposite me and put the coffee and cruller he was holding on the table.

I gazed morosely at my lettuce. I had an hour till my plane was called and I was willing to let him grow tap roots before I said anything more. I ate the rest of my salad, pretending it had a taste. The silence grew long.

"I'm sorry," he said when he realized he was losing. "It's a perfect opportunity. The Director thought you wouldn't mind."

"He was wrong." I held my fork in mid-air and slowly raised my eyes to meet his. "If you make me miss my plane, I'll kill you. Right here. I am not unarmed." I let my eyes shift to my fork, then back to his face. "And I have a knife by my plate. I have the leather strap of my handbag. I know the pressure points of your body and will not hesitate to use my hands. And when I'm finished with you, I'll go kill the Director."

He chuckled. "You're so dramatic."

"I'm not dramatic, I'm on vacation. Vacation means I do not work." I tried another approach. "Please, Jack, let me go in peace. I *need* this vacation."

"I know you do. But this is really important." His voice dripped sincerity. I wanted to throw up. I'd been working almost non-stop for six months on a secret investigation, trying to trace a trail of CIA strategic documents that had turned up in Nicaragua when they shouldn't have; six months of late nights and early mornings that had left me less than jovial. I'd narrowed the list of possibilities down to three men. Then I'd hit a dead end. Whether the spy found out I was closing in or he was taking a breather, I didn't know. But the trail had grown weeds and I was exhausted. I was hoping a weeks' vacation in the sun would unscramble my brains and give me a fresh perspective.

Jack sipped his coffee and I could tell he was settling in for a cosy chat. I looked at my watch.

"Too bad you left the office early yesterday," he said. "We got a break."

"A break?" I ignored the dig about my hours. Besides, it was just my luck that the night I go on vacation, the action heats up.

"Remember the report you gave me last week?" he said.

"You mean the one with my three top choices?"

"Yes. Roger Perry, George Hall, and Dick Armando, if I'm not mistaken."

"It's thrilling to know you read my reports, Jack, but you'd better get to the point. I've got a plane to catch."

He smiled and bit into his cruller. It left a line of crumbs along his upper lip. I resisted telling him, rather enjoying the sight of his face with a cinnamon crumb moustache. It was his most distinguishing feature.

"We got a tip that there is going to be a meeting in Mexico City between the interested parties."

I gave him the fish eye. "A tip from whom?"

He shrugged. "An anonymous call—how do we get most tips?"

I stood up. "I think I hear my plane revving its engines."

He put a hand on my shoulder with such force that it buckled my knees. I sat down again. "A meeting in Mexico City," he repeated. "So I did some checking with the airlines. Both Roger and George flew to Mexico City last night."

"Both of them?"

He licked his lips like a satisfied cat, discovered the crumb moustache and cleaned it off with a flick of his tongue.

"Looks as if you were definitely beating the right bushes."

"Good. Then I can go on vacation a happy woman."

Jack reached across the table and slipped something into my hand. "Verification," he said. "That's all we need."

"I'm not available for work this week, remember?"

"You photograph the meeting with this infra-red camera. That's all you have to do. Then you enjoy your vacation." He shrugged. "Is that so much to ask?"

"Yes!" The miniature camera burned like hot charcoal in my hand. I looked at him defiantly. Jack was the quintessential intelligence officer—thinning hair, grey eyes that never seemed to hold more than a quick flicker of expression, an undistinguished manner of dressing. He was inconspicuous to the point of invisibility. If you looked quickly, Jack simply wasn't there. But he was definitely sitting across from me now, and I didn't know how to get rid of him.

"What are you doing here?" I said. "Didn't you tell me yesterday that you were taking your wife to New York for a romantic weekend at the Plaza?"

He gave me a superior look. "I had to postpone our departure until this afternoon. Company business always takes precedence over my personal plans."

"How noble." I was seething. "Find someone else, Jack," I said, pushing my hand back across the table to him.

A smile barely grazed his mouth and he crossed his arms in front of his chest like a schoolboy. "Can't. You're on your way to Mexico City and the meeting is tonight."

"I'm on my way to Acapulco."

"You're stopping in Mexico City overnight," he said.

I brandished my fork aggressively. "Have you bugged my phone?"

He shrugged. "You're bound to be overheard when you call your travel agent on company time."

What was he doing, compiling a dossier of my faults? "Let's cut the bullshit," he said. "Nobody knows we're on to this business except you and me. We don't know who's involved on the Mexican end so we can't risk bringing in the Mexico City station. You're going to be there; you might as well take the picture. Once we have verification, we can move in."

I sighed. I should have been more enthusiastic about the climax of my own investigation, but the truth was that I was tired of it all. A witch hunt among one's associates isn't pleasant, and the affair had left a bad taste in my mouth. It was easier to let Jack take the glory—he always did anyway.

"Why does the big stuff always go down when I'm trying to get some time off?" I asked.

"You don't have to be there for the action," he said somewhat huffily. "All you have to do is snap the goddamn camera, then go on about your precious vacation. The meeting is tonight and we have no other choices."

He had me and we both knew it, so I listened to his instructions, then beat a hasty retreat to the ladies room. If he or anyone else had any more ideas for my vacation activities, they were going to have to come in and get me.

I made it to the plane without further interference.

The flight was dull with nothing but cloud cover visible beneath us, so I occupied myself by trying to fit the pieces of the puzzle together.

George Hall was in the computer department and had access to the information that was leaking out of the agency, which is why he was on my list, but he was a timid, bookish sort of man, and from the beginning I had trouble seeing him hocking secrets. Still, he traveled frequently on weekends, and lied to the Company about where he had been. He could be making contacts, or he could be cheating on his wife. I knew he had problems at home.

Roger Perry was a top contender straight from Central Casting: he was a private, weasely sort of man, always showing up in odd places. He had few friends at the agency and no one really knew him well. Yet he was devoid of ideological passion and lived modestly. If he was selling secrets, he wasn't getting much out of it for himself.

I was slightly relieved to think the spy might be either Roger or George because Dick Armando was in my department. Jack had been grooming him to take over the Central American desk. He had access to the right stuff, but his record was impeccable. Dick was a nice guy. And drop dead gorgeous. Even Jack had laughed when he saw Dick's name on the list.

If either George or Roger were my man, why had they *both* gone to Mexico City? And who the hell was giving us anonymous tips?

It was a tangle and I had no solutions. I hate having to think when I'm on vacation, and my brain kept veering away from the problem to fantasize about lush Acapulco beaches. I decided to take my picture and let Jack work it out. But I vowed I'd put in a chit for my expenses. That would teach him.

Mexico City was hot and polluted, writhing under the burden of its overpopulation. By the time I reached my hotel I was sorry, in more ways than one, that the direct flight to Acapulco had been filled.

I put on my swim suit and hit the pool, determined, in the face of adversity, to cling to a vestige of my vacation. The local scenery wasn't bad, and all those gorgeous bodies momentarily diverted me from thinking about who, besides me, was going to a late night meeting. Draped on a chaise, I let the sun soak into my bones and tried to ignore the mariachi band in residence by the outdoor bar. I hate Mexican music. I should have gone to Greece.

It was slightly past mid-afternoon when the sun slid behind the west wing of the hotel, throwing the pool into shadow. That was it for the day's recreation. I decided it was time for a little reconnaissance.

In my room, I changed into the peasant skirt and blouse that I'd bought in one of the hotel shops. My hair was several shades too light, but at least from far away I looked less like a gringo than I did in my Ralph Lauren sundress.

I rented a battered car and drove south out of the city. Jack's directions led me to a small, dusty village. As I got out of the car, I was besieged by scrawny little boys begging for the mighty American dollar. So much for my native look. I gave away my small change and shooed them off.

The meeting was scheduled for midnight in the marketplace. I had no trouble finding it. Erected at the base of a hill, behind the main plaza, the market consisted of several rows of long tables divided with boards to form individual booths. It was alive with colorful confusion. Garrulous merchants were selling everything from fresh produce to serapes to "guaranteed genuine" pre-Colombian artifacts. On the hillside, overlooking the entire proceedings, a picnic was in progress.

I wandered about, looking for a vantage point. The most promising place from which to photograph the meeting in the stalls would be from behind a small wooden storage hut wedged against the hillside. I wondered who would arrive tonight—Roger, George, or both?

My mind balked. I was supposed to be on vacation. I didn't care who showed up, one snapshot and I was through. I drove back to Mexico City, immersing myself in the weighty problem of where to have dinner.

The trouble is, once the seed is planted, it invariably grows sprouts. Halfway through a zesty chicken mole, I found myself thinking about what was going to happen tonight. I knew, by the time I finished a flan I hadn't tasted, that I was committed.

I don't mind following orders, but I like to do my own ground work, so I began by checking my facts. I made a few phone calls. I didn't like what I found out. That led to more phone calls, and suddenly it was obvious my vacation was over. I had a lot to do before I went back to the market, and I didn't have much time. I started at the hotel shop, where I bought two shawls and another peasant skirt and blouse like the one I was wearing. Then I went upstairs and started working on the hotel pillows. Pretty soon I had a lumpy senorita dressed in a duplicate of my peasant get-up. She wasn't much in the walking department, but sitting down, on a dark night, she might pass.

The car headlights bored through the darkness as I drove back to the village. The marketplace was dark and silent; the Saturday night merriment concentrated on the streets leading out of the opposite side of the plaza. I parked on a deserted side street, pulled my lumpy pillow-senorita from the car, and walked along the dimly lit street. It was about ten o'clock, but I needed to be there early.

It was hard to believe the deserted stalls were the scene of such frenzied activity only a few hours earlier. Now the merchandise was gone. Only a faint glow from across the plaza barely defined the empty tables from the shadows.

I went straight to the storage hut. The lock on the door yielded to my plastic credit card and I slipped the senorita inside. Then I examined the outside of the structure from every angle. There was a window and the roof sloped down toward the market. A person crouching against the side wall would blend with the shadows, visible only from the hillside behind the market. It was my best shot and I had to take it.

I hurried back to the car and drove to the outskirts of town. My watch showed an hour and a half until the meeting. Jack had said to show up about a half hour early. I made my last phone call from a dilapidated gas station, pulled off the road and waited.

At eleven thirty I again parked the car in the sidestreet. Tying a shawl over my head to match my twin in the shed, I walked toward the empty market. An old truck stood alone in the parking lot facing toward the dark tables. I took a deep breath; if I was wrong, it was going to be a bad night.

No one was in sight. The hillside rose darkly behind the market. Weaving in constant motion, I dodged between the stalls until I reached the hut, where its bulk momentarily hid me from view from the hill. I opened the door. My lady friend was still on the floor. I grabbed her and thrust her around the corner of the hut, into the position I had chosen as my hiding place.

It was the moment of truth. Either it would look as if I had run into the market, paused briefly at the hut, then reappeared crouching at its side in the shadows, or it wouldn't, in which case I was in big trouble.

As quietly as I could, using the windowsill as a step, I hoisted myself onto the roof, staying well below the peak. I waited, lying on my stomach, not daring to breathe.

In the silence of the night, I heard a whizzing spit of sound. I gave a soft, choked scream. Two more bullets from the silenced gun slammed into the side of the hut as my poor lady bucked into the air, then fell in a heap. Then a figure was running down the hillside toward the lump below me.

"Now," I shouted towards the truck in the parking lot.

Bright light washed the marketplace as the truck headlights snapped on. Jack turned with a cry and shot into the light. I jumped down from the roof of the hut, and thrust my gun into his back.

"It's over Jack. Give me the gun."

He turned at the sound of my voice. In the harsh light I could see his eyes were bland even in defeat. He glanced down at the pile of clothing at his feet.

"You tricked me," he said.

"Sorry," I replied as the man I'd called from our local Mexico City office got out of the truck and joined us. He snapped a pair of handcuffs over Jack's wrists.

"How did you know?" asked Jack.

"You were overzealous," I replied.

Jack's expression actually held surprise, and for a moment I looked at him, savoring it.

"It was the tip that both George and Roger were involved." I shook my head. "I had trouble with that. One of them I could buy, but not both. I called the Plaza in New York to speak to you about it. Your room didn't answer, but the desk told me you and your wife had registered Friday night. Bad boy, Jack." I gave him back the superior smile he had bestowed upon me at the airport Saturday morning. "After all, you told me Company business came before your personal life."

Jack avoided looking at me. The surprise was gone and he had retreated again into the anonymity that was his trademark.

"So I asked for a description of you," I continued. "And I actually got one."

Jack missed the joke. "The woman at the desk said you were gorgeous," I continued. "We compared notes on what that meant. It came out Dick Armando. What was Dick Armando doing in a New York hotel with your wife and your name?"

I forgot that Jack never answers a direct question.

"I checked with the airlines," I said. "The passenger manifest showed no record of Roger Perry or George Hall flying to Mexico City. But your name was there, Jack. On the flight after mine Saturday morning."

We had reached the car. The local man said he would drive.

"I admit I was worried," I said as I climbed into the backseat with Jack. "You and I and the Director were the only people who knew about my investigation. And only you and I knew about the names on my list."

Jack wasn't talking, and as we hit the highway back to Mexico City, the silence began to grate on my nerves. The warm, tropical breeze hinted of lazy beaches somewhere where I should be, and suddenly I was angry at the bland, empty face next to me. I grabbed his collar.

"You and Dick Armando had a pretty good system, didn't you? Once you gave him the information, Dick, as Central American liaison, had the contacts to get it out of the country. But then I came along with Armando's name on my list of suspects. You panicked."

Jack's eyes could have been painted on his lids. I pushed him into the corner in disgust.

"I was the only weed in your garden. So you sent Dick to New York with your wife to forge your name on a hotel register. That was your alibi. In a busy hotel like the Plaza, who would remember one more couple? Meanwhile, you could come to Mexico to make sure that I 'disappeared' while on vacation. With me out of the way, you could doctor my report for the Director to take the heat off Dick, and of course, yourself."

Jack looked at me with the shadow of a smile.

"Not a bad scenario," I admitted. "But you blew it two ways."

His eyes went blank again, but his lip twitched. It was my turn to smile.

"Even if she's only a hotel clerk, never underestimate a woman's ability to spot an attractive man," I said.

There was silence in the car.

"And never, ever, interfere with a woman's vacation."

Death in Rocky Falls

Brenda Melton Burnham

FRANK POTEK'S DEATH caused quite a stir in Rocky Falls. Frank had gone fishing in Dinosaur Lake early one February morning and never came back. They found his boat, a little sixteen-footer with a five horsepower motor, floating out in the middle with a bum motor and one oar, but there was no sign of Frank.

Skindivers came over from Beaverton and my husband, Bill, helped organize a search around the whole lake, especially in the remote wooded sections where Frank might have made it to shore and still be in need of help. The fact that it was February made matters worse because of the possibility of hypothermia.

"Couldn't find a sign of him, Gladys," Bill said to me afterwards. "Not a sign. He's gone, all right."

We've lived our whole lives, Bill and me, in Rocky Falls. Bill's been on the police force nearly fifteen years now. I got my diploma from the beauty college down in Beaverton two years ago, right after Jenny, our youngest, started school, and I work three days a week at Ida Schwartz's Pink Poodle Hair Salon.

Anyway, like I was saying, they searched everywhere. But none of it did any good. When Frank's body didn't show up after a reasonable period of time, Louise Potek conferred with the pastor of the Methodist church and it was agreed a memorial service was the way to go.

Since the Poteks lived on our block—three houses down and across the street—all us neighbors took turns bringing food in and helping Louise out the best we knew how.

She took it pretty rough. They'd been married ten years and there was only the two of them. Millie Coughlin, one of my customers, works in Doc Letherby's office and she told Ida and me, in private of course, that Louise had something wrong with her female organs and that's why they didn't have any kids.

"Probably just as well," Ida said, having been married and divorced twice. "It's tough raising kids all by yourself."

"Maybe so," I said, "but I'd still want to have mine anyway." Bill and I had three, fourteen, eleven and seven, and I couldn't imagine life without them.

"He probably didn't have much insurance, either," Ida went on. "What with the auto parts store going through rough times."

So you can imagine our surprise when Norm Clausen, who is Ida's insurance agent too, told us Louise woud get a hundred thousand dollars as soon as the company settlcd.

"It's held up by the fact there isn't anybody, you know," Norm said. He always enjoys being in the position of knowing little things like that and having to explain them to people like us who don't. "I'm doing everything I can, naturally, to expedite matters. Poor Louise has enough on her hands trying to sell the store. That Frank sure left her in an awful position with the store failing and them in debt."

Did I mention that Norm was a bachelor who lived with his mother? Or that Louise wasn't a bad-looking woman? She worked at the BonTon Dress Shop so she got twenty percent off on all her clothes and she wore all the latest styles. She had a standing appointment every Thursday at the Pink Poodle. I'd done her hair once or twice when Ida was feeling poorly, but Louise was particular and thought Ida did a better job. I thought Ida was more willing to put up with her fancy ideas was all. Every other month Louise wanted something new and different and no matter whether the style suited her or not.

"I saw Sue Ellen on Dallas the other night," she'd say. "She had just the cutest little hairdo. All swept back at the sides with a curl right here. What do you think?"

I thought Sue Ellen had a whole lot of people around whose business it was to make her look gorgeous and rich every week and that didn't go for much here in Rocky Falls. But Ida went along with whatever Louise demanded and always managed to find something good to say about it.

Well, Louise got about nine months good run on the poor widow routine before the insurance company finally settled and the auto parts store sold and it slowly began to sink into everybody's head that "Poor Louise" was turning out to be one well-off widow.

"I've been thinking about moving to Beaverton," I heard her say to Ida one Thursday. "They could use a nice boutique there. I don't like to brag, but I do think I have a certain sense of style that's required for a business like that."

I snorted to myself and nearly drowned Elsie Wanamaker whose hair I was shampooing at the time.

"Why don't you open one right here in Rocky Falls?" Ida asked, her fingers busy making little waves at Louise's temples.

"Are you kidding? The locals have no sense of style. They think putting on their pink polyester for Sunday services is the height of fashion. And the tourists are all just fishermen's wives."

I scrubbed Elsie's head so hard while listening to that drivel that she cried out, so I had to pay more attention to what I was doing and didn't hear any more.

One night at dinner, in October I think it was, Bill said he'd had lunch with Arnie Hooper and Arnie had told him he saw a guy who looked just like Frank Potek when he was over in Spokane.

"You're kidding," I said. "Maybe he had family over there and this was a brother or an uncle?"

"Nope. Frank's family's all back in Oklahoma, remember? We did call the Spokane Police Department and have them run a check, but they had no knowledge of any Frank Potek in the city."

"You think. . . ?"

"I don't think anything, except that water was awful cold and that boat was awful far from shore."

"But maybe Frank did get out and he has amnesia or something and doesn't know who he is."

"Well, that'd be one good reason there was no record of a Frank Potek living in Spokane then, wouldn't it? He wouldn't know his own name."

The news was coming on the TV then and Bill went to watch it while I cleared the table.

December is always a busy month at The Pink Poodle because of all the holiday parties, so I was working almost every day and managed to get caught up on a lot more of what was happening around town that way. Louise was naturally a topic of conversation.

"You know who's taking her to the Legion dance this week, don't you?" Millie Coughlin said to me while I was brushing her set out.

"No. How would I know?"

"Norm Clausen." She whispered this loud enough so even Ida, who was some distance away, could hear.

"And good luck to her," Ida said. "He'll never get free of his mother."

"I think it's a good thing Louise is getting out and about," I said. "It must be awful hard, losing your husband like that. I can't imagine what I'd do if something happened to Bill."

"Ha," Millie snorted and her head moved so sharp she almost jerked the brush from my hand. "I'd say your marriage is a little more stable than the Poteks' ever was.

"Not to mention the fact Louise came out of her 'tragedy' with a tidy little profit," she added when I'd gone back to fixing her hair again. "That just might be the magic potion that could tempt Norm from his mama."

I couldn't get Millie's words out of my head the rest of the day. Louise really had been "blooming" lately, as my mother would've said. Now that I recollected, she had done more than her share of complaining in the past about her husband and their money problems, all of which was Frank's fault, naturally.

But still, that didn't have to mean anything. Did it?

In February Ida flew to Salt Lake City to stay with her daughter who was having a baby, so I took over the shop and her customers while she was gone.

Louise hadn't said a whole lot more about moving to Beaverton and opening a boutique. When she came in on Thursday I asked her about it.

"The deal fell through. I'm thinking now I might just go on down to California. Someplace warm. Palm Springs maybe."

"It must be nice, knowing you have that extra money as a cushion."

"Are you kidding? I got so sick of scrimping and saving, just to keep that stupid auto parts store afloat."

"Frank did try awful hard to make a go of it."

She got a sad look on her face immediately and said, "Oh, don't think I wouldn't trade that money in an instant to have my husband back. You don't know what it's like, being a woman alone."

The words sounded good but I couldn't help thinking of my kids and how quick they could change their tune if the one they were playing wasn't working. Sure enough, after a few minutes Louise brightened up and said, "Listen, have you got that new Peach Brandy rinse? Let's try that today."

"Got a big evening planned, have you?" I remarked, trying to crack a little joke. Everybody in town knew she and Norm Clausen were a hot item.

"I certainly have not!" she snapped, and I thought, Boy, see if I try to be pleasant with you again.

While Louise was under the dryer Carrie Walters called and wanted to know had I rounded up a lot of good things for the church's rummage sale that weekend. I said I thought I'd done about all I could, but seeing as how Louise was in the shop now, I'd ask if she had anything we could use.

When I was combing out her hair, I asked her.

"I suppose I have a few old things you can have," she said, as if it would be a real sacrifice. "Drop by the house tonight and you can pick them up."

After dinner, while Bill was watching the news and the kids were doing the dishes, I threw a jacket on and walked down to the Potek place.

· The house was dark, but Louise's new Camaro was sitting in the driveway. I headed for the back door where I could see a light through the window and hear voices.

When I knocked everything got quiet. I waited a few minutes and knocked again. The wind had a sharp edge to it and I wished she would hurry up and answer.

Finally the porch light came on and Louise opened the door a crack.

"What is it?" she demanded, as if I'd offended her in some awful way.

"It's me, Gladys. I came by for the rummage sale things like you told me."

"Oh yes, Gladys. Listen, I haven't had time to do that yet. Pick them up in the morning, all right?"

I said fine, she shut the door in my face and I left. I couldn't imagine why she was being so secretive. I certainly didn't care what she and Norm were up to. At home later, while we were getting ready for bed, Bill listened while I told him how snappish Louise was.

"Maybe you caught her and Norm at a bad moment," Bill commented while he checked his shirt to see if it would go another day before washing.

"It won't," I said, meaning his shirt, and went back to my main topic. "I'm telling you, Bill, there's something suspicious going on there. She keeps talking about leaving town and all the time holding Norm on a leash like her pet terrier or something."

"What's so suspicious about that?" he asked, pitching his shirt at the dirty clothes basket.

"Well, maybe she got rid of Frank. What do you think of that?"

"I think you've been reading too many Agatha Christie books, that's what I think. Can you really see Louise, with her fancy hairdo and frilly dress, out in the middle of the lake? In the middle of February? She wouldn't even get in Frank's boat in July."

He was right. But I still couldn't let it go. "Well, I've had ideas before that you didn't think were all that bad. Remember the time Cliff Bagby's barn burned down and I reminded you how timely it was, him needing money and all? What if. . . ?"

"Gladys, will you stop and come to bed? I'm the cop in the family, remember? Not you." He grinned that little crooked smile he knows always gets me when he says this, so I gave up.

Since I had to be at the shop at nine the next morning to do a perm for Elsie Wanamaker, I stopped by Louise's on my way. This time I went to the front door. She took a long time answering again and when she did she looked awful. The beautiful set I'd done on her hair was a mess and her face looked really bad, even considering she hadn't had time to put her make-up on yet.

"For crying out loud, Gladys, you are a persistent one, aren't you. Wait a minute, will you?"

She walked away, leaving the door ajar and me standing out in the cold. I figured I'd put up with enough of her bad manners, so I stepped into the hall to wait.

The living room looked almost as bad as Louise did. The throw rug was piled up in one corner, her Boston rocker was turned on its side and the couch was shoved up against the wall. No wonder she didn't let me in last night, I thought. They must've been having a wild old time.

Louise came out of the bedroom with an armload of dresses just then and nearly fainted when she saw me.

"What are you doing?" she screamed.

"I'm waiting for the rummage things," I said, dumbfounded.

"Oh God, I can't bear it," Louise sobbed and dropped the clothes in a heap. "Why don't you leave me alone?"

I didn't know what to do. She could still be suffering from grief; I'd read articles that said it could last for years.

"Louise, why don't you sit down?" I said, real gentle-like, starting down the hall to the kitchen. "I'll go make you a nice hot cup of tea."

"Get out of my house! Get out, get out, get out."

She was still screaming when I pulled the front door shut behind me. I got in the car, telling myself the heck with her, but I knew I couldn't leave her like that. I may not have liked the woman much, but she was another human being and she was obviously suffering.

I decided to go next door to Mabel Sorenson's. She and Betty Carver were sharing a pot of coffee when I got there. I told them the problem and they agreed we had to do something. Of course I didn't mention my earlier suspicions; actually, they'd sorta been shocked right out of me.

The three of us tramped back over to Louise's. She was standing at the sink and saw us as we passed the window. By the time we got to the door we could hear her having hysterics.

"Heavens," Mabel exclaimed. "It's a good thing we're here. Gladys, why don't you call Doc Leatherby while Betty and I try to calm her down?"

Mabel opened the door and the three of us rushed in. Frank Potek's body lay on the floor, stiff as an old bear hide. Louise Potek crouched beside him, a meat cleaver in her hand.

It was almost noon before most of the excitement was over and Bill dropped by the shop to bring me some lunch.

"Well, it looks like you were right after all," Bill admitted graciously. "And ol' Arnie Hooper may have seen Frank in Spokane to boot."

I recollected how awful it was when Mabel and Betty and I had gone busting into the Potek's kitchen. "When I saw Frank lying there, my first thought was he'd been there for a whole year."

Bill laughed. "Nope. Nothing like that. Just since sometime last night. Seems they'd come up with this plan for him to fake his drowning and disappear, so they could collect the insurance money. The store was going down the tubes and so was the marriage and they thought this would solve all their problems."

"What happened?" I'd been dying of curiosity ever since I'd had to leave to come down and open the shop.

"After the money finally came through, Louise decided she didn't want to share. She had Norm half-talked into going somewhere else and 'starting over.' And she figured Frank wouldn't have a lot to say about it since he was supposed to be dead. What was he gonna do, sue her?" Bill took a big bite of tuna salad sandwich and chewed.

"What did he do?"

"He harassed her, that's all. Called her at all hours of the day and night, said he was going to turn himself in. She claims when he did show up last night, he threatened to kill her. Slapped her around and tried to choke her. But she managed to get free of him and hit him on the head with that antique doorstop of hers. Says it was self-defense. Him or her. Who knows?"

"But this morning, when we got there, she had a cleaver. . . ."

"We figure she was going to try to cut the body up and get rid of it somehow."

I shuddered at the thought and changed the subject. "Is Norm going to stand by her?"

"Not hardly. He's back-pedaling so fast it makes your head swim. Says he didn't know a thing about it and I reckon that's the truth. Old Mrs. Clausen stood right next to him the whole time saying, 'I told you so. I warned you.' Poor man's practically a basket case."

"And Louise?"

"She's cool as lemonade on a hot day. Now. Self defense all the way. That's her story and she's sticking to it."

I shook my head. I couldn't imagine such a genteel woman killing her husband.

"She sure was mad at you, though," Bill added with a chuckle. "Before she got her act together I heard her mutter, 'If it weren't for that damned Gladys.'"

"I can't imagine why she'd say a thing like that," I said modestly. "All I was doing was collecting for the church rummage sale."

Be Kind to Your
Web-Footed Friends

Linda Wagner

WINTER IN THE CITY of Cleveland, Ohio has all of the charm of
a camping trip during the last ice age. It's not just cold. It's cold and
wet and windy. An icy wind blows off Lake Erie that goes right for
your bones.

As I rode the wind up Ninth Street, I tried to understand why
someone whose parents had a condo in Florida would choose to
stay in Cleveland during the month of January. Was I crazy?

Then I thought about what it would be like to spend a month or
so under the same roof with my mother. Now *that* would be crazy.
I don't know any attorneys with a reputation for getting matricides
off the hook, so I decided that I really was better off here. It was bad
enough that she called me twenty times a week when she was in
town. Ten calls were to kvetch about my profession, (I am a private
investigator), the other ten were to inquire as to why I am, as yet,
unwed. At least, while she was in Florida, she had to call me long
distance. There could be no dinner invitations catching me by
surprise . . . evenings that inevitably turned out to include an eligible
man my age. I had experienced enough of these exercises in
boredom to know that they always ended in weeping, wailing and
gnashing of teeth as they deteriorated into the home version of
Family Armageddon.

The weather suddenly seemed a heck of a lot more palatable.

I was on my way to visit a possible paying client. I don't get too
many, (a situation that my mother never tires of pointing out), so the

prospect was a real treat. It's hard to convince the world at large that a woman can be as good as a man in a profession where the media has shaped the public's perception with the likes of Magnum, P.I.

Apparently some really rich broad had disappeared. The rich don't like bad publicity, so instead of bringing in the police, the husband decided to hire me. He got my name from Harry Wilson, a retired cop who occasionally throws business my way.

I paid off the scary looking parking attendant, got my car out onto the freeway and, dodging the local crazies-on-wheels, I made for the East burbs.

Edith Berlinger Gustafson's money was not terribly old. It had only been around since the forties. She was an heiress to a fortune made in pickles. Don't laugh. Pickles are a serious enough product to make some pretty serious money. Edith's old man founded his company in his basement. Whatever magic he had obtained from the pickle fairy, it worked like crazy. From that basement, John Berlinger went on to build a successful business. Eventually, he was manufacturing all sorts of condimental delights. A huge conglomerate bought the company, leaving Berlinger a wealthy man. While the conglomerate went on to bankruptcy caused by overdiversification, John Berlinger went on to become immensely wealthy through a series of wise, if narrow, investments.

When her father died, Edith inherited the whole nut.

I arrived at the Shaker Heights mansion still referred to as "the Berlinger place." I had barely touched the bell when the door opened and I found myself looking up the nostrils of a very tall man in a black suit. He looked sort of familiar, although I was pretty sure that we had never met before.

"Hi," I said. "You the butler?"

"No, ma'am," he answered. "I am the houseman."

"Oh . . . what's a houseman?"

"Is there something we can do for you, ma'am?"

I didn't see anyone else, so I assumed this must be the editorial "we." "Yeah, uh . . . I have an appointment to see Mr. Gustafson. Is he in?"

"You may wait in the foyer," he said, as if granting a favor. Maybe that had been the royal "we." "Who may I say is calling?"

"Ms. Lewis."

"Miss Lewis," he misquoted.

"No, Starchy, *Ms*. Lewis. Welcome to the latter half of the twentieth century." He looked confused. Maybe he didn't get out much. He inhaled noisily.

"Very good, ma'am."

He left with a sort of silent gliding motion. It was as if he had a miniature hovercraft in each of his highly polished shoes. He really reminded me of someone. Who the heck was it?

I cooled my heels in the marble foyer for the better and worse parts of twenty minutes before he reappeared. "Follow me, ma'am. Mr. Gustafson was on the phone. He asked me to apologize for the delay."

Maybe a houseman was someone you paid to make apologies for you. He led me into a large study. The man behind the huge walnut desk didn't look as if he had ever studied anything other than possibly a racing form. He was dressed in an expensive charcoal gray sports jacket, but he looked as if he would have been more at home in a T-shirt. Preferably one of the stained variety. The porcelain tea cup near his right hand should have been a can of cheap beer. He was short and squat, his head shaped like the proverbial bullet.

"Hey," he said, standing up and holding out a beefy hand. "How ya doin', hon?" He pumped my hand up and down as if he were expecting to produce well water.

"I'm doing fine and my name's not Hon."

"What?"

"My name is Livia Day Lewis. You may call me Ms. Lewis."

"Call me Al," he replied generously.

"Mr. Gustafson—"

"Al. Call me Al. Sorry about the wait. I was on the phone."

"So the butler said."

"He's not a butler. He's a houseman."

"He said that, too. What exactly is a houseman? And how does it differ from a butler?"

"Harry Wilson tol' me he thinks maybe you can find out what happened to Edith."

"Well, I can try." Maybe the "houseman" thing was a secret, like Masonic stuff or something. "Tell me what happened and when."

He motioned me to a chair. I sat while he explained. "Edith makes regular trips to the Cleveland Clinic down in University Circle to keep check on her blood pressure and stuff. Every other

Thursday at one o'clock. Last Thursday she gets into a cab out front and damn if that's not the last time I see her to this minute."

He opened a desk drawer, rooting around in it for several seconds. He pulled out a very large cigar. He fiddled with the cigar and some sort of scissors. I watched in fascination, never having seen a cigar of such size outside of Saturday morning TV. Was he actually going to smoke it? I speculated on what it might smell like. When it was finally lit, I realized that I had underspeculated by quite a bit.

"Let's see," I coughed, "you haven't heard from Edith for the last six days. No ransom note, though, right?"

"That's right."

"Not much to go on." Cough. "Has she ever stayed away before? I mean why did you wait so long to do something?" Cough.

"Well, no, she never done this before. I just thought maybe she decided to go visitin' and forgot to call."

Strange attitude. They say the rich are different. Still. . . . "Okay, well, I'll give it a look. Now as to my fee. . . ." The room had begun to resemble a rib burn-off and it smelled like a toxic waste dump. He waved a hand, moving some of the smoke around.

"Money's no object. Just find my Edith." He gave me an advance check for $500 and I was able to make my escape before I had to be hospitalized for smoke inhalation.

Anyone capable of smoking a cigar the size of the Hindenburg might be capable of anything. That, coupled with the fact that I just plain disliked the man, made me wonder if I really should have taken his check. Well, Livia, I thought, here's where we find out how objective you really are. After all, my calendar was not exactly overcrowded and I had grown fond of such luxuries as eating and paying the rent.

I shivered my way back to the office. The heat in my car was nonexistent. The heat in my office was what you might call occasional. I just hadn't figured out for what occasion it might be turned on. Warmth just didn't seem to be an option for me today. For what it was worth, I was wearing two pairs of socks.

I called the Clinic to establish that Edith Gustafson had, in fact, kept her appointment. She had. I contemplated checking taxi records, always an exciting prospect, if you find being on hold entertaining. In the end, I felt I needed to know more about the woman I was looking for, so I called my friend, Tom Jennings. He was a mostly freelance reporter, who was temporarily subbing for a vacationing editor at the *Plain Dealer,* the city's only remaining daily newspaper. Sad comment on the times, eh?

"Tom, it's Livia."

"Hello, dear, haven't heard from you in a while."

Hearing his slight British accent always gave me a little thrill. As did his attractive blonde good looks. "I know. I meant to call...."

"Of course. You were just so darned busy."

Tom knows how underemployed I am, so his sarcasm had the effect of making me feel guilty. I was, after all, calling for a favor. My mother taught me how to play the Guilt Trip Game at an early age. Indeed, I may be one of the champion players in the world. "No, look, I really did mean to call. I just . . . uh . . . I need a favor."

"Certainly," he said, gently. "Maybe if I do you enough favors, you might give me the time of day." Ouch. Medic! "What do you need, luv?"

"I need to get a bio on Edith Berlinger Gustafson," I said, choosing to ignore the preamble remark.

"Berlinger? The pickle princess?"

"Yup," I said, relieved that we were getting down to business. "It seems she's disappeared. The husband, who, by the way, is a real pip, has hired me to find her."

"Al Gustafson is something of a legend in certain social circles," he said. "Apparently nobody ever understood what they saw in each other. Opposite ends of the spectrum. Bloody strange match. Still, I suppose that even an heiress can be lonely."

"She must have been awfully lonely to marry this guy. He immediately made my list of the ten most obnoxious people I've ever met."

"So what do you need from me?" he asked.

"Maybe you could get me a clipping file on her. I just need to know her a little better."

"Righto. Give me about an hour. Why don't you come by here and pick it up?"

I agreed to be at his office in an hour. Hanging up I thought about all of the times I'd worked with the lanky, laid-back Englishman. I liked him a lot. We'd "dated" for a while, but had decided that a romance would get in the way of the professional teamwork which benefited us both. We worked well together. I wanted to keep it that way. Lately, though, I had been under the impression that Tom was looking for something more. I didn't know what to do about it, so I chose the mature alternative . . . I'd started to avoid him completely.

At the agreed upon time, I arrived at the offices of the *Plain Dealer*. Tom's secretary handed me an envelope with a Post-It note attached.

"Livia," it read, "sorry I had to leave. Something came up. Call you. T."

"Thank Mr. Jennings for me," I told the secretary, trying not to advertise my disappointment. She already seemed a little smug. And it really didn't matter anyway, did it? I headed back to my apartment to learn what I could about the pickle people.

My two cats, Sleepy and Dopey, greeted me at the door with worried meows. Within moments I understood their anxiety. My upstairs neighbors were home. I've never actually seen these people, nor do I know how many of them there are. Every night around eight o'clock it's as if the army were holding maneuvers up there. They run back and forth, they move furniture . . . and they vacuum. The nightly vacuuming ritual is akin to living on a construction sight. The carpeting must be threadbare by now. How much dust could accumulate in a twenty-four hour period, anyway? Myself, I vacuum twice a year, whether it's needed or not. Well, okay, I'm a slob . . . but every night?

I tried to drown out the sound of their activity and turned my attention to the public life of Edith Berlinger Gustafson. Most of the early clippings were pretty standard-issue rich person stuff. Coming out party, junior league, charity work, social appearances. Absent, it seemed, were any courtships. I studied young Edith's picture. She was a handsome woman, but looked a little on the icy side.

She apparently dropped out of the news for a few years. When she surfaced next, she was getting hitched to Mr. Alphonse Gustafson, a man of rather vague background. They had met during a cruise. Something about Al must have gotten to the young heiress. Maybe it was the fact that he was so very different from the other young men she knew.

According to the clippings, not long after the nuptials, old man Berlinger bought the farm with a sudden and massive coronary, leaving the newlyweds with more money than the treasuries of several small countries. There was a lot more society news about this time . . . pictures in which Mr. Gustafson stuck out like a pigeon at a swan convention. The couple made substantial donations to various organizations with idealistic names like Mothers for World Peace and the National Movement Against Nuclear Arms. There were also donations to the usual large national causes, like the March of Dimes and the Red Cross. Tucked among the names of these humanitarian groups was one I had never heard of before, the Association for Animal Equality. It was the only group involving animals, and the bequest mentioned in the article was larger than any of the others. One hundred and fifty thousand dollars to be granted automatically on an annual basis. I pulled out the phone book. Sure enough, the Association for Animal Equality was listed in the white pages, with an office on Payne Avenue in the downtown area. I made a note of the address, and planned to check it out the next day.

Sleepy and Dopey were doing a routine of head bumps and ankle rubs that indicated they thought it was time for bed. I agreed, since even the upstairs neighbors had quieted down. The three of us called it a night.

An ice storm occurred during the night, as we slept the sleep of the innocent. Outside, everything was covered with a coating of sparkling white and silver. I expected to see Jack Nicholson with an ax over his shoulder shuffling into view at any moment. Never mind, I thought, better off here with Jack than in Florida with my mother.

I spent the morning trying to get the building custodian to send some heat up to my office, inbetween calls to taxi companies. In the end, all I had was confirmation that Edith was indeed deposited at the Cleveland Clinic on Thursday afternoon, but if a taxi had picked her up, there was no record of it.

By then it was late afternoon and my nose was turning blue, so I figured I would go outside to get warm. It had to be at least thirty degrees outdoors. It was a short walk to the address on Payne Avenue where I was hoping to find the Association for Animal Equality.

The office building was a little on the seedy side. The directory in the lobby told me that the organization I was seeking, Herman P. Gargoyle, President, was located on the sixth floor, so that's where I headed.

Arriving on six, I opened the door to an office so tiny it would have to take steroids to become a broom closet. There was nowhere for the tall, thin man behind the desk to hide, although he looked around for a place. He was balding, with beady eyes and an Adam's apple that bobbed up and down. He did not seem delighted to be having a visitor.

"Yesss?" he said, all too loudly. "How may I help you?"

"Herman P. Gargoyle?"

"Yesss."

"Association for Animal Equality?"

"Yesss." The man hissed like a snake. I tried my best to look like a mongoose.

"Mr. Gargoyle, I'm investigating the disappearance of Edith Berlinger Gustafson." I flashed my standard issue Junior G-man badge. It may have come out of a cereal box, but it tended to make people feel more like cooperating. I never actually claimed to be anybody special. I let others draw their own conclusions.

"Why would I know anything of the woman'sss comingsss and goingsss?"

"I'm not saying that you do. I'm checking some background facts."

He eyed me suspiciously. "Like what?"

"Mrs. Gustafson made a very generous donation to your organization."

"Yesss . . . she isss a very generousss woman."

"Well, it seems unusual that all of her other donations were on a one-time basis. This bequest was large and automatically extended from year to year."

"Yesss . . . that isss true. Edith and I are old friendsss. We went to ssschool together. The donation wasss for a ssspecial project."

"Which was?"

"Ducksss."

"Ducksss? I mean ducks?"

"Yesss. A ssstudy of migration and ssso forth."

"Oh. . . ."

"Isss there anything else? I'm very busy." The desk seemed to be empty, save for a Spiegel catalog in one corner.

"No. I guess not. Thank you, Mr. Gargoyle. You've been a big help."

As I left the building I had several thoughts in rapid succession. Why had Herman Gargoyle been completely unsurprised by the news that Edith had disappeared? He hadn't blinked an eye, even though a hundred and fifty thousand dollars a year was involved. What about Edith's will, then? If she died and everything went to Al, would the automatic bequest stop? If she disappeared without a trace would. . . ? It was a thought to tinker with.

I decided to do my tinkering at my apartment, which was at least relatively warm. As I let myself in, I heard the phone ringing. I ran for it, thinking it might be Tom.

"Hello?"

"Livia, this is your mother."

I groaned inwardly. "Hi, Ma. How's Florida?"

"Still here. Right where I left it last time. Why are you out of breath?"

"I was just coming in the door. I ran for the phone." I coughed.

"Were you expecting a call?"

"Not really." My upstairs neighbors started banging and pounding on something. Maybe they were making orange crates out of old furniture.

"So . . . why I called, Livia, your Dad and I," she emphasized "Dad" who probably knew nothing about this phone call, "were thinking you should come down here for a weekend at least and—"

"I can't, Ma, I'm working on a case."

"What did you say? The connection's not good." The connection was fine. It was my profession that was not good. "I thought you said something about working."

"Yes. I have a case. I have to work."

"You're kidding!"

"I wouldn't kid you, Ma." The neighbors were in full swing. Sleepy and Dopey hid under the coffee table and glared up at the ceiling.

"Okay," my mother replied, though I could tell that it wasn't okay. "Maybe next weekend."

Yeah, sure. Maybe next incarnation. "Maybe," was all I said aloud. We said our goodbyes and hung up. For possibly the millionth time, I questioned the wisdom of Mr. Bell's invention.

The noise from upstairs continued unabated. "What are they doing up there?" I yelled. Sleepy and Dopey looked at me with reproach, their ears laid back. Cats consider yelling for any reason in very poor taste.

I lit a cigarette, tossed my coat on the chair, tossed myself on the couch and inhaled furiously until I reached a state of semi-calm. I pulled out Edith's file again, wondering about the will. If Al were on the up and up, I could ask him. Compared to Herman P. Gargoyle, Al didn't seem half bad anymore.

I had a glass of sherry, watched some mundane television and looked up the word "houseman" in the dictionary. The definition? "A butler." Go figure.

I turned in around midnight. The cats were restless, but the neighbors had quieted down. As I drifted off to sleep, I thought of Edith Gustafson, missing one more full day.

It was still early when I arrived once again at the Berlinger/ Gustafson manse. Familiar nostrils opened the door.

"Say, howdy, Mr. Houseman."

"Ma'am?"

"Do you have a name?"

"Bentley, ma'am."

"Okay, Bentley, let Mr. Gustafson know I'm here. Ms. Lewis, remember?" He stared at me as though I were a particularly distasteful dust bunny. I suddenly realized who it was that he reminded me of.

"Alfred Hitchcock!" I crowed.

"What?" he said, obviously startled.

"Sorry," I said. I hadn't intended to say it out loud. It just happened.

He gathered his composure, and sucking in a noisy breath said, "Very well. Come in."

I was once again left to do my heel-cooling in the marble foyer. A door opened and closed somewhere. Soon I saw Al bustling towards me.

"Do ya have something?"

Don't bother with hello, Al. He was dressed in a yellow sports jacket and green golf pants today. Oh, Edith, I thought, it's only been a week and already his wardrobe is going to hell.

"Well, not exactly," I replied. "I have a hunch. I need to ask you a couple of questions. Can we go somewhere? It's kind of chilly here."

"Sure thing. Library's this way."

I followed him into a room with expensive mahogany pan-elling. There were many shelves of books, which I was pretty certain that Al had never touched. We settled into a pair of matching leather chairs.

"Hey," he said, "you want tea or something?"

"No, thanks." He looked disappointed. He had remembered his duties as a host and I had spurned his offer.

"Al, I need to know about Edith's will."

"Will?" He said it as if it were a foreign concept.

"Yes. Who inherits all of this if she dies?"

"You think she's dead?" he asked slowly.

"It's very possible. If she had been kidnapped, you would have had a ransom note long before this." He sat quietly, digesting this. "Uh, Al? The will?"

"Will." He was somewhere else.

"Yes, Al. Tell me about Edith's will."

He came back. "Well . . . I guess I do. Inherit it all, I mean." He looked panicky. "Do you think I would do anything to Edith to get money? I would never—"

"No, Al. I think you're eliminated as a suspect for that reason." If Al had killed her for her money, there would have been a body. No body, no official death for seven long years until the court declared her legally dead. It made no sense that he would put himself in that kind of limbo.

"One more question, Al. Outside of Herman Gargoyle, did she ever make any charitable donation on an automatic annual basis?" Something flickered in his eyes. I couldn't read it.

"Herman who?"

"Gargoyle. Association for Animal Equality. Something about ducks."

"I don't know anything about any ducks," he said as I got up to leave. "Miss Lewis?"

I let him get away with it. "Yes, Al."

"I would never hurt Edith. I love her. I know it seems hard to believe . . . we're so different . . . but I do. I think she loves me, too." He was still using the present tense. Not believing in the probability of her death.

It's a rare man who understands his relationship to the universe. Al Gustafson knew that he was something of a blot on his wife's social landscape. I looked at him, sitting there with hurt in his eyes. No one had figured out the reason that Edith and Al were together. It was very simple . . . they loved each other. I didn't bring up the houseman thing. The moment was more profound than that.

"Al," I said gently, "there's not much hope that I'll find her alive, but I will find out what happened to her. I promise you that."

Outside, the air had turned bitter. For Alphonse Gustafson, life was turning bitter. I pitied him.

I phoned Tom from my office, asking him for anything he could turn up on Herman Gargoyle and his alleged organization. He said he'd ask around and call me back. The phone rang a half hour later.

"Herman Philip Gargoyle," Tom said, "that's his real name, by the by, has had quite a career as a petty crook. In fact, it's amazing he's not using an alias or three. He's been arrested eight times. Never convicted of anything. Different kinds of fraud. No one can ever get quite enough on him to convict him. They arrest him, which puts him out of whatever business he's in, but he always walks."

"So, how'd he get his hooks into Edith?"

"Well, he may have been blackmailing her, actually. I called in a couple of favors with the coppers to get this stuff, and something solid came up. Gargoyle was once associated with Al Gustafson. They worked a con together a lot of years ago. It seems that old Al only made one foray into the world of bunko, but maybe Herman shows up one day and tells Edith he's going to make this skeleton public unless she pays. He sets up a charity to explain the payments. If she's the only contributor, who's going to ask to see the books?

"And suppose he decides he wants bigger payments and she says no. In the course of threatening her, he kills the goose that's been laying the golden eggs. If she's dead, no more money. Al doesn't care enough about his social position to be blackmailed. With him in charge of the money, it's over. So. . . ."

"Gargoyle disposes of the body somehow," I filled in. "As long as Edith's missing and not dead, yearly payments continue to be made until she's declared legally dead. That's seven years from now, Tom."

"Enough to be worth. . . ?"

"Could be." I answered.

"What are you going to do, Livia?"

"Why, beard the Gargoyle in his den, of course."

"Not alone, you won't."

We argued about it for a few moments. My feeling was that if Gargoyle was going to admit to anything, he would consider me harmless if I were alone. In the end, I agreed to wear a microphone.

Tom would listen from his car. If it seemed that I was in any danger, he'd be there in a flash.

"I think you're taking lessons from my mother," I pouted. "She almost always gets me to do what she wants."

"I care about you."

"I know. My mother probably does, too."

With Tom in place just outside of Gargoyle's office building, I took a deep breath and got on the elevator, pressing the button marked "six." When I walked into the tiny office, I could have sworn that Gargoyle was expecting me.

"You again." It was a statement.

"Yeah, me. I keep coming back like a recurring nightmare."

"What do you want thisss time?"

"You killed Edith Gustafson, didn't you?"

"Yesss, but you can't prove it." I was amazed by his arrogance. "Ssstupid woman wouldn't give me more money. Ssshe wouldn't have missed it."

Since he seemed in the mood to talk, I pressed him. "What did you do with the body?"

"I cut it into very sssmall piecesss," he smiled. He had obviously been dying to brag to someone. "Then I visited the zoo very late at night."

"You've got to be kidding."

"No, indeed. I am a visionary. I do the necessary. No tracesss will be found." He looked thoughtful. "I did not mean to kill her. We argued. Ssshe lossst her temper. Flew at me like a giant goossse. When I pushed her away, she fell. Hit her head." He shrugged. "Alphonssse would have ssstopped the money. Thisss way, my future isss intact."

It hadn't been about ducks, then. It had been about geese. I never had a chance to respond to Gargoyle. At that moment, the door flew open, almost knocking me to the floor. I looked up to see Al Gustafson, still badly dressed, but with a fashion accessory he hadn't had before. It was a small, shiny revolver. He was pointing it at Gargoyle's chest.

"You son of a bitch. I been outside the door listening. You killed my Edith and fed her to zoo animals? When I heard your name, I knew what you'd been up to. You were always slime."

"Wait, Al," I said, trying to be calm. "Don't do this. It's not worth it."

There were tears in his eyes. He wasn't listening to me.

"Please, Al. It won't bring Edith back. We'll find a way to prosecute him. Stop and think."

Herman Gargoyle simply stared at the gun, his Adam's apple bobbing wildly. A minute went by in silence.

"Gargoyle," Al said quietly, "you're dead." The gun exploded, sounding like a grenade in the tiny room. The president and entire staff and membership of the Association for Animal Equality lay dead at our feet.

Tom ran through the doorway at that moment. "Jesus," he said, "I never even saw him come into the building. I didn't realize he was here until I heard you talk to him."

"Why, Al?" I asked the big man. "We would have nailed him somehow."

"Don't matter." Tears were streaming down his face now. "Edith's dead, so who cares? Not old Al."

He looked sad. He wasn't a killer. It was a moment of vengeance and now it was over. I comforted him as best I could while Tom called the police.

Before they took him away in handcuffs, Al got permission to talk to me in private, one more time. "Please tell Bentley he can stay on as long as I can arrange to have money available."

"Okay . . . uh, Al?"

"Yeah?"

"Houseman's just another word for butler."

He smiled. "Edith thought the word had more class. It was important to her."

After all of the hubbub was over, Tom and I got into his car.

"What a shame," I said.

"Thought you didn't like the guy."

"I changed my mind. Whatever his faults, he was a loyal man."

After a moment of quiet, both of us thinking our separate thoughts, Tom spoke. "Want to go to dinner somewhere?"

"Yeah. But I think it had better be vegetarian. And, please, don't even drive past the zoo."

Lily and the Sockeyes

Sara Paretsky

WHEN CLEMENTINE DUVAL took the job of managing public relations for the Vancouver Sockeye baseball team, the sports side of town buzzed. Nepotism, some said. After all, if her father hadn't been Hall of Fame shortstop Leon DuVal, the Sockeyes would never have talked to her. True, she was an athlete in her own right—women's NCAA strike-out leader when she played softball for the University of Kansas. True, she'd studied journalism and covered sports for several local papers for five years. But still—a woman handling the press for a men's pro team? If Leon hadn't bought a piece of the Sockeyes, the sportswriters said, it would never have happened.

Other tongues clacked about WXJ sportscaster Jimmy-Bob Reedy. Sixty if he was a day, fat, slack-lipped, with hands he couldn't keep to himself, he'd been chased out of Los Angeles by an angry Dodger franchise. Five years later, he had somehow ingratiated himself with the Sockeye front office and was the lead announcer on both television and radio. While loyal fans—and hapless color man Carlos Edwards—flinched, Jimmy-Bob lost track of the ball-strike count, forgot who was at bat, mispronounced names and droned on about his latest fishing trip.

Three WXJ women staffers had quit after doing technical back-up for him. The station and the front office gave handsome severance pay to stop possible attempted-rape charges, but the tales were known widely among sportswriters. How, they wondered, would

Clementine react if Jimmy-Bob copped a feel? Known for her slow curve and her fast temper, she might well break his nose. However much that might please the fans, it wouldn't endear her to the front office.

The team gave Clementine mixed reviews. The fact that her college pitching stats were better than their two-million-dollar Cy Young starter was gleefully repeated in the papers. When Jason Colby gave up a walk and three consecutive doubles in a crucial game with Philadelphia, Jimmy-Bob talked on the air about little else for days.

"Why Carlos," he'd say to his long-suffering back-up, "our cute little Clementine could of got us out of that inning without a scratch. You see her working with the boys at batting practice? You should a caught her from behind on her follow-through." Followed by a wet-lipped laugh.

Clementine had pitched for batting practice a couple of times as a publicity gimmick. She had a decent fastball and a good curve, but no one—least of all herself—thought she was any competition for Jason Colby. But the Cy Young winner was having a bad year, and he couldn't laugh off Jimmy-Bob's sniping. Even though he knew it wasn't Clementine's fault, he reacted by refusing her efforts to set up interviews and keep relations running smoothly with the press until his rhythm returned.

She had more success with young players still trying to prove themselves. She'd bring them over to her father's apartment for dinner, and they would sit stiffly on their chairs listening to Leon discourse on fielding and hitting: it couldn't hurt their chances in the majors for Leon DuVal to know who they were.

The other person who wasn't crazy about Clementine's sports career was her grandmother. Lily DuVal, a notable actress in her day, still carried considerable punch in film and theater circles. She had no use for sports and had never understood why her son wanted to go into baseball when she'd lined up a couple of movie parts for him. Her daughter-in-law had even less love of baseball and had walked out on Leon and two-year-old Clementine. Lily took in her granddaughter and tried to instill in her a hatred of baseball and a love of theater. Alas, neither took.

When Clementine graduated from college, she returned to the city to live with her grandmother in Lily's twenty-room mansion in suburban Fisherman's Cove. Lily, who adored her, swept magnificently through the house in emerald-studded caftans, entertained the theater and the press with panache, and loftily ignored her granddaughter's calling. "Clementine is in entertainment," she would tell people, smiling maliciously.

Lily was a vegetarian and a single-malt whiskey drinker. Loch Ness Distillers flew in crates of twenty-three-year-old Glen Moray whiskey for her from Scotland. Some people said that she and Sir Malcolm Darrough, Loch Ness's chairman, had been more than close friends in the thirties. All Lily would say was she judged a man by his taste in single-malts, not how far he could hit a silly white ball.

Other dear friends said that despite her famed hatred of baseball, Leon got his start with the Sockeyes because of Lily's "friendship" with Sockeye owner Teddy Wolitzer. After Clementine had been around the Sockeye dugout and front office for three months, she naturally heard these stories, which lost none of their zest to the tellers for being forty years old. With the same straight-forward action that characterized her fastball, she asked Lily about it one night at dinner.

"I hope it's not true," she said, her mouth full of lentil salad (with endive, tomatoes and onions—a summer treat, Lily called it). "I mean, he may have been the world's biggest charmer when he was thirty, Granny, but he's almost as disgusting as Jimmy-Bob Reedy. And almost as fat, too. Around the newsroom, they call him Teddy Bear, not because he's cute, you know, but because of his paws. I believe the stories they tell about him and Jason Colby's daughter. He's just the type, you know."

Lily raised her plucked eyebrows as high as the line of her brilliantly dyed turquoise hair. "Really, Clementine. Isn't it bad enough that you bring home earned-run-averages and at-bats, without dredging up all this ancient—and very dull—gossip? Could we change the topic, please? How's your Jock-Talk program going?"

This was Lily's name for Clementine's boldest PR venture to date. Clementine had done the traditional—bat days, glove days, autograph days ad nauseam. But she believed baseball's great untapped market was the woman spectator. In a survey of the ten most popular sports among women, baseball wasn't even ranked, while football was fourth behind tennis, ice-skating and gymnastics. How to get women interested in baseball? She had talked it over with Lily.

"Impossible!" her grandmother had snorted. "The only thing even remotely appealing about baseball is the bodies of the players. And even those are only good on a hit-or-miss basis."

Clementine's eyes lit up. "Granny! That's it! We'll get cameras in the locker room after games. We'll have the jock-of-the-week, and we'll reveal everything about him. Everything!"

In execution, the idea had to be toned down a little. Ballplayers, while as graphic as the next man in their discussions of female anatomy, proved strangely shy about revealing all on national television. In fact, when Clementine came into the locker room for the first time after a brilliant 2-1 victory over Montreal, the speed with which everyone leapt to the nearest towel was twice as fast as they ever ran the baselines.

After overcoming the ballplayers' initial reluctance, the in-depth profiles, done by Carlos Edwards, proved very popular. They couldn't do one every week—there are only so many good-looking jocks, and they produce a limited number of heart-stopping plays. But every two or three weeks Clementine and Carlos Edwards would pick a player and produce an interview accompanied by candid photographs. Clementine's forthright, friendly manner got the men to reveal details about their lives that their wives and coaches didn't always know.

When Jimmy-Bob used his pressure at WXJ to keep the interviews off the air, the *Herald-Star* agreed to run the stories. The sports section included a poster-size picture of the player in uniform. The first thousand women to come to the ball park on the next game day received a free copy of a candid glossy color shot, and the player would meet twenty women for drinks on the first following non-game day. The women's names were selected by a random drawing of their ticket stubs, so they had to come to the ballpark to participate.

The campaign proved so popular that other major-league teams soon started their own copy-cat programs. Lily was proud of her granddaughter's ingenuity. She secretly read the *Herald-Star* sports section on interview days. Teddy Wolitzer bragged openly, as did Leon DuVal.

The only person who wasn't happy was Jimmy-Bob Reedy. He already worried that fans preferred Carlos Edwards's reporting style. Carlos had been a Cy Young winning pitcher himself in a brilliant career with the Kansas City Royals. He not only understood the game well, but could talk about it.

Until the Jock-Talk program started, Jimmy-Bob got his pals in the Sockeye front office to keep Carlos's air time to a minimum. Now, however, the younger man was getting a lot of publicity. The *Herald-Star* articles proved so popular that the paper got their TV station, WSNP, to run tapes of Carlos's interviews. Jimmy-Bob tried blocking this in court, claiming it violated his exclusivity rights for Sockeye baseball coverage. He lost the suit and the newspapers made him look ridiculous.

Angry and humiliated, Jimmy-Bob started ridiculing Clementine on the air. His beady, lecherous eyes had taken in the fact that Carlos and Clementine were spending more and more time in restaurants and bars discussing "Jock-Talk." He even happened to drive "casually" by Carlos's apartment one morning in time to see Clementine come out, laughing, arm-in-arm with Carlos.

The sight added to his rage, because his early amorous efforts with Clementine had been soundly rebuffed. No one ever knew exactly what happened between them in private, but the day after Jimmy-Bob had invited Clementine to stay late to work on publicity, he had taken time off to treat an abscessed tooth. When he finally returned to the studio, his jaw was badly swollen. "It might have been from dental work," one columnist said dubiously. The other sportswriters had a field day ("NCAA Pitching Ace Connects," the *Province* gleefully reported).

Jimmy-Bob hoped that Carlos might react wildly to his attacks on Clementine. Then he could get the Sockeyes to cancel his contract. Or his attacks might provoke a response from Clementine herself that would turn the Sockeye front office against her. So he carolled happily about her possible sex life, insinuating that all women athletes were lesbians, discussed her probable drug habits, and how she wouldn't have a job at all without Leon and Lily's influence. He was even foolhardy enough to allude to Wolitzer and Lily's forty-year-old romance.

Carlos controlled himself with an effort. He had played second fiddle to Jimmy-Bob for two years, maintaining a cheerful camaraderie on the air. He reminded himself of the three years he'd played for a manager who hated him and still won twenty games each season. Off the air, he contemplated lying in wait for Jimmy-Bob and mugging him, or fiddling with the brakes on his car so that he would plunge into Howe Sound when he next went fishing.

Leon DuVal put in his two cents with Teddy Wolitzer.

"Come'n, Teddy. That lump of lard is screwing my daughter on the air. Not to mention what he's saying about Lily, who doesn't take too kindly to insults."

Wolitzer lit a fresh cigar. "Just be glad he ain't screwing her in the press room, Leon. Come'n. This feud is sweet music to my ears. TV ratings have never been better. The fans are pouring into the ballpark. I ain't gonna put a plug in the guy's mouth. He may be crazy, but he's selling ad time for the network."

Word of Jimmy-Bob's attacks reached Lily quickly enough. Not from Clementine, who didn't pay much attention to him—she figured if he got too wild she'd just break the other side of his jaw—nor from Leon, who knew his mother's temper of old. But one or another of Lily's pals in the press corps came out for cocktails or dinner most days. And one of them, a drama critic, brought the word out to Fisherman's Cove.

Lily took the unprecedented step of turning on WXJ. In all the years Leon had played, when he batted .295 and won a Golden Glove three seasons running, Lily had never watched a Sockeye game. Now she spent all of one hot August week watching them in a road series with Chicago. Her eyes began to sparkle dangerously.

Clementine, dividing her evenings between Lily and Carlos—between tofu and hamburgers—came in one afternoon to find Lily pacing the length of the patio, green silk billowing around her as it sought to keep pace with the swift movement of her legs.

"That man is a menace," she pronounced majestically.

"What man, Granny? You don't mean Carlos, do you? I thought you liked him. And don't tell me I'm not old enough—"

Lily cut her short. "Don't be ridiculous. I'm delighted to see you having fun with a nice boy with good legs. I'm talking about that fat, slobbering ape on television."

Clementine's eyes opened wide. "Granny! Don't tell me you've been watching the games! You shouldn't, really. Jimmy-Bob is a jerk. Why, yesterday when Sergio Diaz was batting he called him Manford Yates, and when he took a curve that just clipped the inside of the plate, Jimmy-Bob started yelling that it was high and outside and should have been ball four!"

Lily snorted. "Don't talk like that in front of me, Clementine. You know I don't care for it. I have no interest in anything Jimmy-

Bob might say about any ballgame. It is his personal comments that disturb me."

"You mean because he talks about me being a lesbian-Communist? I don't care. If he bothers me too much, I'll just blacken both his eyes so he won't broadcast for a week."

Lily came to a halt in front of her granddaughter. "No doubt. I expect such a lack of subtlety from someone who eschewed the theater for a baseball scholarship. And what are you going to do to stop his innuendos against me?" Her nostrils widened. "No, I'll think of a different way to cook his goose. Something he won't forget as fast as a black eye or two."

Clementine put an arm around her grandmother. "Whatever you say, Granny. Just don't be too rough with him—I think he's supporting a couple of ex-wives and three or four children."

Lily decided her subtle silencing of Jimmy-Bob Reedy would take place in front of as many people as possible. She would invite the whole Sockeye front office, Jimmy-Bob, Carlos and the rest of the broadcast team, and of course the players, to a magnificent party out at Fisherman's Cove. A blanket invitation was given to reporters and TV personalities in the city.

Clementine told her the Sockeyes had a day off in a long home stand right after Labor Day, so Lily announced that as the party date. Only Carlos knew what she was planning, because she needed his help. He took to spending evenings at the mansion, huddled with Lily. Clementine found herself feeling jealous—after all, Lily had pretty nice legs herself. She might be seventy-five, but yoga and high spirits concealed the fact admirably.

Clementine tried to swallow her hurt feelings and took on her usual role at Lily's parties: managing all the practical details. All Lily would tell her granddaughter about the entertainment was that she wanted four five-foot televisions installed in the ballroom. Clementine sighed resignedly and called electronics shops: Granny only got worse if you acted as though you cared what she was doing.

Lily relaxed her strict vegetarian rules for the occasion, allowing Clementine to order fish and pate to feed a guest list which grew with each passing day. Somehow a film producer just happened to be in town, the publisher of Lily's racy memoirs, the travel editor for the *New York Times*, and so it went. Sir Malcolm Darrough apparently had got wind of the affair and was jetting in on his company plane with a case or two of private-label Glen Moray whiskey. And another old flame, head of a steel company, was flying in from Chicago.

For the bulk of the party, Lily proposed champagne, so Clementine ordered thirteen cases of brut. Lily didn't waste her single-malt on the world at large. "It's not for silly ballplayers who want to get drunk as fast as possible. Only those who have the palate to appreciate it will be given a chance to drink it."

By the day of the party, the guest list had grown to three hundred. Since Lily always had everything her own way, even the weather co-operated: it was a sparkling September day, the leaves beginning to show hints of red and yellow, but the air kissed with the warmth of summer.

Guests began arriving in the early afternoon, laden with swimming suits for use at Lily's private beach. She managed to greet most people as they arrived. "Champagne and food on the patio and in the ballroom. Now you must be in the ballroom at six for the entertainment. It's really special."

Clementine herself served Glen Moray according to Lily's orders. Not even Teddy Wolitzer was allowed any—maybe, Clementine thought, all the tales about Lily and Teddy were so much smoke. Her grandmother's ex-lovers were always treated graciously, and the movie producer, Sir Malcolm, and the head of the Chicago steel company could be seen genially drinking and smoking in a corner together, with frequent visits from Lily herself.

By five p.m., it was clear that the party was one of Lily's major successes. Nine cases of champagne had already been disposed of, along with fifty pounds of shrimp, twenty of salmon, innumerable little cakes and giant bowls of fruit. While Lily, exotic in transparent silk and the emeralds which were world-famous, floated from one happy group to the other, it was Clementine who made the party tick. She kept a scrupulous eye on guests with a potential for battle, separating them dexterously into other groups, seeing that everyone was kept supplied with food and drink.

Jimmy-Bob, who had arrived early and was inclined to be aggressive, presented the biggest problem. Whenever Clementine tried to steer him from some prominent person whom he was offending, he would slip an arm tightly around her, squeeze her, and say, "I'm working to convert our little lesbian here. Me and Carlos are working on it together. Who's winning, Babe?"

Because it was a public occasion, Clementine restrained herself from slugging him. She did once dig her pointed heels into his instep with a happy smile on her face. He winced in pain and loosened his grip so that she could break away from him and redirect the people he was talking to.

At six, Lily and Clementine herded the guests into the ballroom. Lily attached herself to Jimmy-Bob. "Now for my most special guest, a special place of honor." While three hundred people disposed themselves around four wide-screen TVs, Lily made sure that Jimmy-Bob had a front row seat.

The lights went out and the screens came to life. To the strains of "Take Me Out to the Ballgame," the words, "Highlights of the Sockeyes' Man of the Hour" flashed on the screens. Then a close-up of Jimmy-Bob's face, red, veinous, slack-lipped. The crowd laughed. For the next fifteen minutes, they roared at a montage of Jimmy-Bob's greatest blunders, on and off the air.

Clementine watched silently. Lily had surely gone too far this time. Not to mention Carlos, who apparently had raided the WXJ tape library to pull the show together. Clementine wondered what she could do to stop it, and decided there wasn't a thing. She could only hope that Jimmy-Bob would feel too embarrassed to raise a legal stink, but knowing his temper, she didn't have much confidence in that. Carlos would lose his job; she'd probably lose hers, too. So maybe Lily could be persuaded to support the two of them. She was gloomily considering the possibility when a scream rose loud above the laughter, effectively shutting off the noise.

Clementine struggled to the wall where the lights were and turned them on. The ballroom was in total confusion. Some people were trying to leave, others to find what had caused the scream. As they pushed against each other, they created an immovable mass.

Clementine went behind the scenes where the A-V equipment was set up. She found Carlos doubled over with laughter.

"Enjoy yourself today, because tomorrow you're going to be out of work," she advised him shortly, hunting around in the equipment for a microphone.

She switched it on and spoke into it. Using her summer-camp counselor voice, which effectively calmed screaming ten-year-olds, she asked for silence. When the room had quieted down, she explained where she was standing and requested anyone who knew of any problems to join her.

The ballroom promptly began buzzing again, but more quietly.

She saw Leon work his way through the crowd to her.

"It's Jimmy-Bob," he explained when he reached her. "Someone stuck one of the carving knives for the salmon into him. I guess his blood seeped out to where one of the ladies from Los Angeles was sitting and she started to scream. I've already sent a waiter to call the police."

By eleven o'clock the police had sorted through the bulk of the guests and had sent most of them home. The head of the investigating team, Lieutenant Oberlin, had asked Leon, Carlos, Lily and Clementine to wait for him in Lily's front drawing room. Teddy Wolitzer insisted on waiting, too, on the grounds that he needed to know any new developments which might affect the Sockeyes. A uniformed policeman stood guard, trying to control his awe at being with his childhood baseball heroes.

Every now and then, Lieutenant Oberlin sent in an additional suspect to wait. Jason Colby, the Sockeye starting pitcher, was among them. Sir Malcolm Darrough, although given permission to leave, hovered solicitously at Lily's emerald-laden shoulder. Lily herself, while losing none of her vivacity, had stopped trying to entertain her troubled guests.

When Lieutenant Oberlin finally joined them, his voice was hoarse from four hours of interrogations. He sent the uniformed man for a glass of water and settled back to talk to his chief suspects and their hostess.

"From what I have seen of the video, I'm surprised it was Mr. Reedy who was killed instead of you, Mr. Edwards, or—with respect—yourself, ma'am. I'd like to know what prompted you to show a libelous film like that to three hundred people with the subject watching."

Lily's painted eyebrows went up. "My good man—have you ever watched Jimmy-Bob Reedy's broadcasts of the Sockeyes? If you have, you know how he slandered everyone and anyone. I thought it was time to give him a dose of his own medicine."

She turned to Sir Malcolm, who was trying to silence her, and patted his hand. "Don't worry, Malcolm—I'm not telling the man anything he doesn't already know, I'm sure."

Lieutenant Oberlin swallowed some water and leaned back tiredly in his chair. "Now, I know Jimmy-Bob—Mr. Reedy—had been insulting you and Miss Clementine DuVal on the air: I heard him myself a few times. So the two of you were understandably angry with him. And Mr. Leon DuVal wanted Mr. Wolitzer here to take Reedy off the air. And Mr. Carlos Edwards, who's pretty friendly with Miss DuVal, was angry with the deceased for insulting her. So any of the four of you might have been angry enough to kill him.

"Mr. Reedy had also been insulting Jason Colby all year—saying that Clementine DuVal could out-pitch him and that he ought to be sent back to the minors. It's true Mr. Colby has had a bad season. I suppose any athlete should be used to being insulted by the press. But maybe you weren't, huh, Mr. Colby? I have statements from a couple of your team-mates who heard you threatening to kill the man a couple of times."

Colby turned a painful red under his sun-burned skin. "I might've said something," he muttered. "You know, you get hot when you're not performing the way you think you should. But I didn't kill the guy."

"What about you, Mr. Edwards?"

Carlos looked embarrassed. "I agree the video wasn't in the best taste, Lieutenant. But it was such a sweet revenge on that jag-off—better than murder. I sure didn't want to kill him this afternoon—I couldn't wait to see what he was going to do when the lights came up."

Oberlin nodded. "And I think the same could be said for Miss Lily DuVal. But you, Mr. DuVal—you were really angry about the attacks on your daughter's character. You were seen near Mr. Reedy before the lights went down. And as a trained athlete you certainly know enough about the human body to be able to stab a man to death. We're going to take you downtown for further questioning."

Clementine turned pale under her tan. "Wait a minute, Lieutenant. You're forgetting me: I'm a trained athlete, too, and it was me he was insulting. Besides, I live here—Leon doesn't—and I know all the silverware and stuff. I knew which knife to use."

Lily snorted. "Do stop the heroics, darling. Even if you haven't been in the theater, a love of drama must be in your blood."

She turned to the policeman. "Lieutenant—could we use a little common sense? Let's talk about Mr. Reedy for a moment—however ugly a topic that is. Is there anyone in Vancouver who could stand listening to the man? He was disgusting. He apparently tried to rape every young lady who had to work with him—I've heard about pay-offs from Teddy Wolitzer to several women to keep their mouths shut. In addition, according to the boring stories my granddaughter brought home, he knew nothing about the game he was supposed to report on. The fans apparently preferred Mr. Edwards here, and it's not hard to understand why.

"Has it ever occurred to you to wonder why, in face of this concerted dislike, the Sockeyes let him announce their games?"

Lieutenant Oberlin looked at her intently. "Go on, ma'am."

Lily looked at Jason Colby. "I'm sorry to have to bring this up, Mr. Colby. But you have a daughter, don't you?"

Colby looked faint. "Alison," he said hoarsely. "She's eleven."

Lily nodded. "Teddy Wolitzer assaulted the child, didn't he? Last year?"

Jason only nodded without speaking.

"I've known Teddy for forty years now. Not a man who likes things going against him, are you, Teddy? I can guess what happened—he told you if you wanted to continue to pitch in the majors you wouldn't press charges."

Jason nodded again. "We sent her to live with her grandmother in California. But I can't get it out of my mind. My pitching's gone to hell. Then Jimmy-Bob made things worse, harping on and on about my playing. It was driving me off my head, but I didn't kill the guy. If I'd killed anyone, it would have been Wolitzer."

"Yes, dear," Lily said briskly. "Very upsetting. I don't blame you. But your daughter's story wasn't the well-kept secret Teddy might have hoped—Clementine brought home some garbled gossip about it earlier this summer. And presumably if Teddy did it once, there were other incidents with other little girls—right, Teddy? Did Jimmy-Bob find out about it? And use that information to force you to hire him and keep him in the lead announcing position?"

Leon nodded agreement. "Makes sense, Lily. You wouldn't know it, since you don't like baseball, but the commissioner would force him to sell the franchise if the word got out. Moral turpitude. They don't like the all-American game smirched by slime like child-abusers."

Lieutenant Oberlin got up and went over to Teddy. "We have people downtown looking through everyone's private papers for signs of blackmail or fraud involving Jimmy-Bob. So maybe we'll find something in your office, Mr. Wolitzer. Meanwhile, you have the right to remain silent, but if you give up that right, anything you say can be used as evidence against you. . . ."

After the police had left with Wolitzer, Lily leaned back in her chair. "Bring the Glen Moray, darling," she said to Clementine. "I think we all need a little drink."

Carlos followed Clementine from the room. "Listen, Clementine: don't be mad at me—I'm not in love with your grandmother—at least, I am, but not the way I am with you—I just wanted a chance to get revenge on that fat bastard. And you've got to admit—he died embarrassed."

They were gone for a long time. When they finally returned with the bottle, Lily raised her painted brows, but said only, "I thought you knew this house too well to get lost in it, darling."

She waited until everyone's glass had been filled before speaking again. "I spent several months with Teddy Wolitzer in 1946. I realized then what a vile man he was—which is why I never let him near my single-malt: that's for friends and whiskey lovers only." She raised her glass in a salute to them.

They lifted theirs to her.

"Lily," Sir Malcolm said, "you're incomparable."

Contributors' Notes

K.T. ANDERS is a former actress with extensive stage, screen and television credits. Her first novel, *Legacy of Fear,* a spy adventure, was published in 1985. She recently completed her second novel. Several of her short stories have appeared in magazines and anthologies. "Don't Shoot, I'm on Vacation" originally appeared in *Espionage Magazine.*

BRENDA MELTON BURNHAM is a former newspaper columnist for the *Chinook Observer.* She has had short stories and poetry published in a number of journals and she was a finalist in the *Northwest Magazine* 1990 fiction writer's contest. "Death in Rocky Falls" is her first published mystery story. She is currently working on a novel.

HELEN and **LORRI CARPENTER,** a mother/daughter writing team, live and work in central Florida. They have written a number of mystery stories featuring their septuagenarian sleuth, Emma Twiggs, some of which have been published in the first and second *WomanSleuth* anthologies.

LEA CASH-DOMINGO, pseudonym, lives in the Bay Area. She has had short stories published in *Ellery Queen's Mystery Magazine* and has written a book about treatment for adult children of alcoholics. In 1987 "The Cherry on the Cake" won an award from the Northern California chapter of Mystery Writers of America.

CAROL COSTA is an award-winning scriptwriter whose plays have been produced off-Broadway. She lives in Tucson where she is associated with a literary agency and is currently writing scripts for feature films and television. Her Dana Sloan stories have appeared in the first and second *WomanSleuth* anthologies.

ELLEN DEARMORE is currently at work on a collection of mystery stories that feature Gertrude Stein and Alice Toklas as detectives. One of these stories, "The Adventure of the Perpetual Husbands," appeared in the first volume of *The WomanSleuth Anthology*.

GAIL GILES is a native of the Texas Gulf Coast, where she has taught high school for fourteen years. She began writing short stories and young adult novels at the age of forty, and has had a number of stories published in magazines.

JAQUELINE GIRDNER is the author of *Adjusted to Death*, a chiropractic murder mystery (forthcoming in 1991 from Berkeley Books). She lives in Marin County, California.

WENDY HOBDAY HAUGH has published mini-mysteries in *Woman's World Weekly* and has had short stories and articles printed in a number of magazines, including *Mothers Today* and *Children's Digest*. She is the co-author of a non-fiction book, *Sled Dogs*. "Small-Town Ingenuity" is her first mystery story to be anthologized.

NANCY R. HERNDON is a former college English instructor whose first novel, *Wanton Angel*, was published under the pen-name Elizabeth Chadwick. Her second novel, *Widow's Fire*, is scheduled for publication in 1990. She has had short stories published in magazines and anthologies, including *Lighthouse, The West Texas Sun* and *Women of the West*. She lives in El Paso, Texas.

SARA N. PARETSKY grew up in eastern Kansas. Her first published writing, which appeared in the magazine *The American Girl* when she was eleven, told a story of surviving a tornado. She has worked full-time as a writer since 1986. Her novels, *Indemnity*

Only, Deadlock, Killing Orders, Bitter Medicine, Blood Shot and *Burn Marks* all feature V.I. Warshawski, a woman detective who lives and works in Chicago. "Lily and the Sockeyes" first appeared in the Japanese magazine *Suntori Sisters Quarterly*.

ELIZABETH PINCUS is an ex-San Francisco private eye. Her first Nell Fury story, "Trouble on the Beat," appeared in *The Second WomanSleuth Anthology*. She writes movie reviews for *Sojourner* and *Gay Community News*.

JUDITH POST had a short story, "No Handicap," published in the first *WomanSleuth* anthology and two mini-novels published by Penny Paper Novels. She is currently working on a full-length mystery novel.

LYNETTE PRUCHA is a writer and film executive in Beverly Hills. Her first mystery novel is titled *Smokescreen*. She has a Master's Degree in Comparative Literature from the University of Southern California.

CAROLINE STAFFORD has written mysteries, historical/suspense stories and traveller's tales, under a variety of names. She is currently chronicling Mrs. Dunlop's adventures in a series of short stories.

NAOMI RICHARDSON STRICHARTZ was born in Brooklyn. She was a member of Ballet Russe de Monte Carlo and is currently directing the Dance Circle Studio in Ithaca, New York. She has written two children's books, *The Wisewoman* and *The Wisewoman's Sacred Wheel of the Year* (available directly from Cranehill Press, 708 Comfort Road, Spencer, N.Y. 14883). Her first mystery story was published in *The Second WomanSleuth Anthology*.

LINDA WAGNER was born in New Jersey but has lived most of her life around Cleveland, Ohio. A previous story featuring Livia Day Lewis appeared in *The Second WomanSleuth Anthology*. She is currently working on a full-length mystery novel.

IRENE ZAHAVA (editor) has compiled a number of short story anthologies of women's writings, including *Word of Mouth, Finding Courage, Through Other Eyes: Animal Stories by Women, My Father's Daughter, The WomanSleuth Anthology* and *The Second WomanSleuth Anthology*.

Other Titles in the WomanSleuth Mystery Series

The WomanSleuth Anthology, edited by Irene Zahava

The Second WomanSleuth Anthology, edited by Irene Zahava

Angel Dance, by M.F. Beale

Clio Browne: Private Investigator, by Dolores Komo

Footprints, by Kelly Bradford

Murder in the English Department, by Valerie Miner

Paperback Thriller, by Lyn Meyer

Shadowdance, by Agnes Bushell

She Came Too Late, by Mary Wings